COSTING

THE

EARTH

FRANCES CAIRNCROSS

The
Economist
Books

BUSINESS BOOKS

333·7
CA1

First published in Great Britain by Business Books Ltd,
an imprint of Random Century Ltd, Random Century House,
20 Vauxhall Bridge Road, London SW1V 2SA, in assocation with
The Economist Books Ltd.

Copyright © 1991 The Economist Books Ltd
Text copyright © 1991 Frances Cairncross
Charts and diagrams copyright © 1991 The Economist Books Ltd

A catalogue record for this book is available from
The British Library

ISBN 0-09-174918-2

The text, endpapers and jacket of this book are printed on Reprise paper.
Reprise is made of 40% recycled woodfree unprinted waste, 40% recycled
woodfree printed waste, 20% virgin pulp. The case is made from recycled pulp
boards covered in Milskin, which is biodegradable and recyclable, using pulp
from sustainable sources.

Printed and bound in Great Britain by Butler & Tanner,
Frome, Somerset.

06/04/92.

CONTENTS

LIST OF FIGURES

LIST OF TABLES

ACKNOWLEDGEMENTS

For *The Economist* to give space to the environment startles some of its readers. The subject, in the minds of many people, has long been firmly linked with woolly beards and woolly thinking. So my first debt to Rupert Pennant-Rea, the magazine's editor, for having the imagination to see that *The Economist* could make an original and mind-clearing contribution to environmental issues by approaching them from an economist's standpoint; and giving me the job of trying to do so.

As *The Economist*'s first environment editor, I am aware of boarding a bandwagon that has been rolling for some time. But I have been astonished by the generosity of those already aboard in sharing their ideals and knowledge with newcomers. Some of those who helped me most are people who began to work on green issues early in the 1970s, and who went on doing so when that early period of green excitement came to an end. Their persistence has paid off: environmental argument is better informed today that in was 20 years ago.

Although I have acknowledged some of my intellectual debts in the pages that follow, many people who have helped me with facts or (more important) ideas go unnamed. Some, working in governments or in large companies, may be relieved, but to the others I apologise. I am constantly astonished at and grateful for the willingness of busy people to spend time educating journalists. Several people have read all or part of this book, and to them I owe a special debt. They include David Pearce, of University College, London; John Elkington, of SustainAbility; Scott Barrett, of the London Business School; Nigel Haigh, of the Institute for European Environmental Policy; and two of my colleagues at *The Economist*, Nico Colchester and Peter Haynes.

The research department at *The Economist*, under Carol Howard and Peter Holden, saved me from many howlers; Pauline Cuddihy, the systems manager, has rescued me from computer illiteracy; and at The Economist Books, Stephen Brough and Penny Butler have been cheerfully encouraging editors.

Most encouraging of all, though, has been my household. Collin Hawkins has kept us calm and well fed. My daughters, Isabella and Alex, have plied me with hard questions about the mess they see the adult world making of the planet. Above all my husband, Hamish McRae, has provided me with good ideas, disentangled muddled arguments, and kept the show on the road. This book is for him, with love.

PART I

THE CHALLENGE TO GOVERNMENT

INTRODUCTION

(Something extraordinary happened towards the end of the 1980s. People in many countries began to feel unhappy about the way the human race was treating its planet. They began to complain more noisily about filthy air and water, about the destruction of the rain forest and the disappearance of species, about the hole in the ozone layer and the build-up of greenhouse gases.)

(Politicians realised that there were votes to be lost by appearing not to care about the green issues that suddenly preoccupied voters.) In Britain 8,000 people deluged ministers with letters protesting at the devastation in the Amazon area. In America the proportion of those who thought that environmental improvements must be made "regardless of cost" rose by a quarter in a matter of months. Green parties won two dozen seats in the elections to the European Parliament in summer 1989. In Eastern Europe, as the summer wore on, discontent with tottering communist governments centred on green issues: a belching steel works in Poland, a grandiose dam in Hungary. In Bulgaria the main opposition movement called itself "Eco-*glasnost*".

The environmental whirlwind swept through boardrooms, too. Quite suddenly shoppers who had never worried about the origin or the final fate of their purchases began to ask awkward questions about both at annual general meetings. Chief executives who would once have dismissed environmentalists as long-haired radicals suddenly found that their profits depended on knowing whether their products were recyclable or biodegradable, and why it mattered. Environmentalists were suddenly in the queue at the check-out, asking disturbing questions about whether the aerosols contained chlorofluorocarbons (CFCs), or the disposable nappies dioxins. In Britain the proportion of people who said they had bought a product because it was environmentally friendlier more than doubled within a year.

Now, as the illustrations later in this chapter suggest, the first outburst of environmental fervour in many countries has subsided. Some of the green hysteria of 1988 and 1989 has abated. More conventional issues – unemployment, taxes, housing, education – have begun to preoccupy voters more. That does not mean that the pressures for change on governments and companies will vanish. While public interest in green issues may ebb and flow, politicians and businessmen will find some environmental pressure irresistible and lasting. Some of this pressure has noble origins: as people grow wealthier, they will worry more about the world they will pass on to their children. Some of it will be selfish: once an environmental bureaucracy is in place, it seeks out new work to do. Each outbreak of green fever leaves standards higher, and government policy tougher, than before.

Greenery will not go away. Politicians who hope that it will win them votes, though, may be disappointed. The environment is what American public-opinion pollsters call a "consensual" issue: one which a politician can lose votes by being against, but not gain votes by supporting. Moreover, those politicians who try hardest to appear "green" will often be the very ones picked out by environmental lobbying groups and upbraided for not being even greener. Green issues pose immensely difficult questions for politicians.

Why so suddenly green?

In many ways the environment has grown cleaner in the past 20 years, though mainly in the richer countries. Cars are quieter, houses better insulated and machines more energy-efficient. In the 1970s and early 1980s a combination of slower economic growth and tough emission controls led to some striking reductions in air pollution. Several big countries, including the United States, West Germany and Japan, cut their output of sulphur dioxide. Once-filthy rivers such as the Tiber and the Thames carry more oxygen than 15

Table 1 Membership of British environmental organisations ('000)

	1971	1975	1981	1985	1989	1990
National Trust	278	539	1,047	1,323	1,900	2,000
Royal Society for Protection of Birds	121	274	421	475	680	860
Greenpeace	...	...	8	50	300	387[a]
Worldwide Fund for Nature	12	...	60	91	213	231
Royal Society for Nature Conservation	64	107	143	166	205	250
Friends of the Earth	...	5	20	30	180	200
Green Party	...	...	0.5	4	17	16[a]

[a] March 1st 1991.
Sources: Organisations

Table 2 Membership of American environmental organisations ('000)

	1970	1975	1980	1985	1990
National Wildlife Federation	2,600	...	4,600	4,500	5,800
Greenpeace[a]	–	6	80	450	2,000
Sierra Club	114	153	182	363	566
National Audubon Society	105	255	310	425	515
Wilderness Society	66	...	63	97	363
Environmental Defence Fund	10	40	45	50	150
Natural Resources Defence Council[b]	–	15	35	65	140

[a] Founded in 1971. [b] Founded in 1970.
Sources: Organisations

years ago; airborne lead in the United States is less than one-tenth the level of 1975. If a country devotes enough cash and technology to a pollution problem, it can usually clean it up.

So why did environmentalism revive at the end of the 1980s? The answer varies from one country to another. In some countries, especially in Eastern Europe, environmentalism became entwined with nationalism, another growing political movement that also crosses the traditional boundaries between left and right. Elsewhere, it marked a rising concern with public health and particularly possible links between pollution and cancer. Although green issues seemed to attract a wider base of support than in the early 1970s, running across income levels and age gaps, they have been more attractive to women than to men. That may be because, on green issues as on many others, women are more risk-averse than men.

Certainly the public has become more aware of environmental disasters, which seem to occur with increasing frequency. The ten years after the *Amoco Cadiz* spilled its oil on the shores of Brittany brought Seveso and Bhopal, which put the spotlight on the chemical industry; Three Mile Island and Chernobyl which increased hostility to nuclear power; and the *Exxon Valdez*, the most expensive environmental accident ever to befall a company. People have become more willing to see such disasters as the result of bad environmental policies. They have also become more eager to find links between changes in nature and human activities. The drought of summer 1988 made Americans believe in the greenhouse effect; dying seals in 1988 made the British worry about the muck they were dumping in the North Sea; wilting forests persuaded the West Germans to reverse their opposition to curbing acid rain. People protest particularly about what they can see in their own back yards, and what affects their own lives.

Environmentalism has spread to poor countries, too. A mammoth survey conducted in the first half of 1988 by Louis Harris and Associates in 14 countries, nine of them poor, found high levels of alarm about pollution of drink-

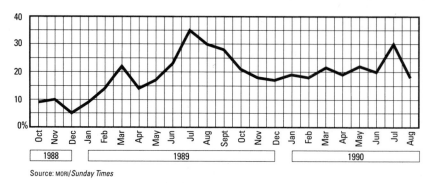

(**Figure 1** % of people who say the environment is the most important issue facing Britain today)

Source: MORI/*Sunday Times*

ing water and of the air and land; majorities of people and leaders in almost every country who thought that pollution would get worse; and large majorities in all countries who saw a direct link between environmental quality and public health. In Argentina, 76% of those surveyed thought their environment was deteriorating; in Kenya, 69% expected air pollution to become a very serious problem over the coming five years; and in India 81% of those polled considered deforestation to be a major cause of environmental damage. Given that the grisliest environmental horror stories come from third-world countries, that may not be surprising: the air is filthier in Mexico City than in Los Angeles, and in Shenyang than in Düsseldorf.

Most significant of all may be the fact that the 1980s, like the 1960s, was an era of rapid economic growth and (from 1986) of falling real energy prices. As growth has accelerated, with more countries and more people joining in, so its environmental side-effects have increased. Falling energy prices have encouraged people to use coal, oil and gas less frugally. The consequence, inevitably, is more pollution. One of the forces which stopped the environmental movement of the early 1970s dead in its tracks was the quadrupling of the oil price by OPEC. With such unwitting conservationists as the oil exporters, people felt, who needs conservation? As growth slows in the 1990s, the high tide of greenery will undoubtedly recede.

Will this wave of environmentalism have more lasting effects than that of the early 1970s? One reason to think it may is a greater confluence of ideas between moderate greens and well-run companies. This has been encouraged by a more broad-minded attitude to economic growth. During the last outbreak of green fever, which reached its peak in 1972, some environmentalists argued fiercely that economic growth was incompatible with wise environmental policies. The most influential book of that era, the Club of Rome's *The Limits to Growth*,[1] was a dire account of the main threats to the environment by a team from the Massachusetts Institute of Technology. "If the present growth trends in world population, industrialization, pollution, food production and resource depletion continue unchanged," it warned, "the limits to growth on this planet will be reached some time within the next 100 years."

The hostility to growth among radical greens sent environmen[...] blind alley. Faced with a stark choice between growth and green[...] people, in most countries, would go for growth. In the early 1970s i[...] better-off who cared most about the environment. Affluent green[...] accused (in the memorable phrase of Anthony Crosland, a British L[...] politician) of wanting to "kick the ladder down behind them". This t[...] there are two differences: environmentalism is no longer a middle-class movement; and some environmentalists have been looking for ways to reconcile greenery with economic growth.

A more important difference from the early 1970s has been the influential concept of "sustainable development". This is a convenient phrase, meaning different things to different people. It was popularised in the report *Our Common Future*,[2] by an international commission set up under Gro Harlem Brundtland, then prime minister of Norway. Its virtue is that it allows people to think of compromises: of ways to temper the impact of growth, without sacrificing it entirely.

Having it both ways

Many people hope that economic growth can be made environmentally benign. It never truly can. Most economic activity involves using up energy and raw materials; that, in turn, creates waste that the planet has to absorb. Green growth is therefore a chimera. But *greener* growth is possible. The whole history of technology has been about squeezing more output from the same volume of raw materials. Governments can dramatically reduce the environmental harm done by growth if they create incentives to use raw materials more frugally. That means harnessing the inventive energy of industry.

"Sustainable development" is a useful concept but from the point of view of a politician it begs lots of awkward questions. Margaret Thatcher can hardly have thought through the telling metaphor she used in her speech to

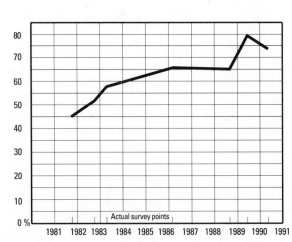

Figure 2 % of people who agree that protecting the environment in the United States is so important, "that requirements and standards cannot be too high and continuing environmental improvements must be made regardless of cost"

Source: *New York Times*/CBS News Poll

the Conservative party conference in October 1988 that marked her transition from Iron Lady to Green Goddess. "No generation has a freehold on the earth," she said. "All we have is a life tenancy – with a full repairing lease." The implications of that elegant metaphor are tremendous. For only government can ultimately set the terms of that "full repairing lease".

Up to now, no generation has carried out its fair share of planetary repairs. Each has ignored the costs that accrue to future generations. To demand that this generation should undertake repairs means making people pay for something which they have previously regarded as free. That is why politicians who take up green causes can suddenly find themselves in dangerous territory.

Painful for politicians

Environmental policy is inevitably interventionist. (Without government intervention, the environment cannot be fully protected.) That was clearly anticipated two centuries ago by John Stuart Mill. "Is there not the Earth itself, its forests and waters, above and below the surface?" he asked in his *Principles of Political Economy*. "These are the inheritance of the human race. ... What rights, and under what conditions, a person shall be allowed to exercise over any portion of this common inheritance cannot be left undecided. No function of government is less optional than the regulation of these things, or more completely involved in the idea of a civilised society." Small wonder that Chris Patten, interventionist environment secretary in Mrs Thatcher's free-market Conservative government, took that passage as the theme of the government's white paper on the environment in September 1990.

Mill saw that environmental policy was ultimately about distribution. But allocating rights and determining conditions drags government, willy-nilly, into nasty questions of gainers and losers that politicians usually prefer to leave alone. The gainers and losers may live in the same town. But the gainers may be rich and powerful; the losers poor and weak. The losers may even be foreigners, if one country's environmental damage harms the citizens of another. Or they may be the weakest of the weak: generations yet unborn.

"Why should I care about posterity?" Groucho Marx is supposed to have said. "What's posterity ever done for me?" Posterity has no votes; yet caring for the environment is often a matter of changing the habits of today's voters for the benefit of future generations. Heating our homes would cost far more if we used only wind power and solar energy, in order to avoid putting into the atmosphere the carbon dioxide that may well cause global warming. Why should politicians ask us to bear such costs? After all, alarming though the speed of global warming may be in terms of the history of evolution, by the time today's politicians retire its results will still be barely noticeable.

Sometimes those harmed by a country's environmental degradation will not be its own citizens, present or future, but its neighbours. Dirt travels across borders. The sewage dumped into the Rhine by the Germans washes on to Dutch shores; the gases from America's power stations may shrivel Canada's trees. One of the new characteristics of environmental issues that preoccupy people now is their international aspect. Increasingly, environmental issues will replace defence as the staple of international negotiations. Diplomats will learn to argue about whether sulphur dioxide or nitrogen oxides causes acid rain, rather than about warheads and troop deployments. Governments that want to be green will have to persuade their citizens to accept costs for the benefit of other countries' voters.

Even within a country, environmental issues may raise awkward questions of justice and rights. Especially in poor countries with weak democracies, those who grow rich by letting the environment get dirty may be few and well organised; those who lose as a result may be poor and have little political clout. The loggers and ranchers who chop down the trees of rain forests are often a more powerful lobby than those who live in the forest; the miners whose waste pollutes rivers or coasts more influential than the fishermen whose living is destroyed.

In place of the market

One of Britain's most radical free-market politicians, Nicholas Ridley, justified state intervention in environmental policy with a telling metaphor. "Pollution, like fraud, is something you impose on others against their will so that you can perhaps gain financial advantage. It is an ill for which the operation of the free market provides no automatic cure. Like the prevention of violence and fraud, pollution control is essentially an activity which the State, as protector of the public interest against particular interests, has to regulate and police."[3]

Only government can right environmental injustice. For it is only government that can decide how much society should value the environment, and how that value should be inserted into economic transactions. The market, that mechanism which so marvellously directs human activity to supply human needs, often has no way of putting a proper price on environmental resources. "Free as the air" is all very well, but it means that factories pay nothing to belch smoke from their stacks. It is easy to put a price on a tree as timber. But that price will take no account of its value as a mechanism for preventing soil erosion, or as a home for rare birds or insects, or as a store of carbon dioxide that might otherwise add to the greenhouse gases in the atmosphere.

To talk of trees in the language of economics seems odd to many environmentalists. The very idea that values can be attached to natural beauty is an affront to those who think that the green world is beyond price. Yet one message of this book is that to think of the environment in economic terms is a useful way to understand green problems. In particular, it is a helpful approach for politicians and businessmen, who are familiar (whether they know it or not) with using economic concepts to analyse policy decisions.

Some environmentalists have grasped this, and realise that governments and companies may become more concerned with green issues if they see that this is in their economic interest.

Because the market does not set prices on environmental resources, the economy is skewed in favour of the things that can be marketed and against those that cannot. A developer who wants to put up a factory in a beauty spot can easily calculate the gain in terms of jobs and production. Those who want to protect the beauty spot have no such numbers. The undeveloped spot has no "output" to set against the products of the factory. It is never easy to argue that the gain to those generations who can enjoy its views will be greater, over the years, than the hard cash that the developer thinks can be earned.

When goods are underpriced, or not priced at all, they tend to be overexploited. When Britain has experimented with the metering of domestic water supplies, people think carefully about running a second bath or turning the sprinkler on the lawn. Where water is thought of as free, or paid for in a lump sum, they do not.

Why are environmental goods so often unpriced or underpriced? Sometimes the reason is cultural: in Muslim countries, many of which are dangerously short of water, people have strong religious objections to paying for a gift from God. More often, the reason is that the resource is owned by everybody or by nobody. Nobody owns the sea or the sky; therefore nobody charges those who overfish the sea or fill the air with ozone smog. Nobody owns quietness; therefore nobody can set a price for nasty noises.

Where nobody owns an environmental resource, the market will not give its usual warning signals as that resource is used up. In the early 1970s some environmentalists fretted terribly about the imminent exhaustion of oil, iron and copper which, they rightly pointed out, were non-renewable. Once all the oil was burned, that was that. They reckoned without the oil-exporting countries, which behaved like any cartel with limited supplies of a product in great demand and jacked up the price. Result: much investment went into energy conservation and into searching for oil in places like the North Sea and Alaska where it would not previously have been profitable. We will never pump the last barrel of oil. We may well, however, kill the last whale, for as that mammal becomes more scarce, so the rewards for catching it increase.

In fact the true limits to growth are not the earth's stocks of natural resources such as coal, oil and iron, which are bought and sold at prices that will rise to reflect their increasing scarcity. They are the capacity of the environment to deal with waste in all its forms; and the "critical" resources – such as the ozone layer, the carbon cycle and the Amazon forest – which play no direct part in world commerce but which serve the most basic economic function of all, which is to enable human beings to survive. It is these two kinds of resources, long treated as free goods, which have been most dangerously overexploited.

Painting markets green

Green lobbyists have wanted to replace markets with government simply because the forces of unfettered markets can destroy the environment. If private enterprise chops down forests, the argument runs, put the forests in the hands of the state. This extreme faith in the benign green role of the state has faded, partly thanks to growing realisation of the scope of environmental catastrophe in the state-run lands of Eastern Europe. Many examples (some set out in Chapter 4, Part I) show that bad government policies may make even more of a mess of the environment than the unfettered market.

A better starting point is to look for ways to improve markets. Some American economists see an answer in better definitions of ownership. If ownership of environmental assets is clearly established, the argument runs, then polluters and the polluted will be able to bargain over a reasonable price for allowing pollution to take place. Sometimes such solutions work. If people have fishing rights in a river which they can rent out to others, they will have a strong interest in seeing that their bit of the river is not overfished. They will also be able to bargain with other owners to prevent the whole river being over-exploited. But often – think of the ozone layer – it is simply not possible to use private enterprise in this way. Establishing ownership is too difficult; the numbers of polluters and of those affected by pollution are too great for bargaining to be practical.

Clear rights of ownership for natural resources may, however, sometimes improve the way they are managed. Chapter 3 (Part I) discusses ways in which conservation may sometimes be helped if local people are given a financial interest in it. Chapter 4 (Part I) looks at a different aspect of ownership: in third-world countries particularly, governments often tend to under-price resources (such as water) and thus encourage overuse. Private suppliers frequently go to the opposite extreme. In Britain the separation of ownership from regulation in several natural-resource industries – gas, electricity, water – may eventually improve the quality of environmental care. That is, of course, likely to be true only where state ownership has encouraged environmentally damaging investment (as with the nuclear power programme) or discouraged green spending (as with water).

Another way to improve the working of the market is to make sure consumers and producers pay the true costs of the environmental damage they cause. Markets work best when prices reflect as accurately as possible the costs of production. So the price of a gallon of petrol ought to reflect the damage caused by exhaust gases, while the cost of running a bath should incorporate the ungreen effects of water extraction and sewage disposal. The main ways in which economists urge politicians to pass such information into pricing is through taxation.

But making polluters pay is easier advocated than done. Once a politician pauses and wonders, "Right: but how much?", a whole new batch of problems appears. It is impossible to estimate exactly the price that a green government should exact from polluters. If that developer who wanted to build a factory in a beauty spot had wanted, instead, to build it where a housing estate now stands, the price of the site would have reflected the price at which houses are bought and sold. There is a housing market, but there is no beauty market. So if government is to make sure that the beauty spot is properly valued, it has to put a price on loveliness. Economists have thought up ways to do this, such as asking people what they would be willing to pay to keep the spot undeveloped. But none has the real-world quality of the price of a house.

The concept of assigning values to the environment irritates many environmentalists, who argue that such values represent no more than a rationalisation of political decisions. Faced with a powerful developer, only a very rash politician would become involved in a fight over the social value of undeveloped land. Yet without some sense of the costs that pollution inflicts on the planet, governments have no idea what price polluters should be made to pay.

Most difficult of all, some environmental damage is irreversible. Clean up the Thames and the fish come back. Increasingly, the green problems that call for government action are ones that are irreversible, at least within any imaginable span of human time. It may take centuries for the hole in the ozone layer to repair itself, or the oil in the sea to degrade, or the greenhouse gases in the atmosphere to fall to levels that no longer threaten global warming. Putting a sensible price on irreversible damage is all but impossible.

That is a counsel of caution, not despair. Simply because environmental costs are so hard to estimate is no argument for abandoning the effort, for two reasons. First, setting a rough value may be a better basis for policy than none at all. Only by groping for values for environmental resources can governments think sensibly about costs and benefits. Scientists who are alarmed by the prospect of global warming tend to argue that carbon emissions must be halted at any price. Wise governments will first ask what the costs of global warming are likely to be, and will then want an estimate of the costs of slowing the build-up of greenhouse gases. Both figures will be wobbly and widely disputed. But without some grasp of costs and benefits, governments are likely to do either too much or – worse – too little.

Most governments, far from making polluters carry the costs of environmental damage, do precisely the opposite. So a second reason to try to put values on green goods is to discourage such perversity. Lots of governments subsidise polluting activities. Many third-world countries in particular hold down electricity prices. That drives up demand. Generating electricity to supply this demand produces more gases, sulphur dioxide and carbon dioxide, both harmful in their different ways. It may mean building more dams for hydro power. It may encourage a country to develop polluting industries.

Such folly is not confined to the poor world. Most rich countries subsidise agriculture. That encourages monoculture – usually more polluting than mixed cropping – and increases the demand for fertiliser and pesticides. Britain subsidises company cars. Germany subsidises coal mining. America subsidises the logging of its ancient forests. Each country has its own madness, often as economically perverse as it is environmentally damaging. Such perversities survive because powerful lobbies back them. Governments, in democracies at least, can rarely do more than their electors want. If this generation of electors is not prepared to foot the bill for that "full repairing lease", governments will find it hard to make them.

Intervene, too

To rely exclusively on the force of the market, however ingeniously harnessed, to clean the environment is as naïve as relying solely on government intervention. For one thing, markets need information. They will need to collect information – or at least, to say clearly what information they require. If polluters are to pay, governments will need to measure pollution. Government will need to punish polluters who cheat, just as Mr Ridley would expect government to punish more familiar kinds of fraud. Monitoring, measurement and enforcement are all jobs that cannot be done voluntarily. They require a legal framework and the sanction of the state.

Governments may sometimes need to make the market work better in other, more subtle ways. If a market does not exist in the first place, giving it green signals will be pointless. The countries of Eastern Europe had elaborate systems of fines and charges to discourage pollution; but, as the fines were rarely collected and the charges were carried by monopolies, pollution simply continued unabated. It is important to worry about creating a market in the first place – getting, say, somebody in the Soviet Union to worry about leaks of natural gas, or somebody in Britain to care about water lost from pipes – before building elaborate schemes to ensure that polluters carry the full costs of environmental damage.

This is important because a characteristic of many of the activities that most affect the environment – energy supply, the provision of water, transport – is that they are highly regulated by the state. Power lines, sewage works, roads and airports are frequently monopolies or near-monopolies. They are often state-owned. It may therefore be difficult to rely on pricing alone, or on market forces harnessed in other ways, to influence the supply of and demand for these services. Raising the price of electricity may encourage consumers to turn off their lights, or it may simply leave them with less cash to spend on other things. Only gradually will it encourage them to buy more efficient central heating or to install double glazing. It may be faster and less painful – and politically easier – if governments intervene to encourage conservation in more direct ways. Some of these may seem corny: Peter Walker, when he was British energy secretary, toured the country inviting businessmen to breakfast to preach the gospel of energy efficiency, and did wonders for the insulation business. Others may be practical, such as setting high standards for insulating new buildings. The principle will remain: where markets work badly, governments have more reason to step in and give them a shove.

Enlist companies

The first half of this book looks at the challenges that environmental policy poses for government. It examines what might be called the "political economy of environmental mismanagement" and the policies which make good sense environmentally and politically. The second half narrows the focus from governments down to companies. Only by enlisting the help of companies, it argues, can governments hope to combine economic growth with good green stewardship.

Electors will not welcome greener policies if those deliver what they perceive to be a lower standard of living. Governments will be able to pursue greener policies only if companies can find ways to give people the level of comfort to which they have become accustomed, in less environmentally damaging ways. The second half of this book therefore explores the incentives for companies to introduce greener products and greener ways of making them.

Companies are more likely to help politicians if politicians take their proper responsibilities seriously. Government must decide environmental priorities; determine what information (as a minimum) needs to be put before the public; government needs to set clear rules; and work out how true environmental costs are to be reflected in costs of production. These are not jobs for companies. Their role is to respond, energetically and inventively, to the framework that government sets out. The better that framework is designed, and the more imaginatively companies use it, the more electors will support green policies.

Environmentalists need to understand this in order to campaign effectively for a cleaner world. If they talk the language of wealth creation, of incentives, of efficiency, of market opportunities, they are infinitely more likely to be listened to by politicians and by businessmen. To say, "We want a green world and to hell with who pays for it," may be good television, but it is ultimately bad politics.

References

[1] D.H. Meadows, D.L. Meadows, J. Randers and W. Behrens, *The Limits to Growth*, Earth Island, London, 1972.

[2] World Commission on Environment and Development, *Our Common Future*, Oxford University Press, 1987.

[3] Nicholas Ridley, "Policies against Pollution", Centre for Policy Studies, London, 1989.

1

THE QUESTIONS
THAT COUNT

In taking decisions about environmental policy, two questions matter right at the start. One is "Ought we to do something about this?" and the other, "If so, what?" This chapter and Chapter 2 of Part I are primarily concerned with answers to the first question. The rest of Part I deals mainly with the second.

Often the answer to the first question is arrived at almost by default. Newspapers, whipped up by green lobbyists, clamour for action; governments publicly accept that a problem exists and announce that they will solve it, without first pausing to see where the road will lead. Are there nitrates in the nation's rivers? Announce that they will be reduced. Is toxic waste seeping from dumps? Announce that dumping will be restricted. Such decisions may lead to a cleaner environment; but not necessarily – and this is a key point – to the cleanest environment that could have been bought for the same expenditure of money and effort.

Setting green priorities is one of the most difficult and essential jobs that governments face. More and more, companies will demand it. Sophisticated green companies, carrying out studies of the environmental impact of their products, will find that the answers are rarely clear-cut. Ought drinks containers to be refillable (which means making heavier bottles, and using more energy to bring them back to the plant)? Or should they be recyclable (which might mean using aluminium cans, with their high value as scrap)? Or should they be biodegradable, so that they will rot quickly on rubbish heaps? The answer will depend on whether governments are more worried about, say, the effect on global climate of using more energy, or the ugliness of more rubbish dumps.

Politicians have frequently turned to scientists to help them answer the question "Ought we to do something?". They are, after all, more likely than anybody else to be able to say whether chlorofluorocarbons harm the ozone layer, or whether pollution causes cancer, or how many species will be lost if the Amazon forest is burnt or chopped down.

But scientists will not necessarily agree with each other – any more than economists, those favoured special advisers of earlier days. For establishing scientific proof of environmental damage is much harder than, say, finding a link between a falling apple and the force of gravity, or even cigarette smoking and lung cancer. Environmental damage may occur far from the original cause. Acid rain in Norway may be caused by British coal-fired power stations or by German cars. It may take place long after the original event, too late for preventative action. Nitrates in the water supply may come from spreading nitrogen fertilisers today, or from ploughing grassland 20 years ago. By the time we know for sure how the greenhouse effect will warm the earth, large amounts of warming gases will already have built up in the atmosphere. The only option for politicians who want to be green may be to pick their scientists, and bet voters' money on the pet view.

Because greenery is fashionable and scientific proof is hard, people may readily assume that pollution causes problems when the truth may be simpler but less welcome. For example, plenty of attempts have been made to link the lower life expectancy of people of Eastern Europe with the high levels of pollution in those countries. Life expectancy is undoubtedly lower (67 years for a male Pole at birth, compared with 74 years for a man in nearby Sweden). It has been declining. Pollution is high and rising. Some links between pollution (especially air pollution) and health clearly exist. But take the facts that 81% of Polish men and 57% of women in their early thirties smoke cigarettes; that cigarette smoking did not decline between the mid-1970s and mid-1980s; that Polish cigarettes are probably more harmful than those smoked in the west; and that cigarette-smoking almost certainly compounds the respiratory harm done by air pollution. If you add all those together, many Poles could clearly enjoy a cheap short cut to better health simply by stopping smoking.

Half an answer is no better than none

In fact, what scientists can say on many environmental issues is important but limited. Even when they can link environmental cause and effect with some confidence, they know only half the reply to the first question policy-makers must answer, "Ought we to do something?". Scientists may have a good guess at the consequences of allowing damage to continue. They can tell politicians that unchecked water pollution may cause illnesses, and that the sea level will rise in a warmer world. But they cannot attempt to put a cost on such damage – let alone (and this is important) set that cost against the costs of taking action. They cannot say: "It would be sad if this species became extinct, but for what it will cost to save it, one could run a hundred hospitals or a thousand schools." Yet such trade-offs, anathema to greens, are what politicians and business people must do all the time.

Nor can scientists easily move on to the second question: "If so, what?". Stopping environmental damage generally means changing human behaviour. That is a matter for social and political scientists. Scientists may judge that, say, fish stocks are dangerously low because of overfishing; they are not good at thinking of ways to persuade people to reduce the amount of fish they catch. Scientists may see that car exhausts cause city smog; they are not equipped to think of ways to make people drive their cars less, or change the kind of car they buy.

Environmentalists are suspicious of economists, reasonably enough: for while environmentalists tend to think in terms of absolutes, economists think in terms of costs and benefits. To an ardent green, no level of pollution is safe; to an economist, the costs of getting rid of a pollutant will rise steeply as it diminishes. Some kinds of pollution, economists will admit, ought to be totally prevented: thus a nuclear power plant ought never to leave highly radioactive waste lying about, nor ought factories to dump cyanide in their local river. Generally, though, economists think that it may be wiser to tolerate some pollution than to try to get rid of it all, whatever the cost.

Governments need to be aware of costs and benefits if they are to answer the first kind of question sensibly. Voters do not always get most excited about the things that do the most environmental damage. This chapter looks at some of the problems involved in deciding how seriously to take an environmental threat.

Into the unknown

The question, "Ought we to do something about this?", is the one governments face when deciding whether to sign the Montreal protocol on CFCs or to pass laws on permitted water pollution. It is also the question they ask when deciding whether to run a road through a beauty spot; and the one that companies broach when carrying out an assessment of environmental impact. The simple answer is: "Yes, until the benefit of an extra little bit of safeguarding the environment is less than the cost of the next step to protect it." Simple, but not usually terribly helpful. To know the benefit of safeguarding the environment means wrestling with two kinds of uncertainty. It means putting a value on what is being protected. And it means deciding whether damage is likely to increase along a smooth path, or in sudden unpredictable jerks.

It may seem pointless, or even cynical, to try to put a monetary value on a beautiful view or a rare species. Certainly lots of environmentalists think it is silly to try. But economists may persuade people to think more clearly by trying to do so. Most real-world decisions involve conflicts of interest: if a view is blocked by a building, those who once enjoyed it lose, while those who rent out the building gain. In a world where money talks, the environment needs value to give it a voice.

Economists use two main approaches to set values on environmental assets. One is direct: they ask people questions. At their simplest, these are along the lines of, "What would you be willing to pay to stop the Grand Canyon being shrouded in smog?" Some answers are shown in Table 3, page 26. Over time, such questions have become more and more refined in order, for instance, to

Table 3 A value on nature: non-use values for unique natural assets ($, mid-1980s)

Asset	Value per adult
Animal species	
Whooping crane	1
Emerald shiner	4
Bottlenose dolphin	6
Bighorn sheep	7
California sea otter	7
Northern elephant seal	7
Blue whale	8
Bald eagle	11
Grizzly bear	15
Natural amenities	
Water quality (S. Platte river basin)	4
Visibility (Grand Canyon)	22

Source: K. Samples, M. Gowen, J. Dixon, "The Validity of the Contingent Valuation method for Estimating Non-Use Components of Preservation Values for Unique Natural Resources", paper presented to the American Agricultural Economics Association, Reno, Nevada, July 1986

try to stop people naming huge sums on the sensible assumption that others will share the bill through higher taxes. Some surveys ask a set of questions once, then give interviewees a pep talk on the environmental issue at stake, and finally ask the questions again. Not surprisingly, such experiments prove the importance of environmental education in raising people's willingness to pay to prevent environmental damage. People name even larger values if they are given a day or two to reflect after their pep talk.

The other approach is indirect. Economists hunt for a real-world market in which to try to capture the value of environmental assets. In developing countries, where the environment is literally what most people live off, such markets are often easy to find. Several examples appear in Chapter 3 of Part I. In richer countries, the link between environmental damage and a real market may be more tenuous. Take the property market. If two identical houses in neighbouring streets sell for widely differing amounts, and the cheaper one stands in the street with the noisiest traffic, it is reasonable to suppose that the price difference may at least partly reflect the value people put on quiet streets. In fact, it may be hard to disentangle environmental nuisance from lots of other factors. A study[1] by economists at Salford University of 3,500 houses in Stockport found that those in the areas most affected by noise from Manchester airport were on average 6% cheaper than others; but most of this price difference could be explained by other characteristics of the neighbourhood and the houses. Even if they had not been under the flightpath, the houses would still have been cheap.

Another kind of proxy price may be reflected in what people pay to visit a particular forest or park. The assumption is that, even if visiting the forest is free, the cost of travelling there gives some idea of the value people put on it. Sometimes environmental damage has measurable costs. When air pollution corrodes stone, the cost of repairs can be reckoned up. That is one way to get at the value of cleaner air. When polluted water makes people ill, economists may try to put a value on the loss of health.

One problem with indirect, or "contingent" valuations, as they are sometimes called, is that they may capture only part of the story. For example, travel costs say nothing about the values of those who might like to travel to a park next year, or the year after, and would pay to keep that option open. Surveys do not have that drawback: what people say they would pay reflects, at least in theory, not just the market value of some environmental assets, for instance the higher price their house commands because it fronts on to an unpolluted river. Surveys also pick up the priceless enjoyment a person might get from fishing on that river, and the value that might be derived by another person, far away, from the comforting thought that the river was clean.

This kind of psychic value is important. One of the advantages of using surveys is that they are the only ways to discover values put on some environmental assets by people who do not actually consume them. People may be willing to pay to ensure the continuing survival of the humpbacked whale or the black rhino even though they never expect to see either creature. They may be willing to pay such an "existence value" for the benefit of posterity, or simply because they feel that animals have a right to exist.

Surveys have drawbacks, too. One is the large differences that regularly appear between the answer to the question, "What would you be willing to pay for a 50% improvement in air quality?" and the apparently similar question, "What would you accept as compensation for a 50% worsening in air quality?". When these very questions were put to 2,000 people in Haifa, Israel, the answer to the first question was about £12 per household per year (1987 prices).[2] But the compensation the households wanted if air quality were to worsen was roughly four times as much.

Sometimes surveys find that people simply say that nothing would be enough to compensate them for an environmental loss, implying that its value to them is infinite. Ask a "What would you pay" type question, and the numbers are always much more modest (Table 4, page 28). One possible explanation is that people feel more strongly about losses imposed on them than about gains which they choose. The loss of something a person already "owns" – like clean air – is valued more highly than a potential gain of something new, like even cleaner air. People feel that they are the owners of an endowment of environmental rights which they are deeply unwilling to abandon.

This may be why companies trying to site a polluting plant seem to find it easier (see Chapter 6, Part II) to give the local community some sense of control over the decision. But the differences between what economists dub

Table 4 Calculation disparities of models in various studies, between WTP, "willingness to pay", and WTA, "willingness to accept" (year-of-study $)

Study	WTP	WTA
Hammack and Brown (1974)	247.00	1,044.00
Banford *et al.* (1977)	43.00	120.00
	22.00	93.00
Sinclair (1976)	35.00	100.00
Bishop and Heberlein (1979)	21.00	101.00
Brookshire *et al.* (1980)	43.64	68.52
	54.07	142.60
	32.00	207.07
Rowe *et al.* (1980)	4.75	24.47
	6.54	71.44
	3.53	46.63
	6.85	113.68
Hovis *et al.* (1983)	2.50	9.50
	2.75	4.50
Knetsch and Sinden (1983)	1.28	5.18

Source: Cummings *et al.* (1984), quoted in David Pearce and Kerry Turner, *Economics of Natural Resources and the Environment*, Harvester Wheatsheaf, London, 1990

"WTP" (willingness to pay) and "WTA" (willingness to accept) questions are interesting from another point of view. Normally, economists draw curves to show how people are willing to trade, say, apples for oranges, or money for matches. They assume that people are willing to move smoothly – "indifferently" – along these curves, trading gradually increasing amounts of apples for rising numbers of oranges, or a few pennies less for a declining number of matchboxes. Some environmental economists argue that the answers to their valuation surveys suggest that this key assumption of conventional economics may be meaningless in the real world. Such curves may simply not exist. People's reactions may depend on whether they are paying to get more or being compensated to accept less.

In the real world, survey evidence faces its own problems. However refined the methods by which economists value the environment, politicians and businesses may take more notice of cash payments than the value people say they derive from this or that aspect of greenery. There may be no mechanism for those who want to protect a resource to compensate those who want to destroy it. Ask English bird-lovers how they value the Highlands of Scotland unscarred by new ski resorts, and they would name a high price; but Highlanders know that another group of people, Scottish skiers, would also name a high price to have the ski slopes developed. More relevant from the point of view of Scottish politicians, Scottish skiers are more likely to put their price into the pockets of Highlanders than are English birdwatchers.

Skiing pays real cash, and is a use value of a sort; birdwatching pays imaginary cash, and has a value assigned by sassenachs who may never come north of the border.

A premium for insurance

Because environmental science is an uncertain art, most policy decisions involve a weighting for risk. Part of the answer to the question, "Ought we to do something about this?" is another question: "How likely is it to happen?" If sulphur dioxide from coal-burning power stations were undoubtedly the cause of acid rain, then the decision to install scrubbers would be a (relatively) simple matter of balancing their cost against the value people placed on forests. But there are probably several causes, one of them nitrogen oxides from car exhausts, and disentangling the main culprit will take time. In the meantime, governments have to decide whether to compel power stations to cut sulphur-dioxide output now, or to wait for harder proof. If power stations are indeed the problem, then the sooner governments take action, the less it will cost; if they are not, then governments are wasting money by making electricity dearer rather than petrol.

Many environmental decisions take this form. Not surprisingly, no single passage in the British government's environmental white paper of September 1990 proved harder to draft than the one laying down the proper approach to uncertainty. In the end, it set out a concept against which the government had previously fought tooth and nail: "Where the state of our planet is at stake, the risks can be so high, and the costs of corrective action so great, that prevention is better and cheaper than cure. Where there are significant risks of damage to the environment, the government will be prepared to take precautionary action to limit the use of potentially dangerous pollutants, even where scientific knowledge is not conclusive, if the balance of likely costs and benefits justifies it."

The "precautionary principle", the precept that it may sometimes be wise to take action before scientific knowledge is sufficiently conclusive to justify it, applies particularly where environmental damage is likely to be irreversible. Clean the sewage out of a river and the fish will come back; stop homes from burning coal and air quality will improve. Lots of important environmental improvements of this very sort have occurred in the past couple of decades. But once the rhino is extinct, no earthly power can reinvent it; once the Amazon forest has gone, it probably can never be replanted; once the world has warmed up, we will have to wait for the next ice age to cool it again; and once genetically engineered organisms have escaped, they may never be recaptured. The problems that most preoccupy environmentalists are precisely the irreversible sort. The stakes are highest, and often the costs of correction are highest, too.

Better than nothing

The greatest environmental dilemma currently facing the world is the question of what to do about global warming. A broad (though not infallible) scientific consensus predicts that the atmospheric accumulation of greenhouse gases will cause the world to become warmer in the next century, and the level of the sea to rise. No such consensus exists on the speed at which warming is likely to occur, or how far its damaging effects on the planet may be offset. Some food-growing parts of the world may see their crops increased, as plants flourish on extra carbon dioxide. Others may starve, if rainfall dries up.

If governments wait until they are sure of these costs before deciding whether or not to try to cut output of greenhouse gases, that output will certainly have increased. Reducing it will be more painful and more expensive. Besides, during the delay, more greenhouse gases will have built up in the atmosphere. Because they will linger there for years, the world will be locked into yet more warming. But it will be vastly expensive to reduce the world's output of greenhouse gases to a point at which future warming is not likely to be faster than the planet can bear. Governments therefore face an immensely difficult decision: to take some action now, and risk wasting money; or to delay, and risk more environmental damage.

Setting the costs against the benefits is hard when making the most important environmental decisions, but is better than nothing. It forces governments and voters to think in terms of broad orders of magnitude. Global warming is no exception. Those who write about climate change are usually more interested in how to set about stopping it than to ask whether it is worth trying to do so. Not many attempts have been made to quantify the costs of preventing global warming. William Nordhaus of Yale University is one of the few who have tried to set out both sides of the balance sheet. His attempt, discussed in Chapter 7 of Part I, has been greeted with horror by greens, but with understandable interest by governments.

Most studies of global warming begin by asking what pace of climatic change the world can tolerate. The answer comes in two parts. Species can tolerate only very slow change: beyond about 0.1° Celsius a decade, some would not be able to shift or adapt and would become extinct. Human beings can tolerate much faster change: their ability to cope will be determined mainly by what happens to world food production and to sea-level rise. To some extent, they may be able to adapt to both. Food output may be sustained either by growing different crops, or by growing crops in different places. Walls can be built against rising sea levels. Both adjustments carry costs, which will be greater for some countries than others.

An alternative approach is to try to quantify the costs of slowing global warming. That is also understandably difficult. Scientific uncertainty (about how fast the world will warm, and where the warming will occur) is compounded by economic uncertainty (about what will happen to world energy demand, economic growth and population increase over the next century).

If estimating the costs of slowing global warming is difficult, estimating the costs of letting it rip is harder still. Professor Nordhaus has tried to sketch in the other side of the balance sheet. He argues that only 13% of America's national output comes from parts of the economy even mildly sensitive to climate change. If sea levels rise, land may be lost and walls will have to be built, but over 75 years the cost would be only 0.1% of cumulative private investment. In the third world some farmland may be lost to sea-level rises and higher temperatures. But the fertilising effect of extra carbon dioxide might increase food output.

Professor Nordhaus's conclusion is that banning CFCs is sensible, and so are those cuts in carbon-dioxide output that might quickly pay for themselves through energy saving. But the sort of goals that European governments have set themselves, of stabilising carbon-dioxide output by the year 2000 at 1990 levels, will cost much more than the world will gain from avoiding global warming, and that is assuming the stabilisation is permanent (a point on which all governments have been remarkably reticent). It is also without making any assumptions about discount rates (explained below).

Greens hate sums of this kind. Professor Nordhaus, they point out, makes no allowance for the irreversible loss of species that will not be able to adjust to increased temperatures, yet many people would be willing to pay something to prevent such a loss. He ignores the possibility of sudden catastrophe, yet many kinds of environmental damage seem to move in steps, rather than along smooth lines. Economists find it hard to evaluate sudden nasty surprises. Most of all, Professor Nordhaus, at least in his earlier work, took no account of the double benefit from some carbon-cutting measures. If the world uses less fossil fuel, not only will carbon-dioxide emissions be reduced, so will acid rain, oil spills, open-cast coal mining, traffic jams, road accidents and city smog. Attach a value to just some of these incidental green goodies, and much of the cost of cutting carbon dioxide has already been met.

Irritating though Professor Nordhaus's arithmetic may be for environmentalists, it ought to concentrate attention on two points. First, as some carbon-cutting measures clearly pass the cost-benefit test (see Chapter 6, Part I), governments need to be persuaded to take these quickly. And second, greens need to ask whether the money the world may yet spend to check global warming might not yield even larger environmental benefits if invested elsewhere: on population control or the preservation of endangered species, for example, both of which yield returns today, rather than half a century hence.

Billing posterity

The passage of time is responsible for many of the complexities that arise in environmental policy-making. The benefits of good environmental policies accrue over time; the bill for setting them in train usually arrives at once. The idea that environmental policy should try to be fair to future generations is captured in the discussion of "sustainable development" in the next chapter. But being fair to posterity, in the sense that environmentalists mean, clashes with the concept of discount rates which economists (and business people) use to look at the value of investments.

Economists like to assume that a benefit today is worth more than the same benefit enjoyed in the future. Jam today is worth more than jam on Tuesday week, let alone jam the year after next. To have $100 today is worth more than having $100 in ten years' time, because today's $100 can be invested and earn a return, or spent and enjoyed at once. The higher interest rates are, the greater the value of $100 today compared with the same sum in a decade's time, and the higher the discount rate applied to the value of the money ten years hence. A business will tie up cash in building a new factory only if the return it is expected to earn when it comes on stream next year will be greater than it could have earned by investing it today.

On this arithmetic, long-term interest rates of 10% a year mean that it is not worth paying more than $73 now to avoid an ecological loss of a million dollars expected to happen in a hundred years' time. Even if interest rates fell to 2%, costs incurred 35 years into the future are only half as important as those suffered now. Using such logic, governments argue that it is more important to use up oil today than to keep it in the ground for future generations; and more important to sell teak forests now than to leave them standing. International aid agencies frequently demand that projects whose costs and benefits can be quantified earn a rate of return of at least 10% a year. One consequence is to rule out any forestry project that involves conserving or replanting mature forests, rather than planting fast-growing species. Trees that take a hundred years to grow make no economic sense at all.

Lots of other decisions with environmental consequences benefit people alive today at the expense of their children or grandchildren. Generating electricity from nuclear power leaves posterity to solve the problem of disposing of radioactive waste; using CFCs in an air conditioner keeps people cool now, but at the expense of a hole in the ozone layer for several centuries to come. The higher the discount rates governments (or businesses) apply, the more they are willing to pass environmental costs on to posterity. Benefits today become more worthwhile, even at the expense of costs incurred tomorrow.

Some economists argue that environmental decisions should enjoy a special low discount rate all of their own. They point out that the discount rate appropriate for individual consumers or companies may not be right for society as a whole. If it were, not a single school might be built, since the return on investing in a child's education would be too low compared with that on junk bonds. Plenty of social investments made by governments would never pass the test of a discount rate. Indeed many people in their personal lives work to make the world a better place for their children and grandchildren, effectively applying a negative discount rate by valuing the future more highly than the present.

But arguments for special "green" discount rates are a slippery slope. When governments have applied low discount rates to their own investment programmes, the effects on the environment have sometimes been disastrous. Roads, power stations and dams which are built by governments or nationalised companies often would never be built by a private company that had to raise its capital in the open market. Governments, which never (formally) go bust, are always able to borrow more cheaply than everybody else. They reward themselves by accepting lower rates of return for their investments. Once environmentally beneficial decisions are taken on special low discount rates, environmentally damaging ones may demand equal treatment.

Besides, for many environmental decisions the whole notion of discount rates is flawed. The return on a cost incurred today may be so distant that no sensible discount rate could justify it. Costs incurred today to reduce the output of greenhouse gases will slow global warming through the second half of the next century. Moreover, where an environmental decision has irreversible effects, the cost to future generations may be infinite.

Ultimately, it is easier to think of environmental issues in terms of ethics than of discount rates. Most people feel comfortable with the idea that their descendants ought to enjoy the same natural inheritance as they have themselves received. One survey[3] found that the most important influence on the environmental thinking of corporate managers, after public opinion, was their family. The best way to appreciate the concept of environmental stewardship is to remember that one's children will eventually inherit the earth.

Wasting money

Most of the time governments undervalue the environment. To the "Ought we to do something?" question, they reply, "No, it's not worth it." Plenty of examples, including many where governments could save themselves money by saving the environment, arise in the next few chapters. Sometimes, though, the opposite happens. Some policies are undertaken on environmental grounds where the costs vastly exceed the benefits. That is particularly true of policies whose immediate costs fall on companies in industrial countries. Companies, after all, do not vote.

Thus about $100 billion a year is spent in America on compliance with federal environmental regulations. The Clean Air Act of 1990 will add around $4 billion–5 billion a year to the costs of controlling emissions of sulphur dioxide from power stations to prevent acid rain. It is not at all clear that the environmental benefits from these measures will justify their cost. A ten-year study by the federal government, through the National Acid Precipitation Assessment Program, found that fewer lakes were acidified than had been feared; that acid rain had virtually no effect on agricultural output, and damaged forests mainly on mountain-tops in the north-eastern United States; and that it was hard to calculate harm to buildings. All these discoveries reduce the benefits to be expected from curbing sulphur dioxide. Paul Portney of Resources for the Future added in something in his study[4] for improved visibility and for a reduction in illnesses due to air pollution. Even then, he guesses at benefits totalling between $2 billion and $8 billion – in other words, maybe half or maybe double the cost of the controls.

Measures to improve air quality in towns by cleaning up car exhausts are included in those figures. These might, he thinks, add $19 billion–22 billion to the annual cost of compliance by the year 2005. The main results might be better health and gains in farm output. Add those together, and the overall environmental benefits might be $4 billion–12 billion a year. Controls to reduce toxic air pollutants from industrial plants will cost anything from $6 billion to $12 billion a year. At the very outside, such controls might prevent 500 cases of cancer a year. Trying to put a value on a human life is always difficult. But if each of those 500 cases were to result in death, the best techniques for valuing life would suggest the total cost might come to $1.5 billion. Add all three new measures together, and Mr Portney concludes that the United States may be committing itself to spending an extra $29 billion–39 billion a year (or $300–$400 for every household) to gain benefits worth, perhaps, around $14 billion.

Why are people willing to accept that? One possibility is simply that they do not realise what the costs are. One of the beauties of regulation, from a politician's point of view, is that its true costs are largely buried and that is even more true if the regulation falls on companies in the first instance, rather than on individuals. Another possible explanation is that people are prepared to pay an extraordinarily high price for each avoided cancer death.

One of the oddities of human behaviour that has played a big part in determining environmental policy is an apparently irrational attitude to risk. Sit next to an official from a green organisation in London and you may be engulfed in a cloud of cigarette smoke puffed by a campaigner berating the British government for doing so little to clean up the water supply. Cigarettes are responsible for 30% of all avoidable cancer deaths (plus plenty of deaths from heart disease and other causes); polluted drinking water, in developed countries, for well under 1%.

Much environmental regulation, especially in the United States, is dominated by a view common in the early 1970s that the "environment" was responsible for 80–90% of all cancers. Since then, epidemiologists have generally become convinced that only a few human cancers are caused by exposure to contaminated air, water or soil. The best estimates suggest that 2–3% of all cancers are associated with environmental pollution, and 3–6% with radiation. Work by the Environmental Protection Agency (EPA) suggests that up to half of all cancer deaths from environmental risks each year may be caused by one factor: exposure to indoor radon, a radioactive gas that seeps into houses through the soil. Just under a quarter may be caused by exposure to ultraviolet light as a result of the depletion of stratospheric ozone.

Work by Michael Gough of Resources for the Future[5] suggests that, at the very outside, regulation by the EPA might be able to prevent about 6,400 American cancer deaths a year. If cancer risks are estimated using a method employed not by the EPA but by the Food and Drug Administration, the numbers are tinier still. On that basis, the entire expensive panoply of EPA regulations might prevent a mere 1,400 of America's 485,000 cancer deaths.

Of risks and rats

Just possibly, the figures are smaller still; or environmental regulations sometimes expose people to greater, not lesser risks. This view has been repeatedly set out by Bruce Ames, a leading American cancer specialist and director of the Environmental Health Sciences Center at Berkeley, California. Environmental regulation has been based heavily on tests carried out on rats and mice. But those tests may be misleading. Of 392 chemicals tested on both rats and mice, 226 were carcinogenic in at least one test, but 96 of these – almost half – were carcinogenic in mice but not rats or vice versa. Common sense and Mr Ames both suggest that if rats and mice, closely related species, react so differently to different substances, then the entirely different human species may react more differently still.

Mr Ames also argues:[6] "Our normal diet contains many rodent carcinogens, all perfectly natural or traditional (for example, from the cooking of food)." Even if a food is natural, he points out, it may still be laced with naturally occurring chemicals that are toxic, as Table 5 shows. Most plants generate natural pesticides as part of their protective mechanism. Americans, he calculates, ingest at least 10,000 times more by weight of natural pesticides than of the manmade kind. Only a few of these chemicals have been tested on rodents, and many of those have turned out to be carcinogens.

Mr Ames is concerned less to stop people from sprinkling their food with black pepper or eating grilled chicken, both effective ways of eating large doses of rodent-killing chemicals, than to restore a sense of proportion to environmental policy. "The total amount of browned and burnt material eaten in a typical day is at least several hundred times more than that inhaled from severe air pollution," he protests. Sometimes, banning a product may prevent some cancers but raise the risk of others. He cites the EPA's decision to ban EDB, the active component in the most commonly used grain fumigant in

Table 5 Natural cancer-causing pesticides found in food

Food	Carcinogen[a]	Parts per m
Celery (stressed)	5-and 8-methoxypsoralen	25
Parsnip (cooked)	5-and 8-methoxypsoralen	32
Honey	benzyle acetate	15
Jasmine tea	benzyle acetate	230
Apple	caffeic acid	50–200
Carrot	caffeic acid	50–200
Coffee (roasted beans)	caffeic acid	1,800
Coffee (roasted beans)	catechol	100
Mushroom (commercial)	glutamyl-p-hydrazinobenzoate	42
Orange juice	limonene	31
Black pepper	limonene	8,000
Nutmeg	safrole	3,000
Mace	safrole	10,000
Cabbage	sinigrin (allyl isothiocyanate)	35–590
Brussels sprouts	sinigrin	110–1,560
Mustard (brown)	sinigrin	16,000–72,000

[a] Cancer-causing in rodents.
Source: Bruce Ames, quoted in *Financial Times*, October 9th 1990

America, after a risk assessment which concluded that, at the very worst, residues in grain might cause 1% of all American cancers. Yet peanut butter is a much more potent source of rodent tumours and remains unbanned. And EDB was banned without any attempt to decide whether the alternatives, such as food irradiation or more mould, might be more hazardous to humans.

Such illogicality in regulators has its counterpart in a deep illogicality in human attitudes to risk. People clearly feel more frightened by the remote risk of a large catastrophe than by the greater risk of an equivalent number of deaths spread out over a long period. Hence the greater fear of nuclear power-stations than coal-mining fatalities, and of aircraft crashes than road accidents. People feel more frightened by risks over which they feel they have no control than by those they inflict on themselves. Hence the greater desire for regulation of pesticide use than of alcohol consumption. One study[7] found people willing to accept risks from voluntary activities (such as skiing) roughly 1,000 times as great as those they would tolerate from involuntary hazards, such as food preservatives, that brought much the same level of benefit — as far as such different commodities could be compared.

Such human foibles will always complicate environmental policy. Better measurement techniques will bring no reassurance: on the contrary, it seems that lots of people find the idea of one part per billion more frightening than one part per million, on the innumerate grounds that a billion is a bigger number. Public education may help; better mathematics teaching certainly would. In the meantime, companies find it impossible to talk sensibly to the public about the concept of "acceptable risk": any cancer risk is unacceptable, which helps to explain the corporate pursuit of the impossible goal of reducing toxic emissions to zero described in Part II.

The people with the greatest power to reassure or to disturb are environmentalists. They have an essential duty to think carefully about environmental costs and benefits before demanding some new regulatory change. Irrational the public may be, but only up to a point. If people suddenly discover that large costs have been imposed on them to achieve environmental goals that have little value, they may revolt against the pursuit of goals that really are worthwhile. To win on toxic waste and lose on global warming would be a hollow victory for greenery.

References

[1] G. Pennington, N. Topham, R. Ward, "Aircraft Noise and Residential Property Values", *Journal of Transport Economics and Policy*, Vol. XXIV, No. 1, 1990, pages 49–60.

[2] Quoted in Per-Olov Johansson, "Valuing Environmental Damage", in *Oxford Review of Economic Policy*, Vol. 6, No. 1, Spring, 1990, page 46.

[3] Tom Nash, "Green about the environment?", *Director*, February 1991, page 42.

[4] P. R. Portney, "Economics and the Clean Air Act", *Jnl. of Environmental Protection*, Vol. 4, 1990, 173–78.

[5] "How Much Cancer Can EPA Regulate Anyway?", *Risk Analysis*, Vol. 10, No. 1, 1990.

[6] Bruce Ames, Renae Magaw, Lois Swirsky Gold, "Ranking Possible Carcinogenic Hazards", *Science*, Vol. 236, April 17th 1987.

[7] By C. Starr, *Science*, Vol. 165, 1232 (1969), quoted by Paul Slovic, "Perceptions of Risk", *Science*, Vol. 236, April 17th 1987, pages 280–85.

2

GREENING GROWTH

Newly green politicians like to tell voters that taking better care of the environment is good for economic growth. Some of them add a rider: poverty is the worst pollutant, and wealth makes it easier to clean up. The implied conclusion is that the richer a country becomes, the better care it will take of its environment. Therefore, growth is good for the environment.

Like many things that politicians say, most of this is too simplified to be true. Ordinary, dirty growth may well be quicker, as conventionally measured, than the cleaner variety. This is because economic activity generally takes little account of the costs that it imposes on its surroundings. Factories pollute rivers as if the rinsing waters flowed past them for free, power stations burn coal without charging customers for the effects of acid rain or global warming. The bill is left for others to pick up, including other countries and future generations. A truly green economy would pay such bills as it went along, instead of slipping them to posterity. To the extent that it had to forgo consumption today in order to bequeath more of the world's resources and rubbish-absorbing capacity to its children, a green economy would grow more slowly than a dirty one. Companies, consumers and countries externalise costs for good reasons: if they paid as they went along, their polluting activities would cost more.

A decision to invest in a cleaner environment is a decision not to invest in something else. Money invested in pollution control is not available for investment in other enterprises; people who run sewage plants are not available to make widgets for export; boffins who spend their days working out better ways to get rid of toxic waste do not invent money-making (and perhaps life-saving) new drugs. Because low-sulphur coal costs more than the high-sulphur kind, preventing acid rain means dearer electricity; because unleaded petrol costs more to refine than the leaded sort, cleaning up city streets means bigger fuel bills for motorists.

Such costs, though real enough, have so far been tiny even in the greenest countries (see Table 6). France and Germany each spend about 1% of GNP on environmental protection. In the United States, where spending on environmental protection is set to double over the 1990s, the cost is still unlikely to be more than 3% of GDP. Even the Dutch, whose national environmental plan is the most comprehensive ever published, expect to spend no more than 4% of GNP by 2010. It is therefore not surprising that the effect of increasing pollution-control spending on the growth of economic output also seems to be small. An attempt by the OECD in 1984[1] to estimate the effect by looking at the experience of some industrial countries found that such spending sometimes seemed to raise output (at most, by 1.5% over ten years in the case of Norway) and sometimes to depress it (at most, by 1% over 18 years in the United States). Either way, the differences were trivial.

The costs may be much larger for individual industries. As the second half of this book points out, the main expense of cleaning the environment in industrial countries has fallen on relatively few industries: chemicals, energy, mining, the motor industry and pulp and paper. The costs may also vary over

Table 6 Who spends what on the environment: abatement expenditure (% of GDP)

Country		1978	1985
USA	Total	1.6	1.5
	Public	0.7	0.6
Japan	Public	1.5	1.2
W. Germany	Total	1.3	1.5
	Public	0.8	0.8
France	Total	...	0.9
	Public	...	0.6
UK	Total	1.7 (1977)	1.3
	Public	0.8 (1977)	0.6
Canada	Public	1.1	0.8
Austria	Total	1.1	...
	Public	0.8	...
Denmark	Public	0.9	0.8
Finland	Public	...	0.3
Greece	Public	0.3	...
Ireland	Public	1.0	...
Netherlands	Total	1.1 (1980)	1.3
	Public	0.9	1.0
Norway	Total	...	0.8
	Public	0.8	0.5
Sweden	Public	0.8	0.7 (1986)
Switzerland	Public	1.0	...

Note: Data cover operating expenses and investment expenditure by government and the goods-producing business sector. In some cases outlays on charges and fees are also included. Coverage of data differs considerably between countries.
Source: OECD, 1990

time. America devoted a much bigger share of GNP to environmental investment in the 1970s, when quite a few green laws were passed, than in the 1980s. The same is true for Japan, where the brunt of environmental investment was incurred in the 1970s.

Figures for lost GNP take conventional measures of output at their face value. But as every undergraduate economist knows, conventional measures leave out lots of things that greatly affect the sum of human happiness, or even social well-being. They give no value to the unpaid labour of housewives, to the undeclared earnings of gamblers or to the unmeasured value of clean air and pure water. As this chapter explains, some economists now hope to find ways to measure national wealth that will concentrate the attention of policy-makers on what effect economic activity has on the environment. But even without greener statistics, it is clear that there is at least one sense in which taking care of the environment may indeed be good for economic growth.

Greenery involves a huge shift in consumer tastes. People want products that they did not want before. They want vegetables grown without pesticides, energy-saving refrigerators, aerosols that contain no CFCs. Such a shift in tastes is a tremendous spur to innovation at every level. It means new investment, new product development, new markets. Nothing is more exciting to industry, especially in the sated markets of the rich world. This shift in tastes may be further stimulated by tough regulations set by green governments. These will be an incentive to industry to develop new technologies in order to comply, which companies may then find that they can export when other countries come abreast. Such a use of regulation is one of the main themes of the second half of this book. Japan and Germany have both built large overseas markets for pollution-control equipment by driving their own companies to meet standards well ahead of competitors.

This source of growth will become increasingly important. Green leaders, whether they be companies or whole countries, will reap big rewards. But where greenery is fostered by regulation, there will be costs, too: dirty companies will shed jobs or close down or move abroad. Indeed, the 1984 OECD study (see note 1) found that the first impact of environmental spending was the most beneficial to an economy. In the short term, more investment in pollution-control equipment boosted output and activity. Only later might lower profits or higher prices erode some of these early gains. Countries may see this as one more reason for constantly tightening the screw. What balance a country strikes between gains and losses will depend on the way it has designed its regulations (as Chapter 5 of Part I explains) and on the ingenuity of its industry in turning those regulations into advantages abroad.

When ungreen means ungrowth

While sound environmental policies may increase output, bad ones may reduce it. They may carry real economic costs. Often the costs of environmental damage are measurable mainly with the ingenious arithmetic described in Chapter 1 (Part I), and often they fall in the future. But there are also costs that are measurable in terms of lost production, wasted investment or reductions in the productivity of labour.

Pulling together a smattering of representative figures (see Table 7), David Pearce comments: "The figures are subject to fairly wide margins of error, but I doubt if they are far wrong in telling us that the rich world is losing income equal to *at least* 1% of its gross national product, and maybe 5%, while the poor world is losing even more through deforestation and soil erosion, without even beginning to count the economic cost of water-borne diseases from water pollution and other environmental stresses."[2]

In industrial countries, the most dramatic examples come from Eastern Europe, where the environment has been neglected for 40 years. The result is ill health, damaged buildings, machinery corroded by polluted water. Most estimates put the total cost of environmental degradation at 10–15% of national income, though that is almost certainly too high, as Gordon Hughes argues forcefully.[3]

The costs of environmental damage are most evident in third-world countries where the environment is what many people live off. Typically, primary production – farming, fishing, forestry, mining – accounts for more than a third of their GNP, more than two-thirds of employment and over half their export earnings. Their natural resources are their main asset. From them, they must feed a billion more mouths every 13 years. Damage to their environment means damage to their largest single source of income.

Indeed, the failure of third-world countries to recognise the impact of development on the environment often renders meaningless the whole concept of economic growth. It profits a country nothing if it cuts down its forests to gain export earnings and extra crop land, only to find that the consequences are soil erosion, shortage of wood for fuel, an increase in floods and

Table 7 The costs of natural resource degradation to national economies

Country	Nature of damage	Year	% of GNP
Ethiopia	Deforestation	1983	6.0–9.0
Burkina Faso	Biomass loss	1988	8.8
Poland	Pollution damage	1987	4.7–7.7
Germany	Most pollution damange	1983/85	4.6–4.9
Indonesia	Deforestation	1984	3.6
USA	Avoided damage due to environmental legislation	1978	1.2
Netherlands	Some pollution damage	1986	0.5–0.8
Indonesia	Soil erosion	1984	0.4
Mali	Soil erosion	1988	0.4

Source: David Pearce, "Global Environmental Change: the Challenge to Industry and Economic Science", 35th Fawley Foundation Lecture, University of Southampton

damage to fisheries. Moreover, most of those costs fall mainly on the poor. So economic growth that relies on destroying the environment may enrich the most powerful, but may impoverish the weak. These uncomfortable truths are slowly beginning to seep into aid policies.

A paper drawn up for the Development Committee of the World Bank and International Monetary Fund in 1987[4] pulls together some examples of the way environmental degradation threatens economic development. Deforestation means that households have to walk farther to look for fuelwood. In the Gambia and Tanzania households already spend 250–300 days a year gathering wood, while in Addis Ababa fuelwood costs a household up to one-fifth of its income. Because wood is harder to find, people burn an estimated 400m tons of animal dung each year. That in turn robs the soil of fertility, and depresses each year's grain harvest by 20m tons. This lost grain, enough to feed 100m people for a year, would be worth about $3 billion in 1987 prices.

Deforestation brings other costs. As the trees go, soil is more easily blown or washed away. When trees are cut down along watersheds, floods become more likely: the flood-prone area in India doubled to 40m hectares between 1970 and 1980. The eroded soil is carried by rivers and chokes harbours and dams. One set of calculations[5] looked at 200 large dams built since 1940 and reckoned that a 1% constant rate of accumulation of sediment each year (probably a conservative figure) would cut the useful storage capacity of the dams by one-third between the mid-1980s and the end of the century. By the year 2000 the build-up of sediment will have cost these dams 148,000 GW of generating capacity. To replace that with oil at the low 1988 oil price of $15 a barrel would have cost more than $4 billion. And this cost of erosion will accrue for a single year – the year 2000 – alone. In each succeeding year this vast burden on poor countries will recur or grow.

Deforestation probably imposes the largest single batch of measurable costs for third-world countries. But nature's nemesis takes other forms. Water pollution is an infinitely greater threat to human health in poor countries than in rich. Pollution of the Rimac river, on which Lima relies for its water supply, has increased the costs of chemicals and disinfectants by almost 30%. Pollution of the Isser in Algiers and the Han in Seoul have both forced municipal authorities to move water intakes upstream. In Shanghai, the cost of moving a water intake for the public supply more than 40 km upstream was about $300m.

Development economists have realised only recently that environmental degradation may be a serious constraint to third-world growth. Aid policies in the past frequently encouraged environmental damage precisely to achieve faster growth. The World Bank, which began to take the environment seriously only in 1987, reviewed the influence of its policies and accepted that it had sometimes encouraged logging as a way to boost export earnings without taking account of the impact on soil, rivers and the livelihoods of people who lived off what the forest produced. But the Bank still finds it hard to lend only to virtuously green projects. It rejects the idea that all its country case studies should show how environmental damage may harm a country's growth and creditworthiness. And it finds that the sheer pressure to lend money means putting cash into ungreen projects.

The availability of water will be an increasing environmental constraint on growth. In parts of the Middle East the World Bank's environment department now sometimes recommends against development projects simply on the grounds that there is not enough water for them to work. The Middle East's water supplies, meagre to begin with, have been reduced by the demands of rapidly growing populations. Jordan and Syria are already close to the limits of their supplies, though Syria's population will treble, and Jordan's quadruple, by 2025. Saudi Arabia and Libya squander irreplaceable fossil water from beneath the desert to irrigate crops that they would do better to pay to import.

But that is not a purely third-world problem. In the mid-western and western United States water shortage is also emerging as a barrier to development. The huge underground Ogalalla aquifer, the great reservoir of fossil water that was discovered after the 1930s dustbowl and helped to restore the region's farming, is likely to be pumped dry in the next 30 years. As a result, rural populations are already falling: North Dakota now has fewer people in it than in 1920. Further west, the waters of the Colorado river are entirely committed; to squeeze another drop for new users will mean persuading some existing users to turn off their taps.

The limit to growth

The proposition that growth is good for the environment (as opposed to vice versa) is one that deep greens have long rejected. Growth, they argue, is the enemy of the environment. "If present trends in world population, industrialisation, pollution, food production and resource depletion continue unchanged, the limits to growth on this planet will be reached some time within the next 100 years." So argued the Club of Rome in 1972. Its report, *The Limits to Growth* (see page 14), took the view that the productivity of natural resources is fixed, and cannot be expanded indefinitely, an idea which has an older lineage. When economists first began thinking about the environment two centuries ago, they called it "land". Thomas Malthus and David Ricardo were both interested in what happened when population growth drove people to cultivate ever more marginal lands. They expected rising rents, diminished profits and subsistence wages. Neither set much store by technology as a way of raising agricultural productivity, by substituting man-made capital for natural resources.

In the event, it was technology that confounded the dismal predictions of these early economists. The invention of the steamship and the railway brought cheap food and raw materials into nineteenth-century Europe from the new colonies. Late Victorian economists such as Alfred Marshall virtually ignored natural resources, and concentrated instead on labour and capital.

The gloomy prophets who published *The Limits to Growth* were also rapidly confounded. One of their main arguments, that the stock of non-renewable raw materials such as oil and coal was being speedily exhausted already, looked silly by the mid-1970s when the price of both had risen dramatically and reduced the growth of energy consumption. They had ignored the ability of the market to increase the price of a commodity in dwindling supply, and thus encourage people to use it more frugally, or to find other sources.

An unrepentant group of economists continues to argue that the environment poses an ultimate limit to economic growth. The natural resources of concern here are not coal, timber or fish. The limits to growth are the capacity of the environment to deal with waste in all its forms, and the threat to resources are those which play no direct part in world commerce, such as the ozone layer and the carbon cycle, critical resources whose economic function is the most basic of all – that of enabling humanity to survive.

Economists such as Kenneth Boulding at the University of Colorado and Herman Daly at the World Bank base their philosophy on the workings of the laws of thermodynamics. The second law says that there will be an increasing tendency to entropy, a state of disorder from which nothing useful can be extracted. By implication, all recycling is inherently inefficient. To the extent that economic growth involves using up larger amounts of materials and energy, it means creating more waste. The only way to short-circuit this process is through recycling, and the second law implies that less and less of any material – or indeed of energy – can be recaptured with each recycling.

Breaking the limits

This glum outlook can be cheered up in two main ways. First, the structure of economic growth may be changed, so that it creates more human welfare from smaller quantities of natural resources. GNP measures any productive activity in which money changes hands, be it logging tropical rain forests or farming organic vegetables; buying a pack of disposable nappies or a ticket for an outdoor concert; working in a coal mine or installing a wind generator. Yet these activities have widely differing impacts on the environment. The extent to which economic growth harms the environment depends on what is growing. By setting prices right, regulation and educating people, economic activity may be channelled into less damaging forms.

It will not be easy. Economists think of three factors of production: natural resources, labour and capital. If natural resources are to be used more frugally without a reduction in conventionally measured economic growth, then one of two things must happen. Either labour or capital must be substituted for them. But in rich countries labour will also be in increasingly short supply. In most industrial countries in the next century, if birth rates do not rise and immigration controls are not relaxed, labour forces will stop expanding. The only source of growth will then be capital. That will be invested in the development and employment of ingenious new technologies to allow production to continue to expand. The companies that develop such technologies will prosper. But it will be difficult for rich countries to squeeze continued increases in GNP from an expansion in the supply of only one factor of production.

A second and related way to allow growth to be green will be by taking some of the proceeds of growth and spending them on protecting the environment. The waste that economic activity creates is not necessarily polluting, unless it exceeds the capacity of the planet to absorb it. By investing in environmental preservation, it may be possible to increase this absorptive capacity. This may mean researching techniques of biotechnology for waste-disposal sites, or installing proper sewage treatment in third-world cities, or building terracing to stop soil erosion. All these investments in environmental maintenance buy a bit of time.

That is essential. For while it will be hard to ensure that growth does not damage the environment, it would be just as difficult to ensure that the environment was unscathed in a society without economic growth. Sometimes, the absence of growth is environmentally benign: compare the largely undamaged rain forests of stagnant Guyana with the devastation in fast-growing Rondonia in neighbouring Brazil. Sometimes, the reverse is true: compare Poland, whose economy contracted in the 1980s but whose air and water still grew dirtier, with the cleaner air and water of most western industrial countries. It matters less whether economic growth is fast or slow than whether it is managed with environmental sensitivity.

Bad economics, bad greenery too

While policies to boost growth may not necessarily be good for the environment, some wise measures are good for both. For example, inflation, which is so damaging for economies, is lethal for the environment. Think of the concept of the discount rate described in Chapter 1 (of Part I) to see one reason. High inflation puts a huge premium on consuming now, rather than next year – let alone leaving something behind for posterity. In particular, inflation tends to drive people out of cash and into tangible assets. Most tangible of all is land, which as Mark Twain noticed, they ain't making any more. Inflation brings land grabs. In developed countries, that generally means property booms. A sharp rise in the value of property gives it an edge over the environmental value of whatever was there before, whether a street of Victorian houses or a piece of woodland. The arbitrary and underdeveloped techniques of environmental valuation have not yet shown that people put higher values on conservation in periods of rapid inflation; inevitably, a property boom shifts the balance in favour of development.

The environmental impact of inflation may be much more damaging for third-world countries. There, land grabs may radically change the way land is used, although the ancient use may have evolved over centuries as the one sustainable way of making the land productive. The best example is the destruction of the Amazon forest. Rain forest frequently grows on poor land, unsuitable for agriculture except in small cleared patches which are left to recover and regenerate after growing a couple of crops. One of the most powerful forces behind tree clearance has been Brazil's stratospheric inflation. Those with cash have bought or grabbed stretches of forest and then cleared it to secure a legal title and to discourage squatters. Having cleared the trees, the land-grabber can sell the land, make a quick profit, and buy or grab another swathe. The cleared land may raise a few cattle for a year or two, but tree-felling has frequently had little to do with agriculture and everything to do with land speculation.

More broadly, macroeconomic stability may be good for the environment. Tony Killick of the Overseas Development Institute argues[6] for two crucial links. First, stability brings confidence in the future. That encourages government, businesses and people to look ahead, and makes possible environmental planning which considers both immediate and long-term issues. Secondly, stability in the economy as a whole brings market stability. Price signals are clearer. It therefore becomes easier to use economic measures to make sure that polluters pay for the harm they do.

In a review[7] for the World Bank of the way economic policies affect the environment, Dennis Anderson concludes: "Ecological damage is sometimes less the result of externalities than of distortions in the structure of macroeconomic policies. However well designed and executed a [development] project may be, and whatever provisions are made for its immediate environment, it is quite possible that ecological damage is unavoidable outside the project's confines, in ecologically sensitive areas, if macroeconomic policies encourage it."

There are other ways in which bad macroeconomic policies can harm the environment, especially in the third world. When rich countries impose tariffs or quotas on the manufactured goods produced by poor countries, they condemn the poor to more environmental damage. Trade restrictions nearly always fall on labour-intensive manufactured goods; hardly ever on non-competing unprocessed raw materials. The effect is to force the poor to earn more of their living by squeezing crops from their land, or selling raw materials, rather than learning to live off the work of their brains or their hands. Conversely, when poor countries hold down the value of their exchange rates, in order to make imports cheap and keep their city-dwellers happy, they penalise those who grow crops for export. But export crops are sometimes (not always) perennials that grow on trees or bushes – coffee, tea, cocoa, rubber, bananas and spices, for instance – whose strong roots may be better at preventing soil erosion than crops such as yams, sorghum, millet or cassava grown mainly for the home market.

Worst of all are the multitude of subsidies with which both rich countries and poor encourage environmentally damaging activities. Chapter 4 (Part I) offers a long list, ranging from logging to electricity generation, in poor countries and rich. All these cost public money and distort economic activity, as well as causing environmental harm. End them, and taxes could be lower or government money spent on things that would increase, rather than reduce, the welfare of all its citizens: better health care, better education or better public transport.

A problem with subsidies is a problem with many bad environmental policies: they hurt the poor and powerless, and benefit the rich and influential. When economic growth has been bought at the expense of the environment, it has often gone hand-in-hand with an increase in inequality. That may be hard to measure, because the value of access to environmental resources may be unquantifiable. But take a couple of examples. In rich countries, the rise in car ownership has brought in its wake losses that have mainly affected the poor, children and the elderly. Public transport has become less economic to run and so has tended to be cut back; streets have become less safe for children to play in or walk along; new roads have been built through poorer areas (because house values are lower, so compensation costs less; and because the poor make less fuss).

More potent examples come from the third world. When logging rights are handed to the president's friends, they inflict floods or droughts on peasant farmers hundreds of miles downstream. When tribal elders privatise common grazing lands, the sufferers are the poor who previously fed their animals there.

In an essay, "The Environment and Emerging Development Issues",[8] two economists, Partha Dasgupta and Karl-Göran Mäler, draw two conclusions from such examples. One is that the commercial production of primary products in third-world countries is often underpriced, in the sense that it imposes environmental costs that are rarely included in the market price. "Countries which export primary products do so by subsidising them, possibly at a massive scale," they comment. "Moreover, the subsidy is paid not by the general public via taxation, but by some of the most disadvantaged members of society: the sharecropper, the small landholder, or tenant farmer, the forest dweller and so on. The subsidy is hidden from public scrutiny; that is why nobody talks of it. But it is there. It is real."

A second conclusion they draw is that "during the process of economic development there is a close link between environmental non-degeneration and the well-being of the poor, most especially the most vulnerable among the poor". When common lands are privatised (or, almost as bad, taken over by the state), often by governments eager to increase productivity, it is the poorest who suffer most. When wood becomes scarce, or wells dry up, the greater burden of walking further to find fuel and water falls on women and children. What looks on paper like faster economic growth may in reality be greater misery among the poorest of the poor.

Development economists have gradually become aware that it is possible to design aid projects for poor countries that meet both economic and environmental objectives. Terraces on hillsides may stop soil erosion and benefit farming; stopping industrial water pollution may improve fish catches. Above all, policies that help to reduce population growth mean a slower increase in the future pressure of people on land, and fewer people for governments to educate and care for.

A sustainable world

The idea that economic growth and environmental protection can be compatible has been captured in the phrase "sustainable development". Brought into debate by *World Conservation Strategy* in 1980[9] and the Brundtland report,[10] the appeal of the phrase is that it means so many different things to different people. Every environmentally aware politician is in favour of it, a sure sign that they do not understand what it means.

Although Mrs Thatcher came closest to a definition of it in her now famous phrases (see pages 15–16), Mrs Harlem Brundtland defined the idea less poetically as "development that meets the needs of the present without compromising the ability of future generations to meet their own needs". A British economist, John Pezzey,[11] has come up with an array of definitions culled from two dozen sources.

The main difference among the definitions is the extent to which man-made assets can be substituted for natural ones. Take the example of an entrepreneur cast away on a desert island which, by happy chance, lies on a busy trade route, in a convenient time zone. The entrepreneur cuts down all the trees and exports them to Japan, sells off the coral for jewellery and drills out all the oil. The proceeds are reinvested in building schools, homes and factories for a new Hong Kong, where everybody lives prosperously ever after on the products of their brains, high technology and imported raw materials. Is that sustainable development or not?

Certainly not, would be the reply of the three British environmental economists who wrote the Pearce report:[12] "We can summarise the necessary conditions for sustainable development as constancy of the natural capital stock; more strictly, the requirement for non-negative changes in the stock of natural resources, such as soil and soil quality, ground and surface water and their quality, land biomass, water biomass, and the waste-assimilation capacity of the receiving environments." Professor Pearce and Mr Markandya have also argued: "Sustainability ought to mean that a given stock of resources – trees, soil quality, water and so on – should not decline."

Others would disagree. Robert Repetto of the World Resources Institute says, "This does not mean that sustainable development demands the preservation of the current stock of natural resources or any particular mix of human, physical and natural assets. As development proceeds, the composition of the underlying asset base changes." Messrs Dasgupta and Mäler take the argument further:

When we express concern about environmental matters we in effect point to a decline in their stock. But a decline in their stock, *on its own*, is not a reason for concern .... There is nothing sacrosanct about the stock *levels* we have inherited from the past. Whether or not policy should be directed at expanding environmental resource bases is something we should try and *deduce* from considerations of population change, intergenerational well-being, technological possibilities, environmental regeneration rates and the existing resource base.

In other words, it all depends. Those who think that physical assets can indeed be substituted for natural ones tend to take a rosier view of technology than the Pearce school does. They point out that technology has steadily reduced the extraction costs of raw materials and increased the efficiency with which they can be used and recycled. Look, they say, at what happened to the gloom of Malthus or of the Club of Rome. As a natural resource becomes scarcer, its price rises, and more investment goes into conserving it and finding substitutes.

Economists describing the limits to substitution put less emphasis on the planet's stock of oil and copper, and more on its reserves of elephants and ozone. No technological fix (not even dark glasses and sun-block) is a satisfactory substitute for a damaged ozone layer. Nor does it make sense to talk of substitutes for extinct species. Moreover, says the greener type of economist, to use up unrenewable natural resources is to take a decision on behalf of posterity. Even if the proceeds are invested in manmade capital, posterity may still feel the decision was the wrong one. True fairness to future generations requires that we leave our options open as far as possible. But we cannot do that if a decision to deplete resources is irreversible.

No amount of political agreement that sustainable development is a good thing can gloss over other problems. How should resources be shared between this generation and its successors? The authors of the Brundtland report argued that sustainable development ought to mean not just intragenerational equity (fairness to our contemporaries) but intergenerational equity (fairness to posterity). But in the third world the very idea of intragenerational equity may be meaningless. In a poor African country, growing food today may mean leaving a desert for tomorrow. Does that mean today's farmers should starve, to leave something for their children?

Indeed, to bequeath to future generations the resources to meet their needs is easier to imagine in those rich countries where populations are no longer expanding. In Western Europe, where the population in 2025 may be smaller than it is today, the phrase may have some meaning; in Kenya, which will have more than three times as many people, it does not. Ought today's 5.5 billion people assume that they leave the 10 billion of 2050 the same stock of resources in absolute terms? Or per head, which means somehow increasing it while the demands on the planet mount?

Called to account

One way for governments to discover whether or not their policies are truly sustainable is by devising national income accounts that value natural resources properly. Conventional measures of national income ignore the value of the environment. They have no way to indicate that industrial expansion may involve air pollution, which may harm health and spoil views. Worse, they may lead governments to think that using up natural resources – by logging, for example – is a way of becoming richer when it may really be a way of becoming poorer. To tackle these drawbacks, economists have been trying to build systems of environmental accounting. Some accountants (see page 234) think that companies might eventually do the same.

Environmental accounts have so far developed along at least three distinct lines. One approach, pioneered in Norway and built on in France and Canada, tries to measure the stock of a country's natural resources, mainly in physical units such as acres, pounds and gallons, and to estimate changes in that stock over time. Norway's physical accounts, which have been published since the early 1970s, show levels of stock, discoveries, depletion and deposition of the country's main natural resources: fish, oil, forests, and so on. France has a more ambitious exercise, its Natural Patrimony Accounts, which try to measure not only stocks and flows of physical resources, but the way they are distributed by region and the way they are used by companies, individuals and government.

Such "satellite" accounts have certain shortcomings. If they are highly aggregated, they may lump together in a single acreage or tonnage wood from a variety of different species of trees whose ecological value is different; or they may describe in a single set of figures coal or minerals from whose mines costs of extraction vary considerably. But if the figures are disaggregated, they produce too much information to be easily used. Not surprisingly, it has proved easier to measure the quantity of physical resources than their quality.

Physical accounts are not generally intended as the basis for adjusting GNP. But they are the prerequisite for more sophisticated exercises aimed at creating a new kind of economic account. Here economists have taken two main approaches. One has been to try to extract resource depletion from GNP. If a country cuts down and sells its forests, conventional GNP figures register a rise in income, when in fact natural wealth has been depleted. The second is a broader exercise that involves trying to attach monetary values to all natural resources, whether or not the market place offers guide prices.

All monetary approaches run up against problems. To some extent, all involve putting a direct value on environmental quality or on changes in that quality. The problems with environmental valuation (see Chapter 1, Part I) are formidable enough when applied to an individual bit of greenery. To apply them on a national scale is even more daunting. On the other side of the balance, there is the question of how to treat spending designed to prevent or cure environmental damage. The effect of the *Exxon Valdez* spill was to increase America's recorded economic growth. The money spent on cleaning up Alaska was treated as an increase in national income; the environmental damage was unrecorded. How should "defensive" expenditures such as the *Exxon* cleaning bill be counted? Leave them in and the result is a kind of double-counting: national income accounts record as "growth" both the rise in aircraft traffic and the sales of double-glazing firms, or the sales both of pesticides and of water filters. But treat them as a negative and other questions arise, since most kinds of spending by the final customer are "defensive" in some sense. As one economist put it, "Food expenditures defend against cold and rain ... medical expenditures defend against sickness, and religious outlays against the fires of hell."[13]

Of the two main monetary lines of approach, the first is more limited but more practical. It takes its inspiration from the idea of income as defined by the late, great British economist, Sir John Hicks. He argued that income was the most that could be consumed in a given period without leaving a person or a country worse off than before. On that definition, true national income is "sustainable" income. National accounts capture that concept of sustainability where investment in manmade capital is concerned through the concept of depreciation. As the value of a factory or a piece of machinery declines over time, it is written off against the value of production. If a country's manmade assets depreciate faster than they are being replaced, it is clearly living beyond its means.

No such concept applies to natural capital. As it is used up, national accounts show no charge against current income to reflect the fall in future potential production. When Britain discovered North Sea oil, its accounts did not register a huge increase in its assets. Britain's exploitation of its oil has been measured in terms of barrels sold as an income gain, rather than a drawing down of capital. Had the national accounts treated North Sea oil as a stock of capital, they would have concentrated attention on the extent to which that asset had been drawn down to provide income, or to pay for reinvestment in manmade capital.

Such a measurement would have been useful for British voters in judging where their higher incomes were coming from in the 1980s. For developing countries, largely dependent on exploiting natural resources to survive, sums of this sort are vital. National accounts that ignore their natural resources effectively ignore their main assets. Mr Repetto sums it up: "Soils, water, forests, the gene pool and other natural resources are economic assets, in that they can generate a flow of future income. Mistaking a decline in that wealth for a rise in income is a confusion likely to end in bankruptcy."

Mr Repetto gives an example of a country where this danger is a lively one. The Philippines, now struggling with unemployment and foreign debt, has chopped down 90% of its old-growth hardwood forests since 1960. It has thus wiped out a resource that could have yielded valuable income in perpetuity, had the woods been carefully replanted as they were felled. Wood exports, the country's main foreign-exchange earner in the 1960s and early 1970s, have fallen abruptly, leaving the country with the prospect of a deficit through the 1990s. On conventional measurement, the economy of the Philippines grew by an average of 5.9% a year between 1965 and 1980. Some of this growth reflects merely the destruction of a resource, which has left the country with over 12m acres of denuded hillsides, releasing floods and silt into rivers and irrigation canals, and reducing food production and fish catches. What sort of growth is that?

Mr Repetto and his colleagues from the WRI have conducted an exercise in Indonesia to show how a developing country can make a start in measuring what is really happening to its natural wealth.[14] Indonesia is a country where primary production accounts for more than 40% of gross domestic product, more than 80% of exports and more than half of all employment. Indonesia's GDP (see Figure 3) grew on average by 7% between 1971 and 1984, making it one of the most successful middle-income countries.

Look again, said the WRI. Take three natural resources: oil, timber and soil. Put a simple market value on them, that of standing trees, of proven oil reserves and of productive land. Look at the rate at which those resources are being depleted – by logging, by oil sales and by soil erosion. Build that back

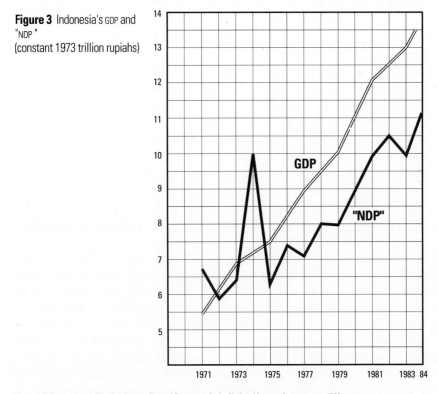

Figure 3 Indonesia's GDP and "NDP" (constant 1973 trillion rupiahs)

Source: R. Repetto et al., Wasting Assets : Natural Resources in the National Income Accounts, WRI, 1989

into the accounts to produce a concept of "net" domestic product. The results appear in Figure 3: a sharp rise in two years of big oil finds, but otherwise a slower growth than the unadjusted figures suggest. Suitably "greened", Indonesia's 1971–84 output growth falls to about 4%, still impressive, but more modest. For farming in particular, apparent growth has been won at the expense of future catastrophe. On overcrowded Java, where 100m people live in an area the size of Greece or of New York State, the soil swept away every year is worth 4% of annual farm output. The capitalised losses in future productivity are some 40% of the annual value of the output from upland farms. "If erosion losses are regarded as the cost of obtaining the current year's livelihood from vulnerable upland soils, then these estimates show the bargain to be harsh," comments the WRI study. "Nearly 40 cents in future income is sacrificed to obtain each dollar for current consumption."

A great virtue of the WRI exercise is that it stays close to the market place. Measuring the depletion of trees and oil is relatively easy. Measuring the value of lost soil is more difficult: it involves estimating erosion rates and then trying to piece together the impact of erosion on soil productivity. But by and large the study looks at market prices to make its point. It does not try to build into the value of forests a figure for their value as a habitat for species or a nice place to walk. That is a great strength over the attempt to measure the value of natural resources more broadly, ascribing values to resources that may play no direct role in the economy.

One example of this approach, developed by Henry Peskin,[15] treats environmental assets as though their contribution to economic activity were similar to that of conventional, marketed assets. The environment produces inputs (such as mopping up pollution), which are consumed by other productive economic sectors (such as companies), and generates outputs, many of them recreational services (babbling brooks, bosky woods), which are consumed mainly by households. The environmental damage that so often results from consumption is set off against the output side of the accounts. This kind of approach, though intellectually sophisticated, is less likely to be used by individual developing countries to examine the true environmental costs of economic growth. It may be more important in developed countries, where environmental damage frequently affects people's health and happiness in more indirect, intangible ways.

The main argument for trying to keep track of how economic activity affects the environment is that, as management consultants like to say, what is not measured does not happen. Governments that learn to measure economic achievement purely in terms of GNP may make awful mistakes. The more dependent their economies are on natural resources, the worse those mistakes may be. Rich countries need good environmental statistics; but for poor countries they may be a matter of life or death. In rich countries popular concern for the environment has in effect made the inadequacy of GNP as a measure of welfare a big political issue. If a building boom means the destruction of familiar countryside, or if increased car ownership makes towns less comfortable for pedestrians, then something unmeasured has been lost, offsetting some of the gains in measurable output. The voters in rich countries may increasingly prefer their growth to be greener, whatever the cost to the crude statistics. For poor countries, old-fashioned figures for growth – and for income distribution, too – mean nothing without some account of how environmental assets are being used, and who uses them. Before politicians make claims for the compatible merits of growth and greenery, they first need to know what is happening to their country's natural inheritance, and why.

References

[1] OECD, *Environment and Economics*, Paris, 1984.

[2] David Pearce, "Global Environmental Change: the Challenge to Industry and Economic Science", 35th Fawley Foundation Lecture, University of Southampton.

[3] "Are the Costs of Cleaning Up Eastern Europe Exaggerated? Economic Reform and the Environment", Centre for Economic Policy Research, Discussion Paper 482, London, 1990.

[4] IBRD (World Bank) and IMF, Development Committee, "Environment, Growth and Development", Paper No. 14, Washington DC, August 1987.

[5] David Pearce and Kerry Turner, *Economics of Natural Resources and the Environment*, Harvester Wheatsheaf, London, 1990.

[6] Quoted in Dennis Anderson, "Environmental Policy and the Public Revenue in Developing Countries", IBRD Department of Environment Working Paper No. 36, Washington DC, 1990, page 15.

[7] *Ibid.*

[8] Paper prepared for the Plenary Session of the World Bank's conference on development economics, April 1990.

[9] Published by the International Union for the Conservation of Nature, Gland, Switzerland.

[10] World Commission on Environment and Development, *Our Common Future*, Oxford University Press, 1987.

[11] John Pezzey, "Economic Analysis of Sustainable Growth and Sustainable Development", IBRD Department of Environment Working Paper No. 15, Washington DC, 1989.

[12] David Pearce, Edward Barbier and Anil Markandya, *Blueprint for a Green Economy*, Earthscan Publications, London, 1989.

[13] Comment by George Jaszi, quoted in Peskin and Lutz (see note 15).

[14] Robert Repetto, William Magrath, Michael Wells, Christine Beer, Fabrizio Rossini, *Wasting Assets: Natural Resources in the National Income Accounts*, World Resources Institute, Washington DC, 1989.

[15] Henry Peskin with Ernst Lutz, "A Survey of Resource and Environmental Accounting in Industrialized Countries", IBRD Department of Environment Working Paper No. 37, Washington DC, August 1990.

3

MAKING CONSERVATION PAY

Extinction is a chilling word. It is the ultimate in irreversible environmental damage. Technological ingenuity may clean dirty rivers; with changes in human behaviour, global warming may even be reversed. But the elephant or the whale, once gone, will be gone for ever. No miracle of genetic engineering is likely to recreate them, any more than the pterodactyl or the dodo.

And indeed, there in a phrase is the question. Why would any scientist struggle to bring the dodo back to earth? Like many wild creatures and plants, its value to mankind might be only as a curiosity. Humanity is no poorer, in harsh financial terms, for its passing. (Although even the dodo had its value. Most of the Calvaria trees of Mauritius were at least 300 years old, and seemed sure to die out. How to rescue the species? An ingenious botanist guessed that the trees' large, tough seeds had to pass through the gizzard of a big bird to germinate. Force-fed turkeys finally filled the dodo's ancient role and saved the trees.)

After years of arguing for conservation for its own sake, some environmentalists have changed their tune. They have begun to realise that the prospects for conserving species and wild lands are better if people can be persuaded that conservation can pay. However hard economists struggle to ascribe option, bequest or other values to nature (as described in Chapter 1, Part I), people are more likely to take conservation seriously if they see that failure to do so will cost them real money, while success will bring real rewards. In particular, local people will become the allies of conservationism only if they can see that it will increase their incomes to do so.

Disappearing diversity

This change has been prompted by desperation born of the realisation that species are vanishing at an unprecedented and accelerating rate. Calculating the pace of extinction is complicated by the difficulty of working out how much there is to be lost in the first place. Informed guesses at the number of species on earth, from monkeys to mosquitoes and from mackerel to mosses, range from 5m to 30m. Of these, only 1.4m have even been named and described. Many of those that are vanishing have not yet been discovered by man. A survey of 19 trees of the same species in a forest in Panama found 950 species of beetles, over three-quarters of which had never met a scientist before. That rather confirms the view of J.B.S. Haldane, the distinguished biologist who, when a theologian asked him what his studies revealed about the nature of God, replied that He appeared to have an inordinate fondness for beetles.

This biological wealth is now disappearing faster than ever before. Some reckon that 5–15% of all species will go between 1990 and 2020. Indeed, the number may be larger still if the destruction of tropical rain forests continues at the breakneck speed of the late 1980s. In tropical rain forests live at least half – maybe three-quarters – of all the species that creep or run, swim or fly, including 90% of the earth's insects. The Amazon forest alone contains one-fifth of all the bird species in the world, and in its rivers swim at least eight times as many fish as in the Mississippi and its tributaries. A small area of Malaysian jungle may contain more than 800 species of woody plants, about as many as live in the whole of North America. That is why saving the remaining tropical rain forests has become the top priority of many conservationists.

Earth's diversity of life increases hugely from the poles to the equator, with the result that nature is most varied in the very countries where human numbers are growing fastest and the pressure on land is greatest. The causes of extinction have altered as the human population has swollen. In the past, the introduction of new species and excessive exploitation were just as important a cause of extinction as the loss of habitat. People bring cats and rats which catch creatures unused to predators; they bring pigs and goats which eat plants previously ungrazed. Hunters despatched the dodo and almost killed off the sea otter. Animal and human predators are still great exterminators: one-fifth of all vertebrate species are currently threatened by new arrivals; one-third by over-exploitation.[1]

But loss of habitat has now become far and away the biggest threat. One sign is the way species are now being extinguished on mainlands. Three-quarters of the extinctions of birds and mammals between 1600 and 1950 were of island-dwelling species. Islands, where creatures can evolve and diversify in isolation, are especially rich in species not found elsewhere. Now, however, two-thirds of species known to be at risk are found on mainlands, and especially in tropical forests.[2] The great danger is to creatures that need a large range: big cats, bears and some tropical trees all need huge territories. Species that are found only in small areas or that are highly choosy about where they live are also at risk when their territory disappears. Often the survival of one species depends on several others. As a result, conservationists have shifted their attention from preserving individual species (such as the panda) to trying to save entire "eco-systems", with their intricate networks of insects, plants, birds and animals.

Why worry?

We might miss the panda, but it has no obvious economic function. Nor do all those beetles that vanish when trees disappear. Lots of people would sympathise with Ogden Nash's bewilderment:

> "God in his wisdom made the fly
> And then forgot to tell us why."

Conservationists turned economists reply that losses of biological diversity are economic losses, sometimes in a rather airy-fairy sense but sometimes measurable in real or potential reductions in people's cash incomes. Arguments like that tend to carry more weight with governments in poverty-stricken but species-rich countries than ethical exhortations to conserve for the sake of conservation.

Often natural resources have values that can be measured either in one of the ways described in Chapter 1 (Part I), or in still more direct ways. The products of wild nature are harvested commercially. Examples range from animal skins, ivory, fish and timber to resins, rattans, mushrooms and game. The cash value of these wild products is often the only way in which biological resources appear in national income accounts. In some countries their impact on the economy may be considerable. This is especially true for countries with forests: timber from wild forests has been Indonesia's second biggest source of foreign exchange, and teak is now providing Burma with a way to earn hard currency. Other kinds of forest products may also be important exports: two-thirds of India's forestry exports in the early 1980s came from products other than timber. That might be true for other forested countries, if statistics were available, but in practice figures on the value of forest products other than timber are rarely collated.

Local people may use wild nature as an important source of food[3] that may well pass through no market, and so not appear in national accounts. Without wild protein, firewood, medicines and building materials, though, people would be poorer; and it is possible to calculate with some precision just how much poorer they would be. For example, one study[4] by the New York Botanical Gardens of the net present value of fruit, latex and timber from a patch of Amazon rain forest looked at the price of these products in local markets. Using those values, it reckoned that a hectare of forest was worth $9,000 (but only $3,000 if destroyed and used for cow pasture). The timber alone was worth only 10% of the total, and if cutting down a tree for timber killed latex or fruit trees, that wiped out the gain from logging.

Forests are a source of food, fuel and furniture for the world's 500m forest-dwellers. In many African countries wild food is an important part of diet, especially for the poor. In Ghana, for example, three-quarters of the population depends largely on wild foods such as fish, caterpillars, maggots and snails. In Zaire, three-quarters of the animal protein that people eat comes from wild sources.

Amazonia is not the only place where the value of products harvested from the wild exceeds the value of the same land when used for unfamiliar domesticated animals. In developed countries the value of wild food may be tiny compared with the value of the industries that grow up around hunting and fishing. The market value of the hooked salmon or shot pheasant is a fraction of the amount their human predators frequently pay to catch them. Robert Scott, a rancher from western Montana, dreams of turning the cattle off the Montana great plains, where they have grazed for not much more than a century, and replacing them with species that preceded them. He yearns to persuade the owners of 12m acres, on which live 3,000 people and 350,000 cattle, to pool their land which now brings in a net agricultural income of less than zero (offset by the government subsidies on which people live). Fences would fall, cattle would go, and in their place would be wandering bison, elk, antelope, bighorn sheep – and hunters. The revenue from hunting fees, plus guiding, accommodation and butchering, would bring in perhaps $60m. Conservationists would have a wilderness, hunters a paradise and landowners a genuine income.

Wildlife tourism is another way in which protected nature can earn a cash return. Tourism, mainly to see wild animals, is Kenya's biggest foreign-exchange earner. One estimate gives each lion in Amboseli National Park a value of $27,000 a year in visitor pulling-power. The park's net earnings, mainly from tourism, runs at about $40 per hectare per year, a net profit 50 times as high as the most optimistic projection for agricultural use.

Nature as intermediary

Some of the functions of wild nature have enormous value in making possible other kinds of economic activity, but are nonetheless hard to quantify. Wild trees may pollinate domestic ones; wild birds may keep down pests. If either go, the cost will be lost crops, or money spent on developing manmade alternatives. One example is the brazil nut, which needs a particular species of bee to pollinate it, and a forest-dwelling rodent called the agouti to open its hard shell and allow the tree to seed itself. As the bee needs pollen from a forest orchid to mate, and the orchids need insects or humming birds to pollinate them in turn, the continued production of brazil nuts needs enough forest to accommodate bees, insects, humming birds, orchids and agoutis.

Other examples are marshes and wetlands, rich homes for wildlife, which often play an important role in purifying water supplies or preventing floods. One study[5] estimated that retaining a swamp outside Boston, Massachusetts, saved $17m in flood protection alone. In other countries coastal mangroves and coral reefs provide barriers against the fury of the sea and at the same time sustain valuable fisheries.

The functions performed by trees are even more profuse and valuable. Their roots stabilise soil and regulate the run-off of rainfall. Streams in forested areas continue to flow in dry weather and are less likely to flood when storms come. Their enormous value in preventing soil erosion has been recognised in Venezuela where the government recently tripled the size of Canaima National Park, which safeguards a watershed that feeds some of the country's most important hydroelectric facilities. In Honduras the 7,500 hectare La Tigra National Park guards over 40% of the water supply for Tegucigalpa, the country's capital. Rain forest has an even more important economic function, that of feeding rainfall as well as absorbing it. Cut down the trees and nearby regions suffer higher temperatures and more drought. The destruction of Africa's rain forests may well have caused the Sahara to advance, fatally impoverishing millions; destroy the Amazon, and large tracts of central and northern Brazil might suffer the same fate.

Making money from daydreams

Most of these uses for wild nature accrue locally. A price can be put on them without too much ingenuity. But there are other, less quantifiable ways in which natural resources may have considerable value to the human race as a whole, but where it is much more difficult to turn that value into earnings for the country which has to preserve species.

All those would-be tourists who will never go to Amboseli reward television companies, not Kenyans, when they watch nature programmes. Many medicines on the shelves of Western chemists have been developed from plants or (more rarely) animals and bugs. In the mid-1980s the value of prescription and over-the-counter plant-based drugs in OECD countries was put at about $43 billion. Tropical species are especially useful because they are often chock-a-block with poisons for scaring off predators. Those poisons – like curare, used by Brazil's Yanomani Indians to tip their arrows, and by doctors as a muscle relaxant – may be the active ingredient in modern drugs. But drugs companies have rarely put money into drug research in developing countries.

Wild species also play an essential role in restoring or replacing domesticated ones. The tiny group of domesticated species which account for most foods on supermarket shelves need to be able to draw on the gene pool in their wild relatives to maintain or increase yields. Ever since 1845, when potato blight wiped out the Irish potato crop, people have been aware that the genetic uniformity of cultivated plants makes them highly susceptible to disease and pests. Stripe rust in American wheat was defeated in the 1960s with germ plasma from a wild wheat found in Turkey. Russ Mittermeier, a former official of the World Wildlife Fund (WWF) in Washington DC, used to thrill American audiences by pointing out to them that: "Democracy in Latin America may depend on conservation in Madagascar. If rust hits the coffee crop, the continent could lose its main source of income. There are 50 species of wild coffee, many of them caffeine-free, in the rain forests of eastern Madagascar." The audiences particularly liked the bit about "caffeine-free".

Some primitive farmers recognise the importance of genetic diversity for agriculture by planting several varieties of a crop in the same field. Modern farming uses plant breeding for the same effect. Most domesticated plants and animals come from countries other than those in which they are most used. In America, for example, at least nine out of ten of commercially grown species are not native. They rely on wild relatives growing in other countries for periodic reinforcement. Only a small proportion of the wild relatives of many commercial crops have been collected and stored in seed banks (see Table 8).

Little-known plants, fish and animals sometimes turn out to be valuable foods. In Panama and Costa Rica attempts are being made to domesticate the endangered but edible green iguana. Quinua, once a staple grain of the Incas, now turns out to be one of the world's most productive sources of plant protein. Teosinte nearly followed the dodo. That is the name local people gave to a species of maize found in 1979 on a small hillside in Mexico that was being cleared. Unlike other known species of maize, this was a perennial, and it is now being used to develop a perennial hybrid for commercial cultivation.

But however valuable teosinte may turn out to be for commercial agriculture (and one study hazarded a figure of nearly $7 billion for the discovery), not a penny is likely to go back to the owner of the Mexican hillside. A recur-

Table 8 Wild species in the bank

Crop	Wild species held in all seed banks as % total holdings	Estimated % wild species still to be collected
Cereals		
Rice	2	70
Wheat	10	20–25
Sorghum	0.5	9
Pearl millet	10	50
Barley	5	0–10
Corn (maize)	5	50
Minor millets	0.5	90
Root crops		
Potato	40	30
Cassava	2	80
Sweet potato	10	40
Legumes		
Beans	1.2	50
Chickpea	0.5	50
Cowpea	0.5	70
Groundnut	6.0	30
Pigeonpea	0.5	40

Source: International Board for Plant Genetic Resources, estimates 1988

rent problem with all these returns on biological diversity is the virtual impossibility of turning these values into cash in the hands of people who might see it as an incentive to continue conserving. In the past the royalties on medicines made from useful medicinal plants have accrued to drug companies, not Yanomani. Several western schools of botany – including the New York Botanical Gardens and the Royal Botanic Gardens at Kew – now insist, before they will undertake a research contract on medical applications of tropical plants, that the companies which commission it agree to pay a share of any royalties to support research by local scientists. That is a big advance. But drug companies are rarely likely to use for long a plant that must be collected from the wild. Supplies are likely to be too erratic. Instead, they usually either cultivate the plant nearer home (which means in the developed world) or synthesise it. Either way, the plant's native country loses income.

Of all the ways in which nature makes possible more measurable economic activities, none is more important than its role in regulating the planet's life support system. Plants and plankton help to recycle oxygen, absorb carbon dioxide and regulate rainfall. Individual countries may make this possible by the way they preserve their natural resources; all humanity gains. As Chapter 7 (Part I) describes, one of the great dilemmas of the coming years will be to find ways to reward poor countries for their contribution to this public good.

Valuing existence

The most metaphysical of all the values that conservationist economists attach to nature are those that reflect the benefit people draw from simply knowing that wild things continue to exist. People in industrial countries especially may put a value on a species or a habitat they may never see – even if they know they will never see it. They may take pleasure in knowing that the oceans still contain whales and the Himalayas snow leopards. They may even attach value, however hazily, to the notion that these creatures will continue to exist long after this generation of human beings has passed.

One symptom of this is the size of voluntary contributions people are prepared to make to conservation bodies that hope to save wild species and places. The WWF, largest of all, receives nearly $100m a year. Another is the effort that people in rich countries particularly will put into conservation campaigns. More people in Britain protested about the blazing Amazon rain forest in 1988–89 than ever wrote about starving Ethiopians, suggesting that the British place a higher existence value on Brazilian trees than dying Africans.

In many ways, nature's benefits have a value not only for present generations but also for those as yet unborn. Extinction shuts doors. Plants that might have contained valuable drugs vanish unexamined; animals that might have been domesticated will never appear on any menu. The dodo, fat and flightless, might have made a better Christmas lunch than the turkey. In losing the dodo, we lost for ever the option to discover.

The economics of extinction

In the days of the dinosaur, extinction was an act of God. Now, it is generally an act of mankind. Understanding the economic forces that cause the loss of species is an essential first step to deciding what to do about it.

Hunting or fishing a species need not necessarily drive it out of existence. Although extinction can be caused by overharvesting, nature's renewable resources can be increased as well as decreased. However, no species (not even human beings) can increase to levels greater than the carrying capacity of the forest or ocean in which it lives. Human beings can harvest species because they can increase, and can continue to harvest them indefinitely.

As long, that is, as human beings do not become too greedy. A plantation of trees or a herd of deer reaches a point at which the harvest it yields is the largest that can be sustainably produced. That will not necessarily be the point at which the owner of the plantation or the herd harvests it: that will depend also on the costs of culling. For trees of a commonplace variety growing a great distance from the nearest road, those costs might be so high that the plantation would be left to grow beyond the point at which the yield was the biggest that could be sustainably reaped; for deer commanding a high market price and grazing next to an abattoir, culling rates might be higher than the maximum sustainable yield – though not necessarily high enough to wipe out the herd. The yield, in other words, might still be sustainable, even if it were not the maximum.

Such logic is fine for natural resources which have a single owner, whose rights of ownership are clearly defined and easy to enforce. But cut a hole in the fence surrounding those deer, or graze them on common land, and that will change. Just as a product that makes a high profit attracts new entrants eager for a bit of the gain, so a valuable natural resource can attract poachers. Once that happens, the danger of extinction hugely increases. It does not become a certainty. That will happen only if harvesting is costless – conversely, if the poachers risk a term in prison, the deer are more likely to survive – or if harvesting is persistently above the natural rate of regeneration.

That second condition is more likely to exist if a resource takes a long time to be replenished. If the trees in that plantation were not lodgepole pine but slow-growing mahogany, the owner would feel all the ungreen logic of discount rates discussed in Chapter 1 of Part I. The way to maximise profits might well be to chop the whole lot down, and replace them with fast-growing eucalyptus.

How do these conditions apply to species that are vanishing? Many can be "harvested" extremely cheaply. The elephant is a good example. Before most countries agreed to ban imports of ivory in 1989, four-fifths of the world's traded ivory came from poaching. Moreover, poachers have extremely high discount rates: they have little desire to curb their killing to stop a species from being wiped out. This is even more likely to be true if the poachers are poor and their quarry is valuable.

Sometimes a species may become extinct not because it is so valuable but because it appears to have no value at all (like all those rain forest beetles). Then, a habitat may be destroyed because it is worth something in its own right (as when a forest is cleared); if the forest contained something worth harvesting, it might stand a better chance of protection. With its habitat gone, the species goes too.

The threat of extinction may be greatest for places or crops that have no clear owner. Elephants in the wild belong to nobody; nor do whales. The ownership of tropical rain forests, where species extinction is fastest, is unclear. Where ownership is vested in the government, the effect may be to speed up destruction: no individual or group of people has clear responsibility for conservation. When ownership rights are weakly enforced, those who are able to pay most are those who exploit the resource, not those who value it most. That is why conservation, like so many environmental issues, has strong undertones of social justice.

From existence value to hard cash

Conservationists need to keep such points in mind when trying to slow down extinction. Conservation is a sort of investment: and like all investments, it carries costs. The trick is not just to draw attention to the many values of biological diversity. Conservation, for those who actually undertake it, is a matter of setting benefits against costs. If the benefits, as perceived by those who do the conserving, are smaller than the costs, then species will continue to vanish. In theory, the benefits may look promising: the countries with the greatest natural wealth are frequently the poorest, their people struggling to survive on subsistence agriculture. Surely it should be possible to live off all those valuable natural resources? In reality, the problems are often immense.

Some of the problems are created by governments. Many countries offer subsidies, set prices, or give tax reliefs in ways that positively encourage the destruction of a country's natural heritage (discussed in Chapter 4 of Part I). But even without perverse government intervention, it is often hard to devise effective incentives for conservation.

One of the most important things that has dawned on conservationists in recent years is that, while governments have tremendous powers to encourage the destruction of natural resources, the co-operation of local people is usually essential to conserve them. As Jeffrey McNeely's excellent study *Economics and Biological Diversity*[6] points out,

> Biological resources are often under threat because the responsibility for their management has been removed from the people who live closest to them, and instead transferred to government agencies located in distant capitals. But the costs of conservation still typically fall on the relatively few rural people who otherwise might have benefited most directly from exploiting these resources. Worse, the

rural people who live closest to the areas with greatest biological diversity are often among the most economically disadvantaged – the poorest of the poor.

Schemes to encourage conservation increasingly shy away from non-use. Instead, attempts are made to find sustainable uses that will bring in revenue for local people. When national parks are set up, people may find themselves driven out of land that they have traditionally harvested, while revenues from tourism go to the faraway government. In Zimbabwe's Matobo National Park, for instance, villagers are crammed on overgrazed lands around the park boundaries. Some villagers lived on the park lands until the mid-1950s, and their descendants regard the land as still theirs. Thatch is Zimbabwe's main roofing material, but overgrazing has damaged supplies. In the park, thatching grass grows so well that managers periodically burn it off to prevent a dangerous fire. In 1962 the park authorities agreed to let local villagers cut grass in the park, in exchange for agreeing not to poach wildlife or graze cattle illegally. A group of villagers is allowed to cut an annual quota of thatch. One bundle in ten goes to the park authorities (on the principle that people tend to undervalue "free" goods) and is used by them to thatch park buildings. A valuable crop of thatch has been cut by local people each year. Trespassing by cattle herders has been reduced and poaching minimised.

A more recent Zimbabwean experiment, in the dirt-poor northern district of Nyaminyami, began in 1988. Central government handed over to local people the right to manage the region's wildlife – and to keep the profits. In 1989 the district council hoped to make some Z$500,000 ($220,000) from sales of surplus game and licences for safari hunting. Within five years, it is hoped that sum will double. Meat from culling impala is sold cheaply to villagers, or used to rear crocodiles whose skins are exported lucratively to France and whose tails are served up in local restaurants.

In some schemes there have been attempts to bribe people more directly. The Wolong nature reserve in China is an important habitat of the giant panda. To try to reduce human pressure on the area, the government provided some $770,000-worth of food rations to 3,400 local people in return for carrying out one of a number of activities, including patrolling the reserve to feed starving pandas, building new free houses to resettle families from the most important parts of the reserve, and planting abandoned farm land with varieties of bamboo that pandas are known to like.

Of tusks and trees

Can the concept of sustainable use, rather than conservation, save two of the world's most endangered and precious natural resources, the large mammals and the tropical rain forests? Perhaps, though old-fashioned conservationists are sceptical. Take the example of the African elephant, whose numbers have been halved by poaching, falling from about 1.2m in 1981 to just over

600,000 by 1989. In some countries (see Table 9, page 65) the decline has been even more appalling: Kenya's elephant population fell by two-thirds between 1981 and 1989, Zambia's and Tanzania's by almost three-quarters. The beasts have been killed mainly for their ivory. So, in the hope of stemming the slaughter, a decision was taken in October 1989 to ban trade in ivory. The richest of the final consumers of ivory – the United States, the EC and Japan – all banned imports.

Splendid, said conservationists. In the wake of the ban, the price of ivory plummeted and poaching fell sharply. The elephant, it seemed, might possibly have been saved. Since trade in the skins of wild cats, including leopards, was banned, their numbers have greatly revived. On the other hand, since the black rhino was given the same protection in 1975, its numbers have dropped from 500,000 to fewer than 40,000.

Which fate awaits the elephant? The most convincing answer comes from a group of economists at the London Environmental Economics Centre (LEEC) in a study[7] they carried out in 1988–89 as part of the groundwork for the conference that eventually banned the ivory trade (see Table 9). They argue powerfully that a ban may eventually speed up the disappearance of the elephant from the wild, because it destroys one of the main ways in which governments could – if they chose – earn back the costs they incur in conserving the species. They suggest that the ivory trade has not caused the elephant's decline. The key factor has been the failure of African governments to use the world ivory market to their best advantage. A ban on the trade will not help, for two reasons. First, the effect will initially be to cause a sharp drop in ivory prices. That will encourage a new demand for ivory among potential importers previously priced out of the market, such as South Korea, Taiwan and African countries themselves. This trade will be unmonitored, because these new importers have not subscribed to the international convention that governs trade in endangered species.

Secondly, a ban destroys a possible incentive to preserve elephants. If elephants are to survive, they must be seen in Africa as an immensely valuable source of foreign exchange. The problem for the elephant is not that it lacks value. If it did, then arguments for saving it would be harder to maintain. Its trouble is that it is too valuable, and that it is, in effect, available to anybody who wants to risk killing it.

But conserving elephants has huge costs. Even if the ivory trade were indeed to be stopped effectively by the ban, elephants might still continue to vanish. "If they are not killed for their ivory, they will be killed for the land they occupy," argue the LEEC economists. Conserving elephants not only means forgoing the use of the land on which they forage. It also means spending hugely on preventing poachers. Zimbabwe reckons that it costs $200 per square km to protect wild elephants from illegal hunting. For Africa as a whole an effective war against poachers might well cost $80m–100m a year.

With a ban in place, only a few countries have an incentive to conserve,

Table 9 Elephant numbers: regions and selected countries

	1981	1989
Zaire	376,000	103,000
Central African Republic	31,000	27,000
Congo	10,800	25,000
Gabon	13,400	92,000
Central Africa total	**436,200**	**278,100**
Kenya	65,000	18,000
Tanzania	203,900	75,000
Sudan	133,700	21,000
East Africa total	**429,500**	**125,600**
Botswana	20,000	58,000
South Africa	8,000	8,200
Zambia	160,000	45,000
Zimbabwe	47,000	49,000
Southern Africa total	**309,000**	**203,300**
West Africa total	**17,600**	**15,700**
Africa total	**1,192,300**	**622,700**

Source: African Elephant and Rhino Specialist Group

and they are the ones whose tourist trade has been built on showing wildlife to visitors. Elephants are one of the mainstays of the Kenyan tourist trade. Properly exploited, they might bring in even more than they do. A back-of-an-envelope survey of tourists in Kenya, by Gardner Brown of the University of Washington in Seattle, found that the average tourist was happy to pay a $100 surcharge to protect the elephant. Even allowing for exaggeration, that suggests Kenya's 1m game park tourists could bring in an extra $20m a year in revenues, one-third as much as all Africa gets from killing the beasts.

The elephant's best hope of survival in other countries still lies mainly in its tusks. The aim should be to cull elephants at a sustainable rate and use the revenue to help to pay for conservation. One intriguing study (see Table 10, page 66) in Botswana compared the value of managing elephant herds just for the enjoyment of tourists wanting to view wildlife, with the value if tourism is combined with elephant cropping. The cropping reduces yields from tourism by about 10%, but leads to other gains, such as tanning elephant hides, ivory carving and producing meat for crocodile farming. The extra benefits almost double the total economic value of a herd.

Even larger revenues may be raised by selling hunters from rich countries the right to kill their own big game. The value of an elephant to a party of German sportsmen hugely exceeds its value to an ivory poacher. Zimbabwe has long found big-game hunting a lucrative use for its elephants. A group of

European or American hunters stalking one of the 100–200 elephants a year that are allowed to be killed this way can easily spend $15,000 all told, some of it going to local people who work as guides and bearers. That is perhaps five times as much as those same people could make by poaching an elephant themselves. Some hunters argue that their very presence, armed to the teeth with guns and field glasses, is a deterrent to poachers. They are probably right.

Above all, local people need to see the elephant as a source of income. As the LEEC economists argue:

> The history of wildlife conservation efforts in Africa has been dominated by a universal approach of divorcing local communities from any control or rights of exploitation of their wildlife. Wildlife utilisation, except perhaps for tourism and limited safari hunting, has been discouraged, and any safari and tourist revenues have gone to the state, not to local communities. The state's objective is to manage elephants and other wildlife for the benefit of the whole nation, whereas the local communities are denied access to protected areas and even to the right to hunt in areas neighbouring them. The incentives for the local population to engage in or assist in poaching increase, while their incentives to co-operate in reducing poaching or aiding conservation efforts decrease.

The best hope for conservation is to try to make sure that more of the gains from conservation come to local people. To achieve that, it is important to try to create clear ownership rights over elephants, preferably giving a big share in them to local communities. Up to now, conservation efforts have cut links between local people and the wildlife they once hunted; restore some of those

Table 10 Economic benefits of different elephant management options, Botswana ($1 = 1.8 pula)

Option	Net present value @ 6% (m pula, 1989)		
	after 5 years	after 10 years	after 15 years
1. Game viewing with no consumptive uses	34.7	98.1	160.6
2. Game viewing with elephant cropping	91.2	198.4	288.9
Difference (2–1)	56.5	100.3	128.3
Net benefits from consumptive uses[a]	60.0	110.1	144.4

[a] The difference between options 1 and 2 is only an approximate indicator of the net benefits from consumptive uses, as the introduction of elephant cropping reduces the benefits from game-viewing tourism by 10%. By allowing for this reduction, the net benefits from consumptive uses can be calculated.

Source: John Barnes, Department of Wildlife and National Parks, Botswana; quoted in Edward Barbier, Joanne Burgess, Timothy Swanson, David Pearce, *Elephants, Economics and Ivory*, Earthscan Publications, London, 1990

links, and hunting may return to sustainable levels. If local people have the promise of hard currency from the tusks of some of their elephants in future, they have less incentive to kill them before they reach maturity and breed. Better still, if governments can turn potential poachers into effective game-keepers, they save some of the cost of game-keeping.

Whose wildlife is it, anyway?

Because the African elephant is being driven to extinction by an international trade, its conservation needs an international solution. Many of the people who put the highest value on the elephant's survival, at least metaphysically, do not live in Africa. But with elephants, as with other wildlife valued by for-eigners, there arises the question of sovereignty. If the world regards ele-phants as something whose preservation is important to the whole human race, then a tussle may arise between the attitude of individual African coun-tries to their elephants, and that of the world at large. Richer countries may say, in effect: "If those are everybody's elephants – if they are a public good – we will accept a duty to help meet the costs of conserving them. If they are just your elephants, you cannot expect us to help."

Something of this emerged in the discussions over the ban on the ivory trade. Those countries that have been most successful in conserving their herds, South Africa, Botswana, Malawi and Zimbabwe, opposed a ban. They argued that their herds are not declining, and that one reason is that they are able to pay for conservation partly from the revenue they earn from exporting ivory and elephant hides from periodic culls. (Although conservationists argue that Zimbabwe makes most money from organising hunts for rich tourists. The ban on the ivory trade does not stop the huntsmen taking their trophies home.)

The LEEC economists vigorously support these countries, which have made a large investment in conservation, and now see the return on it under threat. To raise the yield from elephants further requires not the banning of the ivory trade, but its control. African countries are lucky enough to have a product for which demand in some rich countries is highly inelastic: in other words, even if the price rises, people will continue to buy enthusiastically. Exporting countries could easily increase their takings even without selling more ivory.

It would make sense for African governments to join together to form a sort of ivory OPEC, a cartel which closely controlled the offtake of ivory. That way they would gain a number of advantages. They could drive up the price, taking advantage of the inelastic demand. They could eliminate middlemen, who now take a large share of the profits of illegally exported ivory. They would have a new source of cash to help to pay for conservation. And they would make sure that the elephant survived, to earn money for future genera-tions. Such a cartel might stand a better chance than OPEC of surviving, because it is not in the long-term interest of the consumer of ivory to exter-minate the elephant. On the contrary, consumers may be happy to ensure the survival of the elephant by helping to make controls on the ivory trade water-tight, if they receive a constant but restricted flow of ivory in exchange. Only those who carve ivory, who make more money the more tusks they handle, have little interest in making constraints on the trade work.

With the ban, however, the elephant's future is uncertain. Temporarily, the collapse of demand in the rich industrial countries will discourage poaching. The price of ivory within Africa has fallen dramatically. Large new dollops of aid from the west are helping to improve the pay and equipment of park guards. The danger is that poaching will revive. New markets will be developed. Some people who in the past bought ivory legally will now buy it illegally. Some of the legal demand, in other words, will overflow into the illegal market. That will drive up the black market price, raising the profitability of poaching and increasing the risks that poachers are willing to take.

Returns on rain forest

The logic that applies to Africa's elephants is also being turned to try to save the world's vanishing rain forests. The core of the problem is similar. Rain forests have no clear owners; they are slow growing and expensive to guard; once gone, they appear to be irreplaceable; their trees, left standing, may yield long-term benefits to local people and to the countries in which they stand, but chopped down they yield quick profits to a lucky or ruthless few.

Forests are more valuable than elephants. A single species may be an essential link in a biological chain, as the dodo was for the Calvaria tree. But a habitat is home to a whole group of species, which is why conservationists now worry more about habitats than about individual species. Rain forests have all the values that elephants enjoy; they are valuable as a source of timber, for other forest products such as fruit and resins, and as a way to earn tourist revenue. They also have grander functions. They are home to many species of creatures and plants, as well as to indigenous people who frequently know far more about the use of species than do professional botanists. They protect watersheds by anchoring the soil. They store carbon dioxide, the main greenhouse gas (and release it when they burn). And they may influence rainfall in the lands around them.

Forests have been vanishing almost as alarmingly as elephants (see Table 11, page 69). Precise figures are hard to come by: just as counting elephants is often a hazy matter of checking piles of dung or of patchy aeroplane sightings, so deciding the precise extent of a rain forest and pronouncing the moment when degraded jungle becomes deforestation is a fine judgment. One set of guesses puts the annual rate at the end of the 1980s at 14m–17m hectares a year, out of a remaining 8m square km.

But why are forests burnt or chopped down? To manage them in a sustainable way for their timber is likely to be generally less profitable than clearing them and growing trees for pulp in their place. Pulp trees simply grow faster and are simpler to harvest. Timber alone, though, is not the only cash crop of

Table 11 Rates of tropical deforestation (m ha per year), 1980s (closed forest only)

	Late 1970s[a]	Mid-1980s[b]	Late 1980s[c]
S. America	2.67	9.65[d]	6.65
C. America	1.01	1.07	1.03
Africa	1.02	1.06	1.58
Asia	1.82	3.10	4.25
Oceania	0.02	0.02	0.35
Total losses	6.54	14.90	13.86

[a] Late 1970s data for the 34 countries covered in Myers (see below) from FAO, *Tropical Forest Resources*, Rome, 1981.

[b] Various years to 1986, taken from World Resources Institute, *World Resources 1990–1991*, Oxford University Press, Oxford, 1990, Table 19.1. In turn, the estimates are based on FAO sources, including an update for some countries of the 1981 estimates, and some individual sources. Note that the estimates cover closed forests only. Closed forests refer to dense forests in which grass cover is small or non-existent due to low light penetration through the forest canopy.

[c] N. Myers, *Deforestation Rates in Tropical forests and Their Climatic Implications*, Friends of the Earth, London, December 1989. Myers's estimates cover 34 countries accounting for 97.3% of the extent of tropical forest in 1989.

[d] Myers estimates 5 m ha per year loss for Brazil in 1989: the WRI figure for mid-1980s is some 8m ha per year for closed forest loss.

Source: David Pearce, "An Economic Approach to Saving the Tropical Forests" in Dieter Helm (ed.), *Economic Policy Towards the Environment*, Blackwell, Oxford, 1991

a forest. As the study by the New York Botanical Gardens (page 56) showed, non-timber products may be even more valuable. Some botanists hope that, by adding together the value of sustainably managed timber and non-timber products, they can show governments that rain forests standing are worth more than rain forests destroyed.

One of the most energetic proponents of this view, Ghillean Prance, is director of the Royal Botanic Gardens at Kew, in west London. Professor Prance has worked hard to help the Body Shop find forest products to sell. In one project, the University of Belem, at the mouth of the Amazon, is searching for seeds and plants for pot-pourris and aromatic oils; in another an Indian tribe is being asked to harvest brazil nuts. But processing the nuts and bringing them out of the forest will be costly. It will take at least five years for the Body Shop to make a profit on either venture.

Another enthusiast is Jason Clay, research director of a Massachusetts-based charity called Cultural Survival which has set up a company to buy and market rain-forest products. Mr Clay has found one eager customer in the Body Shop and another in Ben & Jerry's, a Vermont ice-cream manufacturer, which has launched "rain-forest crunch" made with rain-forest brazil nuts and cashews from nearby cashew plantations. Mr Clay has opened a small nut-processing plant in Xapuri, which is in the heart of Chico Mendes's rubber-tapping country. He hopes other products will follow. At present, not one factory in the Amazon area processes local fruit for export. He wants the processing and distribution to be owned and run by those who gather forest products.

In this way the concept of extractive reserves has gathered strength: tracts of forest set aside for sustainable activities such as rubber tapping, gathering fruit and nuts, hunting. Such ideas have their critics, who point out that such reserves will not preserve the full diversity of plants and creatures that exist in untouched forest. And while they may provide livelihoods for the families who still make their livings from traditional activities in forests, they do nothing for the many more families who scratch a living from unsustainable agriculture on cleared land. Rather than confusing conservation and capitalism, say these critics, better to go back to the idea of national parks, aimed simply at conservation, and to look for less damaging and more lucrative things for peasant farmers to do.

Even more risky – but also more lucrative – is to develop "eco-tourism". Costa Rica, for example, earned $138m from what was mainly nature-based tourism in 1986. The number of tourists arriving in Manaus, the largest city in the central Amazon, increased from 12,000 in 1983 to 70,000 in 1988. In the 1990s tourism is expected to become the largest single source of income in Amazonas state.[8] Clearly not every country is likely to be attractive to visitors (most would probably prefer to visit Costa Rica than Zaire). But most rain-forest countries have hardly begun to think of their trees as tourist earners.

It may be possible to harness market forces to save large tracts of rain forest. That is far more likely to happen, though, if governments do not give incentives to cut them down. As Chapter 4 (Part I) explains, governments have long encouraged deforestation in a number of ways: by giving tax credits which allow land speculators to offset the costs of clearing forest land for cattle ranching against income tax; by providing subsidised credit for crops and livestock; and by building roads. Underpriced electricity encourages countries to build dams to provide hydroelectric power. Mechanisation of agriculture, sometimes paid for by foreign aid and often supported by government grants, drives people from the land: in Brazil soya farming displaces 11 people for every job it creates. Some of the jobless head north, to the Amazon, seeking cheap land.

Poorly defined ownership adds to the pressures for clearance. Establishing legal title to land is often cumbersome. A Brazilian law (now rescinded) long allowed a farmer who cleared an acre of land to claim title to two acres. When Brazil first threatened to repeal this provision (and tax credits for cleared land, too) in 1987, the result was a surge of deforestation as farmers rushed to fell trees and grab extra land while they could. When agricultural colonists can win tenure this way, it is hardly surprising that they tend to win legal battles (and the more physical kind) against indigenous people. Some other far-sighted governments are now trying to give native forest people firm title to the lands in which they live, reckoning that this will encourage conservation. In 1989 Colombia bravely added some 23,000 square miles to 46,000 square miles already in Indian hands. The title to half the country's rain forest is now legally owned by indigenous Indians. Colombia's reasons are not purely altruistic: the indigenous lands are sparsely settled, inaccessible territories, mainly bordering Brazil. One foreign observer has described it as a strategy to "sandbag the border with Indians".

Transferring to forested countries the cash value that the rest of the world puts on their trees, might be the biggest incentive of all for conservation. A study[9] by Professor Pearce has a stab at estimating some of these values. He explores the possibility of paying a "carbon credit" to forested countries, to represent the value of protecting the earth from global warming by allowing growing trees to lock up carbon from the atmosphere. Attempts to estimate the damage likely to be done, mainly by sea-level rise, by global warming come up with a figure of $13 per tonne of carbon. Tropical forests appear to sequester 100 tonnes of carbon per hectare per year. That could be the basis for paying a carbon credit of $1,300 per hectare a year to countries in which trees were left standing.

But it seems that people in rich countries may be willing to pay something just to keep them standing. Professor Pearce reckons that the appropriate amount might be around $8 per adult per year, at least among the world's richest 400m adults in Western Europe, North America and Australasia. If all that money were paid into an Amazon Conservation Fund, the resulting $3.2 billion would be a quarter of the entire GNP of the Amazonia region.

Paying the preservers

These calculations may yet form the basis of policy. National governments will start to look for ways to pay exploiters to become preservers. In Britain the Country Landowners' Association has already thought up an ingenious scheme under which governments are invited to pay landowners for their contribution to conservation. The British government has already introduced a more modest scheme, under which farmers in areas designated as environmentally sensitive are paid to conserve stone walls, bogs and other uneconomic but ecologically benign aspects of their land.

The idea behind such schemes is that the countryside is a consumer good; consumers are the majority of taxpayers who live in towns; some of the prettiest countryside, which is what these consumers want, is created by uneconomic farming. So farmers can justifiably claim to be rewarded by taxpayers for preserving it. The snag, of course, is that schemes are hugely complicated to administer (in the British government's scheme officials are sent to hunt through meadows for wild flowers before deciding whether to award a grant), and are likely to bring counter-claims from other conservationists. Those who fail to knock down their medieval cottage may wonder whether they too ought to receive a reward from the taxpayer each year for their forbearance.

Such national preoccupations may eventually become international ones. People have begun to think about a bio-diversity convention, an international treaty which would, in some yet unspecified way, confer obligations on countries to preserve nature's wealth of biological diversity. Such a treaty would inevitably involve payments from rich countries to poorer ones in order to reward them for failing to destroy their natural bounty. But poor countries might find such payments led to a change in the way their natural treasures were regarded. No longer would the Brazilian government be able to insist that the Amazon was its national heritage, to plunder or preserve as it chose. The counterpart of receiving international aid would be the recognition that the Amazon was an international treasure. Brazil held out for some time against offers by first-world conservation organisations to swap its debt for money to be spent on saving forests. Such "eco-colonialism" is the counterpart of being on the receiving end of the metaphysical values that the citizens of other countries put on your natural resources. Developing countries may in time find it lucrative; they will not necessarily find it comfortable.

References

[1] Walter V. Reid and Kenton Miller, "Keeping Options Alive: The Scientific Basis for Conserving Biodiversity", WRI, Washington DC, 1989, pages 50–51.

[2] *Ibid.*, pages 41–45.

[3] This chapter draws extensively from Jeffrey A. McNeely, *Economists and Biological Diversity, Developing Incentives to Conserve Natural Resources,* International Union for the Conservation of Nature, Gland, Switzerland, 1988.

[4] C. M. Peters, A. H. Gentry and R. Mendelsohn, "Valuation of an Amazonian Rain Forest", *Nature*, Vol. 339, June 29th 1989, pages 655–56.

[5] Quoted in David Pearce and Kerry Turner, *op.cit.*, pages 332–33.

[6] *Op.cit.*, page xi, note 3 above.

[7] Edward Barbier, Joanne Burgess, Timothy Swanson and David Pearce, *Elephants, Economics and Ivory*, Earthscan Publications, London, 1990.

[8] See Dieter Helm (Ed.), *Economic Policy Towards the Environment*, Basil Blackwell, Oxford, 1991.

[9] "An Economic Approach to Saving the Tropical Forests", in D. Helm, *op.cit.,* note 8 above.

4

WHERE
GOVERNMENTS FAIL

Governments that are ideologically hostile to the idea of intervening in the market place sometimes see the environment as a left-wing plot to extend the role of the state. After all, one of the main reasons for environmental damage is the failure of markets to provide the right signals. Because clean air is a public good – nobody can be excluded from using it – nobody has any incentive to pay to use it. Governments therefore have to step in and set standards. Because Antarctica undeveloped is not a commodity that can be bought or sold, only government fiat can ensure that it remains undeveloped.

Thoughtful right-wingers like Mr Ridley (see page 17) accept that government has a stewardship role, which extends to the environment. Mrs Thatcher brought herself to accept the need for government intervention by drawing an analogy with monetary policy: just as government has a duty to ensure the stability of the value of the currency, so it has an ethical responsibility "to look after our planet and to hand it on in good order to future generations" (see also page 15–16).

Fallible government
A more down-to-earth point is that, while government may indeed often need to step in to make sure that polluters take full account of the costs of their actions, just as much environmental damage is done by government intervention as by the lack of it. In every country, governments deliberately subsidise the wasteful use of natural resources. This chapter looks at four examples: water, energy, agriculture and forestry, drawing on a series of studies[1] by the Washington-based World Resources Institute (WRI). By removing ungreen subsidies, governments would save their taxpayers money, and reduce environmental damage. Two for the price of one. Ending such subsidies ought to be a matter of commonsense economics. That ought to be consoling. But when did governments ever practise commonsense economics?

Such misdirected subsidies are most common wherever markets are most heavily administered. When government intervenes in an effort to set prices throughout an economy, it is usually tempted to set the lowest prices for the things which are seen as most basic. That explains why water, energy and agriculture are most likely to be subsidised. In the centrally planned economies of the erstwhile communist block, this natural tendency was further encouraged by the Stalinist emphasis on developing heavy industry. By channelling investment into heavy industry and energy production, the governments of the communist countries hoped to stimulate the rest of the economy. The main thing that was stimulated was pollution. Third-world countries make similar mistakes, although they tend to subsidise farming, especially by underpricing irrigation water and holding down the prices of fertilisers and pesticides. Western countries sin in rather different ways: they tend to use agricultural protection to subsidise agriculture, and tax reliefs to hold down energy costs. The effect, though, is the same: an incentive to environmental damage, provided at a cost to the taxpayer.

Watery grave

Of all nature's resources, none is more likely to be consumed at less than it costs to deliver it than water. True, people are as likely to expect the air to be free as to see water as a natural gift. But to breathe the air requires no piping or sewage treatment; water is rarely consumed without some intervening technology. And the costs of installing and maintaining that technology, almost invariably provided mainly by the state, are rarely recouped in full from consumers.

That is particularly true of domestic consumers. No European country yet charges all its households for the amount of water they use, although France and the Netherlands are moving that way. Yet the amount of water people use is closely related to the amount they discharge. If water were metered, more people would continue to wash their dishes by hand rather than buy dishwashers, or would buy washing machines with an economy cycle. But industrial customers are also frequently charged in a way that does not reflect the full costs of treating the sewage that their activities generate. In America the federal government began in the mid-1950s to pay subsidies to help meet the capital costs of building sewage facilities. Legislation in 1972 set the level of subsidy at 75% of capital costs. This has since been reduced, and is planned to be abolished by 1994. Not surprisingly, the effect of the subsidy was to encourage municipalities to build larger, more sophisticated sewage works rather than to press for better ways to reduce or recycle effluents.

An even more dramatic example of undercharging for water is found in irrigation, both in the United States and in many third-world countries. As irrigated agriculture accounts for about 70% of the world's use of fresh water, it needs to be efficient. At the moment, only one-third of the world's irrigation water helps to grow crops. The rest is wasted, often because farmers are not made to pay a price that properly reflects water's scarcity. Undercharging for irrigation does not merely mean an unjustifiable burden on taxpayers. It may mean that countries where water is scarce grow less food than they would do if water were shared out in a more efficient manner.

It is hard to see how the world's burgeoning population could have been fed without a huge expansion of irrigation in the second half of this century. A third of the world's food comes from irrigated land, although the area of cropland under irrigation is barely one-fifth. It has trebled since 1950, making possible the green revolution (two-thirds of all irrigated land lies in Asia). In the rest of this century, the proportion of food coming from irrigated fields will increase.

If, that is, there is enough water to go round. Irrigation has absorbed vast quantities of investment. Since 1940 irrigation projects in Mexico have taken up 80% of all public investment in agriculture. Aid agencies pour money into developing water for farming: irrigation mopped up 28% of all World Bank agricultural lending during the 1980s. In current prices, WRI calculations suggest, $250 billion has already been spent to create irrigation capacity in the third world alone.

Yet public-sector irrigation projects perform badly. They frequently take longer than expected to build, they have higher maintenance costs and they produce lower yields than those who plan them generally expect. Above all, they are a drain on government budgets. Virtually everywhere, the costs of installing, operating and maintaining irrigation systems are carried largely by the taxpayer.

Revenue down the drain

One study[2] of six Asian countries – Sri Lanka, Indonesia, South Korea, Nepal, the Philippines and Thailand – estimated that receipts from public irrigation projects covered on average less than 10% of the costs of the service (see Table 12, page 77). In Pakistan, the corresponding figure was 13% in 1984; in Mexico, 11%; in China, even after a sixfold increase in water charges, farmers pay less than a quarter of the average supply costs. Nor is this true only in the third world. In the western United States failure to recover more than a fraction of the costs of irrigation projects administered by the federal Bureau of Reclamation means that farmers have enjoyed in the 1980s an implied subsidy of $1 billion a year. In California's Central Valley, farmers pay less than 10% of the average supply cost of irrigation water. America's National Wildlife Federation, which has lobbied to abolish this subsidy, claims that approximately 40% of the subsidised water is used to irrigate crops that are already in surplus.

Everywhere, the consequences of undercharging are, predictably enough, overuse. A 1981 study of irrigation in the western United States found that over 30% of the area irrigated with federal water was planted with low-value crops such as hay, alfalfa and other pasture. Another study[3] found that almost one-third of the water used for irrigation by the Bureau of Reclamations leaked and was wasted: not surprising, as a survey in the 1970s[4] found that 85% of the Bureau's 14,000 miles of canals were unlined. Everywhere future supplies are jeopardised by using water extravagantly. In recent years the world's two main food producers, America and China, have both experienced unplanned declines in their irrigated cropland (of 7% in America and 2% in China). Overuse of irrigation water means that saturated land becomes water-logged. The salts carried in irrigation water are deposited on the soil as the water evaporates, eventually leaving the land too saline to cultivate. The dams needed to increase supplies alter the flow of rivers and may harm fishing. Wetlands and bogs that may be rich in wild fowl are unnecessarily drained, or contaminated (as in a notorious case in California) by salts flushed from over-irrigated land.

Subsidising irrigation penalises future generations as well as existing taxpayers. In 1986 the American Department of Agriculture said that more than a quarter of America's 8.5m irrigated hectares were being watered by pulling down the water table. Under parts of the north China Plain, around Beijing and Tianjin, the water table is dropping by 1–2 metres a year. In the Soviet Union the area covered by the Aral Sea has shrunk by 40% since 1960, mainly because of irrigation from the rivers feeding it. World Bank projects for intensifying agriculture, especially in the Middle East, are being stymied by water shortages.

Plenty of evidence assembled from the third world by the WRI study shows that farmers use water less efficiently when they are sold it cheaply by the government than when they pay an economic price to a private irrigation scheme. Often, charges are based on the area irrigated rather than the amount of water used: a farmer pays nothing extra to flood a field. Inevitably, when supply is not rationed by price, it is rationed by availability: farmers at the far end of a canal are starved of water while farmers at the near end have plenty. Rationing by availability gives power to those who control the rationing who are often local administrators or politicians. As farmers downstream would willingly pay more for their water than they are officially charged, to ensure a steady supply, there is lots of scope for corruption, and every incentive to clamour for lots more cheap irrigation.

Water for the wealthy

In a dry land, a supply of cheap irrigation water is obviously an important part of the value of a farm. In the United States, for example, a 1985 study found that the subsidy enjoyed by farms irrigated by Bureau of Reclamation schemes was worth 56% of the average market value of the irrigated land. Not surprisingly, one kind of corruption found both in the United States and in the third world is a tendency for big farmers to do best out of subsidised irrigation. A survey[5] by the US Bureau of the Interior in 1981 found that the largest 5% of farmers creamed off half the total irrigation subsidy, while the

Table 12 Cost recovery through direct and indirect irrigation charges relative to recurrent and total costs of public irrigation systems

Country	1 Actual revenue from farmers $ per ha	2 Operation & maintenance costs	3 Total capital & recurrent costs Moderate est.	4 High est.
		_as % of column 1 _/		
Indonesia	25.90	128	735	1,490
South Korea	192.00	107	550	881
Nepal	9.10	181	1,388	2,270
Philippines	16.85	83	443	984
Thailand	8.31	362	1,818	3,276
Bangladesh: major surface systems	3.75	500	1,000	...

Source: Robert Repetto, *Skimming the Water*, WRI, Washington DC, 1986 (see note 1)

smallest 60% of farmers were left with only 11%. An attempt to cap the size of farm eligible for subsidised water has failed: one 20-square-mile ranch in California was split into 15 units, all operated as one farm with a single loan, but each receiving federal water worth a total of $500,000 more than they paid for it.

These wealthy farmers in America and in the third world make up a formidable lobby for the continuation of subsidised irrigation. An attempt in Congress in 1990 to stop subsidised water being used to grow crops already in surplus was watered down. The forces that may ultimately bring sense to irrigation subsidies are not environmental. In California, where the rice crop consumes as much water as three cities the size of Los Angeles, water shortage is starting to hold back industrial development. In third-world countries the drain on the budget has become unsustainable: several Asian countries have privatised public-sector schemes; some other governments have begun to demand that irrigation agencies repay cash they have borrowed to finance new projects. The Philippine government cut grants to its irrigation agency, forcing it to depend on fees collected from users. In China local goverments have been made responsible for financing irrigation development. Poverty may drive third-world countries to pursue good economic sense, even if it cannot influence the United States.

Wasted energy

While subsidies for irrigation water probably enjoy the most cast-iron political protection, underpricing energy follows close behind. Indeed, more countries probably underprice energy than any other natural resource. It is not just that current energy prices do not reflect the many environmental costs of energy consumption: global warming, acid rain, oil spills, smog, and so on.

Frequently, energy is sold below world-market price, or below its long-run marginal cost of production. The effect may not be a drain on the national budget, in the way that undercharging for irrigation schemes may be, but it may mean that imports of energy are higher and government revenue from energy taxes are lower than economic efficiency would imply.

A study of over 30 countries conducted by the WRI in 1987[6] found that almost all countries intervened to influence energy prices through taxes, tariffs, subsidies and price controls (see Figure 4). Different countries tended to underprice different kinds of energy. Petroleum products, which account for two-thirds of the commercial energy needs of the third world (excluding China) were most persistently underpriced by third-world oil exporters. China and India account for 70% of third-world coal consumption; in both, it is heavily subsidised. Electricity prices are below long-run marginal costs in almost every country in the world. In the United States and a number of other countries, they are set to recover average costs plus a guaranteed rate of return, an approach which fails to reflect the cost of providing new generating capacity. One study[7] reckons that the reductions in economic subsidies that would accrue from proper electricity pricing in the United States are more than four times those that could be made in China and India together. Prices do not even recover average costs in Brazil and India.

Some supposedly green European countries devote large sums of taxpayers' money to supporting their coal industries, even though coal-burning is a large source of atmospheric carbon dioxide, the main manmade greenhouse gas. Before unification West Germany pumped DM12 billion ($7 billion) a year into its coal industry, by forcing power companies to buy coal from min-

Figure 4 Commercial energy efficiency and energy prices, 1983

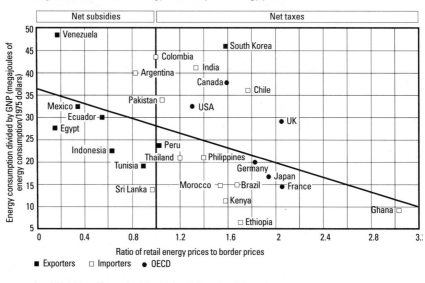

Source: Mark Kosmo, *Money to Burn? The High Costs of Energy Subsidies*, WRI, 1987

ing companies at prices well above market level, and reimbursing them through the *Kohlenpfennig*, an 8.5% levy on consumers' electricity bills. Another huge subsidy induces the electricity industry to buy expensive coke. Britain's government also effectively subsidises coal by forcing the electricity industry to buy the expensive output of British Coal. Spain, France and Belgium also subsidise their coal industries, thwarting the EC Commission's attempts to build a single market for energy and mocking the Community's commitment to tackle global warming.

Energy subsidies do not always take the form simply of holding down prices by administrative fiat. In poor countries energy consumers rarely pay tax but in rich countries, where most motorists do, governments often use the tax system to reduce prices to favoured motorists. Thus Germany gives tax relief to those who commute by car to work and in 1989 the Dutch government fell as a result of its attempt to remove such a tax relief from its commuters. In Britain drivers of company cars are taxed on the value of their cars at a rate that still makes it an attractive part of any pay package. Britain, alone among EC countries, charges no VAT on domestic energy; although (as the Association for the Conservation of Energy, which represents the energy conservation industry, frequently complains) building insulation does carry VAT. Sometimes the subsidy may take the form of limits to liability for damage (as with nuclear power programmes, whose liability for accidental damage is usually restricted by national law) or of cheap access to capital. France's EDF has embarked on a huge programme of building nuclear power stations, assisted by borrowings that amounted in 1990 to one-fifth of the entire French national debt.

Underpricing has a number of predictable consequences. First, it means higher levels of energy intensity. Low energy prices tend to encourage people to use more energy. One study estimated that prices explained roughly half the difference in energy intensity between countries: the remainder could be put down to differences in climate, wealth and industrial structure. The most striking examples of these differences come from Eastern Europe. There, energy prices were held down in the mid-1970s as a deliberate act of policy. When oil prices rose in the West, Soviet prices were held down. Communists regarded this as an advantage. In fact, development stultified. Just one example: cheap energy has meant that the open-hearth furnace, an energy-wasteful technology now largely abandoned in the West, still accounts for roughly half of Eastern Europe's production.

As Figures 5 and 6 show (pages 80, 82), cheap energy and the preoccupation with heavy industry means that Eastern European economies (including the former East Germany but not counting Albania or Yugoslavia) use more than twice as much primary energy per dollar of national income as even the more industrialised countries of Western Europe (and therefore cause more pollution). Poland, with on some counts a GDP smaller than Belgium's, uses nearly three times as much energy; Hungary, whose GDP is supposedly only a

Figure 5 Energy intensity, 1987 (gross energy consumption, kg of coal-equivalent per head)

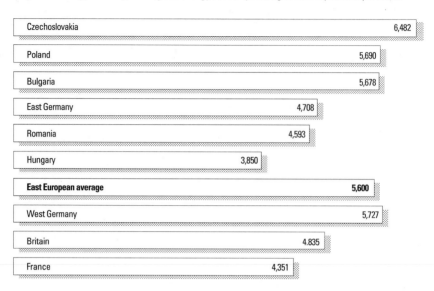

Czechoslovakia	6,482
Poland	5,690
Bulgaria	5,678
East Germany	4,708
Romania	4,593
Hungary	3,850
East European average	**5,600**
West Germany	5,727
Britain	4.835
France	4,351

Source: World Bank

fifth of Spain's, uses more than a third as much energy. Yet these are countries where car ownership is still lower than in Western Europe in 1970. Almost all the energy is used to generate electricity, drive machinery or to heat homes.

A second effect of chronic underpricing is loss of government revenue and of foreign exchange. In China, energy subsidies equal 7% of GDP and 20% of export earnings. In Peru, petroleum subsidies equal nearly three-quarters of the country's oil-export revenues. In Egypt, where energy prices are a ludicrous 20% of the world average, petroleum subsidies cost the government even more: in 1985, as Table 13 (page 81) shows, they totalled twice the value of the country's petroleum exports. Egypt uses massively underpriced electricity (generated partly by the Aswan dam) to support an aluminium smelting industry, even though it has no bauxite of its own. Energy subsidies mop up 13% of the country's GNP, making even China look a model of good sense.

Investment skewed

A third consequence of underpricing is that cheap energy creates economic distortions. It encourages capital-intensive industries at the expense of labour-intensive ones: foolish for countries with big, poor populations. It also diverts investment into building new generating capacity rather than using existing supplies more efficiently. Amory Lovins, director of research at the Rocky Mountain Institute in Colorado and a passionate advocate of energy conservation, reckons that expanding American electricity generating capacity costs $60 billion a year in private investment and federal subsidies. That is

Table 13 Energy subsidies and energy exports in selected oil-exporting developing countries, 1985[a]

Country	Energy subsidies ($m)	Energy exports ($m)	Energy subsidies / Energy exports (%)	Energy exports / Total exports (%)	Energy subsidies / Total exports (%)
Bolivia (1983)	224	329[b]	68	42	29
China	5,400[c]	6,600	82	24	20
Egypt	4,000	2,000	200	44	88
Ecuador	370	2,000	19	64	12
Indonesia	600	9,000	7	66	5
Mexico	5,000	15,000	33	70	23
Nigeria (1984)	3,000	13,000	23	90	21
Peru	301	410	73	20	15
Tunisia	70	690	10	41	4
Venezuela	1,900	13,000	15	95	14

[a] Economic subsidies = (average border price – average retail price) * (total consumption of petroleum products). Average border and retail prices are based on a weighted average of the prices of gasoline, kerosene, diesel fuel and heavy fuel oil.

[b] Primarily (99%) natural gas exports to Argentina.

[c] These are subsidies for fuel oil and crude oil only. Estimate excludes $10.4 billion in coal subsidies and $8.9 billion in electricity subsidies.

Source: Kosmo, *op.cit.*

about the same as the total annual investment in all durable-goods manufacturing. If conservation could keep electricity demand constant, then the capital available for those industries (or others) would be doubled.

For third-world countries, desperately short of investment capital, underpricing energy is especially dangerous: investing in new energy supplies leaves less cash to invest in other, more productive industries. In Colombia, for example, debt incurred by the power sector accounts for almost a third of all government-guaranteed debt. Yet petroleum products in Colombia sell at less than world-market prices. Multiplied on a world scale, potential savings from energy conservation are immense. A study[8] for a meeting of the Energy Sector Management Assistance Programme (ESMAP) in 1989 reckoned that, if 20% of commercial energy could be saved, total gross savings for developing countries would come to around $30 billion a year. That would be about 60% of the net flow of resources out of developing countries for debt service in 1988, and about two-thirds of official aid from OECD and OPEC countries in 1987. Those calculations take no account of the costs of making the savings: but ESMAP reckoned that about 10% of energy use in many developing countries could be saved in industry at no cost at all, and a further 10–15% by investments with a payback period of 1–2 years.

Finally, underpricing energy causes environmental damage. Eastern Europe's cheap power helps to explain why, as Figure 6 (page 82) shows, Comecon countries have an output per head of sulphur dioxide more than double that of the EC – and four times higher relative to GDP. (Another consideration is the prevalence of lignite, or soft coal, which accounts for high

Figure 6 Sulphur-dioxide emissions per head, 1984 (kg)

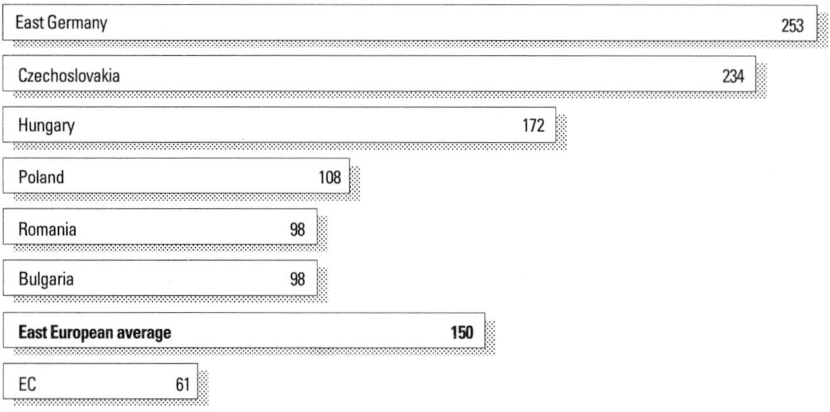

East Germany	253
Czechoslovakia	234
Hungary	172
Poland	108
Romania	98
Bulgaria	98
East European average	**150**
EC	61

Source: Zbigniew Bochniarz, University of Minnesota

proportions of energy use – 60% in Czechoslovakia – and which has the highest concentration of sulphur dioxide of any fuel in common use.)

Underpriced power in Brazil has played an important role in destroying large tracts of the Amazon area. Electrobras, the Brazilian government's power monopoly, has plans to build 18 dams by 2010 in the Amazon basin to provide hydroelectric power. A further 62 dams are planned later in the next century. All told, the 80 dams would flood roughly 100,000 square km in a region with one of the highest concentrations of indigenous people. Power tariffs in Brazil are, on average, much lower than the cost of energy production. This has inevitably helped to build up a concentration of energy-intensive industries: aluminium smelting, for example, is favoured with a rate for electricity that is roughly one-third that charged to domestic consumers.

The most lunatic electricity-generating project of all, the Balbina dam, has flooded 2,360 square km of tropical forest to generate an average of only 112.2 MW of electricity for the town of Manaus in the heart of the Amazon. "Were electricity sold at a rate reflecting its cost," argues Philip Fearnside of the National Institute for Research in the Amazon,[9] "people and industries would probably leave Manaus, thus eliminating the need for additional generating capacity." Instead, the power from Balbina will largely benefit international companies that have set up factories in Manaus, at the expense of Brazil's taxpayers.

Underpriced power does environmental damage on an even grander scale. Burning fossil fuels give off carbon dioxide, which builds up in the atmosphere, trapping the sun's returning rays and helping to warm up the planet. If carbon-based fuels were priced to reflect the private opportunity cost of producing them (world prices, in the case of traded fuels, and long-run marginal cost in the case of electricity), then less carbon dioxide would be sent into the atmosphere. People would use fuel more sparingly.

How much more sparingly? In 1990 Joanne Burgess did some rough sums for 11 countries, mainly in the third world, but including United States, China and India.[10] Looking only at the electricity industry, she found that the total annual reduction in carbon dioxide for those countries that would be achieved by pricing to reflect private opportunity cost would come to 145m tonnes, or just under 3% of the global total of carbon dioxide given off by burning fossil fuels each year. Such pricing would still be too low to reflect the costs imposed by burning fossil fuels on the environment. But the figures suggest that energy pricing that makes sense economically also starts to make sense environmentally.

Farming on the cheap

Once, farmers seemed the natural stewards of the land. The romantic vision, fostered by all those childhood books about charming farmyard animals, and those television advertisements for country-fresh margarine, has become increasingly at odds with farming in the first world. The apparent harmony between caring for nature and feeding the populace has made farm subsidies far harder to eradicate than protection for nasty, dirty industry. Only slowly have people in developed countries begun to feel that the urban majority has rights to the countryside, too, and to realise that the kind of countryside that taxpaying townspeople want may be harmed by the way farming is subsidised.

Governments subsidise farmers in many ways. In poor countries they frequently receive cut-price credit, pesticides and fertilisers. In rich countries, they get grants or – harder to value but often more valuable – trade protection. The way the state gives cash to farmers influences the way they farm, and therefore the effect they have on the environment.

To squeeze more output from their soil, farmers in both rich and poor countries have applied increasing quantities of pesticides and artificial fertilisers. The damage done by agricultural chemicals to human health is easily exaggerated. Figures are hard to come by, but deaths from pesticide poisoning seem to be between 3,000 and 20,000 a year, almost all of them in developing countries. Artificial pesticides and fertilisers have between them saved from starvation many more lives than they have cost through misuse. But farmers in first-world countries increasingly worry about the contamination of rural wells. And other kinds of environmental damage may occur if chemicals are wrongly used.

The chemical treadmill

Thus excessive use of pesticides puts farmers on a chemical treadmill: bugs and weeds become more resistant to poisons, and so next year's poisons must be more lethal. Use of artificial fertilisers may make possible the growing of single crops without allowing the ground to recover in traditional ways, by rotating crops or allowing the land to lie fallow. Crops grown in monoculture tend to be more susceptible to pests – and thus to need more pesticides – than those grown in more old-fashioned ways.

Failure to rotate crops may also may make soil erosion worse; although in the United States, where soil erosion has been studied most carefully, the evidence is mixed. A study in 1982[11] found that about one-fifth of cropland was losing topsoil at a rate likely to cause a decline in productivity; though a subsequent study, by the Department of Agriculture in 1989,[12] found that even in the north-east, the area worst affected, productivity had fallen by only 7% in a hundred years. That is less than four years' growth of productivity. More important than loss of soil productivity may be the effects of erosion on streams and air, both of which are likely to be polluted in ways that raise society's costs, but not those of farmers.

The use of artificial fertilisers and pesticides in rich countries and poor has been rising. A study by the OECD[13] pointed out that fertiliser use has trebled in the United States over the past quarter century, doubled in Denmark and increased in the Netherlands by 150%. The quantity of pesticides applied has risen, too: by 69% since 1975 in Denmark, for example, with a rise of 115% in the frequency of application between 1981 and 1984. As Figure 7 shows, pesticides and fertilisers account for over half the cost of American corn crops.

Recently pesticide use has begun to level off or fall in developed countries, as chemicals with more precise effects have become available. America's pesticide consumption dropped 20% between 1973 and 1983. But farmers still frequently spread more chemicals on their crops than they need. A study[14] by America's National Research Council (NRC), published in 1989, reckoned

Figure 7 Average American cost of pesticides and fertilisers, seed and fuel as % of total variable and of total variable and fixed costs by crop, 1986

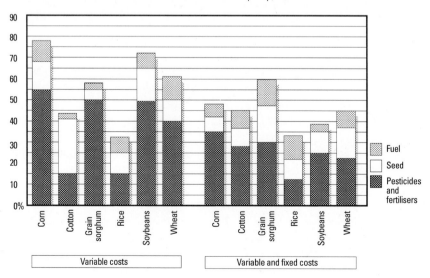

Source: National Research Council, *Alternative Agriculture*, Washington DC, 1989

that 25–70% of the nitrogen spread on crops was absorbed by plants. Much of the rest ends up in rivers and lakes.

What causes such waste? For waste is what much of it is. Over half the nitrogenous fertilisers applied to crops in America's corn belt are not needed to achieve maximum profits. A study[15] by the International Rice Research Institute of pesticide use by farmers in the Philippines found that even moderate applications of pesticides on pest-resistant varieties of rice frequently cost farmers more than they saved.

The answer usually lies mainly in the system of farm support. Pesticides are heavily subsidised in most developing countries. That kicks away any incentive to develop more labour-intensive ways of dealing with pests even though these may, in the long run, be more effective and may make better sense in the labour-rich countries of the third world. A study of nine developing countries by the WRI[16] found the median level of subsidy was 44% of the total retail cost. In Senegal, where subsidies were highest, they accounted for an average of 89% of the full retail cost. Like water subsidies, such subsidies go mainly to bigger farmers. That is especially true in countries outside Asia, where pesticides are mainly used on cash crops, which tend to be grown on big estates. And of course, it is usually hired landless labourers who get poisoned.

The cost of such subsidies falls on taxpayers. As low prices encourage farmers to use more pesticides, so the burden on the taxpayer rises. In Indonesia, where the WRI study estimated that subsidies for pesticides used on food and other annual crops accounted on average for 82% of their retail price, pesti-

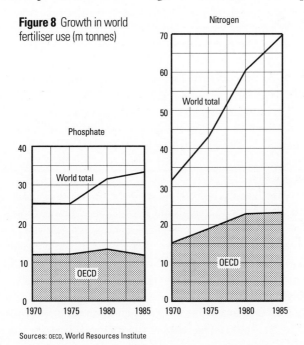

Figure 8 Growth in world fertiliser use (m tonnes)

Sources: OECD, World Resources Institute

cide use trebled between 1978 and 1982. In 1985–90 subsidies were expected to cost the government at least $1 billion.

Artificial fertilisers also tend to attract heavy subsidies, often from aid donors. In developed countries, the aid donor tends to be the agriculture department or – in the EC – the Common Agricultural Policy (CAP). It may be that farm support inevitably encourages monoculture, with its attendant rise in chemical use. Fear of fluctuating prices once led farmers to hedge their bets, keeping pigs in their orchards and cows on their stubble fields. Simply by providing farmers with the insurance against loss of income that once came only by raising lots of different crops, farm support removes some of the need for diversity. That in itself can be environmentally harmful.

Ungreen support

Certainly, the pattern of farm support frequently rewards high yields per acre, regardless of the effect on the environment. By supporting the prices of agricultural products, governments do not ensure that farmers get higher incomes – or not for long. Subsidies and price supports are quickly capitalised into the value of agricultural land. Buying a farm becomes tantamount to buying the right to receive a subsidy. Farmers must squeeze every last drop of output from their land in order to earn back the large investment that they now have to make to buy the land. That may mean draining wetlands, destroying woodlands, cutting down hedgerows or closing footpaths. Capital grants and tax reliefs encourage more capital investment – including farm buildings, which in Britain are not controlled by planning regulations – than would otherwise occur. Farming becomes more capital-intensive, less labour-intensive. By raising the value of farm land, price supports drive up the cost of not maximising the cash return on it, that is, the crops it produces, plus the subsidy it attracts.

The cash crops from a farm in the shape of food and subsidies are frequently substitutes for what one might think of as environmental services: public access, woodlands, hedgerows, unsprayed corners of fields. As the return on the cash crops rises, so the cost to a farmer of producing these non-cash crops increases. The lost income is greater. So the more a government spends on price support, the less willing farmers are likely to be to farm in environmentally friendly ways.

More intensive farming has helped to wipe out habitats and rare species. Almost all the dry chalk grasslands of Champagne in France have disappeared over the past 30 years; in Germany grassland intensification threatens 45 species of butterflies; in Britain 80% of chalk downland and half of all lowland bogs and marshes have vanished or been damaged since 1945. Most of these losses are due to more intensive farming. Not surprisingly, the Council for the Protection of Rural England and the WWF have begun to attack the CAP. They point out that all this environmental damage is expensive for taxpayers and shoppers alike. The costs of the policy to Britain, in government revenue and in cheaper food forgone, are double the benefits; while for the EC as a whole costs exceed benefits by 30%.

Price supports also indirectly encourage the use of fertiliser. Agriculture in the developed world is one of the most energy-intensive and chemical-intensive industries, and any pressure to increase output is likely to raise the use of these crucial inputs. Fertiliser is, in a sense, a substitute for land: if farmers cannot raise their output by buying extra fields, then applying more fertiliser is a partial alternative. High land prices, by raising the incentive to increase output, encourage the application of more fertiliser. One study[17] estimates that a 1% rise in the price of land relative to the price of fertiliser increases fertiliser use by 1.4% in the United States and by 0.4% in Japan.

The way agricultural support is administered in the United States has almost certainly aggravated soil erosion. As the NRC report pointed out, farm support has been based on the average acreage devoted to a particular crop over the previous five years. That is a powerful disincentive to rotating crops and avoiding erosion. Between 40% and 45% of the American maize crop is now grown in continuous monoculture, planted on the same tired land year after year. Not surprisingly maize, together with wheat, accounts for half of all the nitrogen fertiliser used in the United States.

By paying farmers for higher yields, agricultural support effectively tips the balance in favour of farming today and against farming tomorrow. It makes it more attractive for farmers to use up soil fertility now, rather than farming conservatively. Indeed, it would be entirely rational for any farmer who had watched negotiations to curb spending under the CAP, or under the GATT Uruguay round, to farm even more unsustainably, on the grounds that the present rate of farm support will probably not last. Better make hay while the sun shines and grab as much support as possible today, accepting that in future the rate of return may be lower. Thus do farm ministers exacerbate the environmentally unfriendly workings of high discount rates (explained in Chapter 1). As Alan Winters put it in an article in OECD *Economic Studies*,[18] "By far the easiest way of reducing pressure on the soil would be to reduce the incentive for intensive, and especially capital-intensive, farming methods. Moreover, this should be done quickly, for it is anticipated price falls that most encourage over-exploitation."

In time, farm support may play another part in the environmental debate. One of the most potent greenhouse gases is methane. That is given off by coal mines, rubbish dumps and leaking gas pipes – but also by farting animals and stewing rice paddies. Cattle account for three-quarters of the methane given off by domestic livestock. This is partly because they eat more, but also because more of what they eat is converted into methane: up to 9% of their gross energy intake, compared with an average of 1.3% for pigs. One study[19] argued that a 50% cut in beef consumption in the first world and a corresponding rise in consumption of pork would allow a 40% cut in methane production from the developed world's farms. It urges a climate tax on beef consumption. After the collapse of the GATT Uruguay round in late 1990 and the opening of negotiations on a treaty to deal with greenhouse gases, American climate negotiators have begun to talk darkly about cuts in EC agricultural support as part of a package of measures to reduce Europe's output of greenhouse gas.

Governments in Europe have begun to try to counteract the most damaging influence of farm support on the countryside by giving another set of subsidies, this time attached to environmentally friendly behaviour. The greater the damaging influence of the first set of subsidies, the larger the second set has to be in order to have any impact. The EC now allows, at the behest of the British, payments for farmers in areas designated as "environmentally sensitive" if they reduce stocking rates, repair old stone walls, and so on. Another subsidy goes to farmers in areas where heavy ploughing of grassland and use of fertilisers has helped to pollute streams with nitrates. This bribes farmers to use techniques that release less nitrogen.

Although such policies may sound crazy, they may be easier for governments than taking the sensible course of reducing agricultural protection. Cuts in farm support mean, inevitably, a reduction in the prosperity of farmers. Like doctors, farmers are skilled at tugging at the public heartstrings. The first whisper of reform fills newspapers with sad stories of (in Britain) upland sheep farmers struggling to survive, or (in America) westerners fighting for a living on a plot their grandfather settled. Subsidies become rights – rights to pollute, perhaps, but rights nonetheless. Any government that threatens such rights runs straight into powerful, articulate and well-organised lobbies; the beneficiaries of reform are invariably many, but their benefits are more thinly spread and less easily discerned than the losses of the lobbyists.

Down in the forest

The destruction of the rain forests, so important for conserving species and carbon dioxide alike, has taken place partly at the expense of taxpayers in the countries that have lost them. Governments have lost money not just by paying for unneeded hydroelectric projects in forests, but by subsidising forest clearance and by grossly undercharging for logging rights.

The most glaring example has been Brazil, home to 30% of the world's tropical rain forest. A study for the World Bank in April 1989[20] drew attention to three instances. First, agricultural income is virtually exempted from income tax, making farming a tax shelter (though income from non-farm activities could not be offset against gains from farming). That encourages urban investors and companies to buy up land, pushing up its price. Where land happens to carry forest, it is cleared to qualify. Because taxes are so low on farm investments, farmers have an incentive to undertake projects with a lower rate of return than they would otherwise contemplate. And because tax relief stimulates a demand for land and thus pushes up its price, it becomes harder for the poor (who pay no tax and so get no relief) to buy a holding. That in turn gives them a greater incentive to settle and clear frontier lands.

Second, subsidised credit for farmers also helps to reduce the rate of return that cleared land needs to earn, and helps to drive up the value of land (just like those Californian water subsidies and EC farm price guarantees). Third and most damaging, SUDAM, the government agency charged with development in the Amazon region, and other government lenders have in the past offered special tax credits for corporations. A large share, which cost more than $1 billion in 1975–86, was used to encourage forest to be cleared and stocked with cattle. These ranches have produced no more than 16% of their expected output. Many cleared the land, took the tax credit, but never raised a single joint of beef. As a second World Bank report[21] put it, "More than two decades of experience have shown that livestock projects have been responsible for much environmental damage and yield little in the way of production or employment ... most of the benefits have accrued to a small group of wealthy investors who have used these resources to appropriate large tracts of land on the agricultural frontier."

Some of these damaging policies have now been dropped. In 1989 new tax credits were suspended although projects already begun continued to be subsidised. Cheap loans have been scaled down. And the rules that made land title conditional on forest clearance have been repealed. At the same time, Brazil's financial difficulties have virtually stopped new road-building in the Amazon. As a result, the rate of deforestation has dropped dramatically: from 80,000 square km in 1987 to an estimated 20,000 square km in 1990.

Lumbered

Mad though Brazil's policies may seem, lots of other countries share the madness. While more deforestation has been caused by farming than by logging in Brazil, the reverse is true in Asia and in parts of Africa. There, the problem is a different one: governments undercharge for logging licences, discouraging loggers from putting a proper value on the trees they chop down. None does the sensible thing and auctions off logging rights as Britain and America auction oil-drilling rights. If such auctions were held, conservationists could bid, too. If they succeeded, they could choose to leave trees uncleared; either way, the government would gain extra revenue. As it is, underpricing means that loggers tend to cut more trees than they would otherwise do, and have little incentive to spend money on replanting or on taking care of surrounding forest when they take out trees.

Third-world countries say, with some justification, that first-world countries have made most of the mistakes for which they now blame the poor. That is certainly true of forests. The Brazilian provision that clearing land established title to it had its equivalent a century ago in the laws that helped to clear North America's forests. Even now, America subsidises the harvesting of timber in its national forests. For many years the Wilderness Society has been campaigning to end the subsidies that the American Forest Service pays to logging contractors. Each year, the American taxpayer provides $100m to pay for harvesting timber too cheap to cover its costs. The environmental damage enrages American environmentalists. The most heavily subsidised logging is on land too arid and cold to reforest. That often means taking the trees from mountain ridges which are visible from miles away. Worse, subsidies are encouraging logging in America's last great temperate rain forest, the Tongass in Alaska.

In Britain government forestry subsidies have had the opposite intention – to encourage tree-planting – but the same effect: vehement environmental opposition. Forestry in Britain has long been a tax shelter, just as farming is a tax shelter in Brazil (except that in Britain, unlike Brazil, income from activities other than forestry could effectively be set off against losses in forestry). Rich individuals bought cheap hill land, setting off the costs of the purchase and of planting it against income tax. When the trees matured, a quirk of financial law allowed the landowner to sell the land to a financial institution, paying capital gains tax on the land but not on its crop of growing trees. Taxable income could thus be converted into untaxed capital.

By the late 1980s the cost to the Treasury in lost income-tax revenue amounted to £10m–15m a year. Because the tax relief was determined by the cost of planting, it provided an incentive to buy land as cheaply as possible. That meant buying moorlands, whose previous use had been for sheep-grazing. But moorlands, like America's forested ridges, tend to be conspicuous; they also tend to have more than their fair share of rare wildlife. Planting them with subsidised trees destroyed those habitats.

Because tax relief was automatic, neither central government nor local authorities could control where planting took place (although foresters who wanted a top-up grant had to abide by rules laid down by the Forestry Commission). And because the relief was simply attached to tree-planting, regardless of the kind of tree, many foresters planted the trees that gave the fastest returns: mainly imported species of sitka spruce and lodgepole pine. An industry of subsidised tree-farming grew up, with all the disposition to monoculture and high use of chemical fertilisers and pesticides of other kinds of subsidised farming.

In the 1988 budget the government abolished the special tax treatment of forestry and replaced it with grants. Forestry is still subsidised, but in a way that gives the government more control over where the subsidies (and the forests) go. The environmentalists are still worried: applications to plant, which had diminished for a while, began to increase again in 1990.

Pay a proper price

Realising that environmental damage typically resulted from market failure, environmentalists have traditionally seen the cure as government intervention. That ignores the fact that intervention has costs of its own: justified only if the costs of market failure exceed the costs that may come from badly directed actions by the state. The example of British forestry is telling: in theory, subsidising forestry ought to be a thoroughly environmentally friendly thing to do. In practice, the policy has done great harm. Governments that see tree-planting as the easiest way to mitigate the effects of global warming (trees lock up carbon dioxide as they grow) may find that their policies, unless designed with extreme care, similarly backfire.

Government subsidies sometimes do environmental good. But environmentalists and economists alike would be wise to approach such claims with caution. Plenty of green lobbyists, for example, would like to see more state money spent on public transport. That, they argue, would wean people away from their cars, and reduce all their nasty environmental side-effects such as congestion and smog. Sadly, there is little evidence that subsidised public transport is an efficient way of discouraging car travel.

One study of 15 industrial countries by the British Transport and Road Research Laboratory found that a 10% subsidy to urban public transport seemed to result in a 5% fall in fares (the rest was swallowed up in higher costs and lower productivity), and in a 2–3% rise in the use of public transport in the long term. But public transport tends to be used by different groups of people from cars, and for different kinds of journey. Much of the increase brought about by subsidies may come from existing users of public transport, rather than from drivers encouraged to leave their cars at home. While subsidised fares may not lead people to abandon the car for a bus, raising the price of petrol is much more effective, especially once car drivers have had time to adjust. In the long term, a 10% rise in the price of fuel may lead to a 5% fall in its consumption.[22]

The cure for market failure, in short, is not necessarily state intervention. The cure may be to make the market work better. One interesting example has been privatisation. The industries that governments have transferred to private ownership in the course of the 1980s (mainly in Britain, of course, but in other countries, too) have often been those that are most environmentally sensitive: transport, energy, water. Privatisation alone will not necessarily improve (or worsen) the impact of a given industry on the environment. It will[23] put greater weight on profit as an industry goal and less on output. To the extent that more output means more pollution, a greater emphasis on profit may make the privatised industry greener.

The distancing of regulation from ownership may be more important. Before the British water industry was privatised, ministers argued in private that the strongest reason for selling it off was the extreme difficulty of persuading the Treasury to allow enough spending on environmental improvements. That argument clearly could not be used in public. Now that the government is answerable for water quality, but not responsible for the industry's finances, ministers may find it much easier to raise standards. Shareholders in the water industry and its customers may squeal; but the

Treasury, infinitely more powerful, will keep quiet.

The moral of this chapter is that governments do not necessarily need to undertake sophisticated calculations about the costs of environmental damage, nor to devise ingenious pollution taxes (discussed in Chapter 5 of Part I) in order to combine an improvement in their environmental policies with a gain in revenue and in economic efficiency. Here is one of those rare occasions in public life where politicians can enjoy two gains for the price of one. They will need to stand up to the lobbyists who have enjoyed government protection in the past and have come to regard it as their right. Those lobbies may be immensely strong, which is why governments so rarely stand up to them. But good green governments now have a new ally: environmental pressure from their citizens. They have a wonderful chance to spend their taxpayers' cash more sensibly, and to improve the way their citizens use water, energy and soil – all in a single swoop.

References

[1] Robert Repetto, *Skimming the Water: Rent-Seeking and the Performance of Public Irrigation Systems*, Research Report No. 4, WRI, 1986; Mark Kosmo, *Money To Burn? The High Costs of Energy Subsidies*, WRI, 1987; Robert Repetto, *Paying the Price: Pesticide Subsidies in Developing Countries*, Research Report No. 2, WRI, December, 1985.

[2] Quoted in *Skimming the Water*, pages 4–5; see note 1 above.

[3] *Ibid.*, page 18.

[4] *Ibid.*, page 17

[5] *Ibid.*, page 18.

[6] *Money to Burn?*, *op.cit.*, see note 1 above.

[7] Joanne C. Burgess, "The contribution of efficient energy pricing to reducing carbon dioxide emissions", *Energy Policy*, June 1990.

[8] "Energy Efficiency Strategy for Developing Countries: The Role of ESMAP", Background Paper for ESMAP's annual meeting, Paris, 1989, page 2.

[9] "Brazil's Balbina Dam: Environment versus the Legacy of the Pharaohs in Amazonia", *Environmental Management*, Vol. 13, No. 3, 1989.

[10] *Op.cit.*, note 7 above.

[11] US Department of Agriculture, *Agricultural Resources – Cropland, Water and Conservation – Situation and Outlook Report*, Economic Research Service, Washington DC, 1987.

[12] US Department of Agriculture, *The Second RCA Appraisal*, Washington DC, 1989.

[13] *Agricultural and Environmental Policies, Opportunities for Integration*, Paris, 1989.

[14] *Alternative Agriculture*, National Academy Press, Washington DC, 1989, page 42.

[15] Robert Repetto, *Paying the Price*, pages 12–15, *op.cit.*, see note 1 above.

[16] *Ibid.*

[17] Quoted by Alan Winters in "The So-called 'Non-Economic' Objectives of Agricultural Support", in OECD *Economic Studies*, No. 13, Winter 1989–90, page 257.

[18] *Ibid.*

[19] Florentin Krause, Wilfred Bach and Jon Kooney, *Energy Policy in the Greenhouse*, Earthscan Publications, London, 1990.

[20] Hans P. Binswanger, "Brazilian Policies that Encourage Deforestation in the Amazon", IBRD Department of Environment Working Paper No. 16, Washington DC, 1989.

[21] Dennis J. Mahar, *Government Policies and Deforestation in Brazil's Amazon Region*, IBRD, Washington DC, 1989.

[22] David Sawyer, "Taxes good, subsidies bad", *Financial Times*, July 31st 1990.

[23] Dieter Helm and David Pearce, "Assessment: Economic Policy Towards the Environment", *Oxford Review of Economic Policy*, Vol. 6, No. 1, pages 1–16.

5

MAKING POLLUTERS PAY

Governments almost always tackle environmental damage by telling companies or individuals to stop it. They pass laws, set standards, promulgate bans, enforce regulations. Such policies present a paradox. For although they are so popular, they are rarely the most cost-effective way to clean up. Other policies, for example taxes and tradable permits, deliver more greenery at lower cost. Governments have begun to look at such market-based instruments. Wise ones will find strong arguments for preferring them to regulations.

Why do governments need to intervene at all? The answer is that in environmental affairs the invisible hand of the market fails to align the interests of the individual or the individual company with those of society at large. Individuals may drive their cars to work, rather than take a bus; companies may use chlorofluorocarbons in their commercial refrigerators. In both cases, the costs to society at large, from traffic fumes in one case and from a damaged ozone layer in the other, exceed any private cost to individual or company. That is inefficient. Governments need to step in to align private costs with those to society at large.

The phrase that embodies this concept is the "polluter pays principle", that polluters ought to meet those costs of their actions which at present fall on society at large. The industrial members of the OECD adopted this as a guide to proper environmental policies in 1972. The principle, it was argued, would make sure that polluters carried the full costs of their actions. It would thus improve economic efficiency. In practice, the principle is frequently broken by, for example, policies that subsidise polluters to clean up. In the real world, and particularly (as later chapters argue) in international agreements, victims of pollution seem to be just as likely to end up footing the bill for reducing it as the perpetrators.

As earlier chapters have argued, environmental policies may cost dearly in terms of the loss of conventionally measured national income. It is therefore

extremely important to design policies that achieve their goal as cost-effectively as possible. The policies that politicians find easiest to sell to their electors may well not be the ones that deliver the greatest greenery with the least
loss of economic growth.

The trouble with standards

The way in which governments have traditionally aligned private and social
costs is by setting standards. Companies agree to drain waste water into rivers
only when it can be diluted to a prescribed amount; or to build cars that meet
set targets for fuel consumption or exhaust emissions. Standards have some
important advantages, especially in the eyes of industry and politicians; but
they also have drawbacks, some of which have become more apparent as the
nature of pollution problems has changed.

One important weakness is that they aim to make all polluters clean up to
the same extent, regardless of what it costs them to do so. That is one reason
polluters often like standards: they know where they are, and they know that
all other polluters will have to meet the same target. That seems fair. In reality, it may not be fair at all, for some polluters will inevitably find it cheaper
to apply a given standard than others. For example, it is usually cheap for
owners of new cars to have them converted to run on unleaded petrol. For
owners of elderly jalopies, though, it is far more expensive. If a government
were simply to pass a law insisting that all cars be converted within a certain
time, it would inflict huge costs on owners of older vehicles. Instead, some
governments have chosen a sensible economic instrument: a higher rate of
duty on leaded than unleaded petrol. That allows owners of some oldish cars
to weigh the benefit of cheaper petrol against the cost of converting their car.

Such considerations frequently make it impossible to apply uniform standards. A factory with five-year-old machines may not want to scrap them,
even if they make more mess than new ones. So regulators will generally have
to compromise. That is why Britain's new pollution regulations include the
concept of BATNEEC, "best available technology not entailing excessive cost".
Pollution inspectors and companies will have scope to haggle over what
involves "excessive cost" and what amounts to "best available technology".
BATNEEC is an attempt to tailor the cut in pollution each firm delivers to its
particular cost structure. It will inevitably be labour-intensive.

In America, where pollution regulation is a less cosy affair, there have also
been plenty of compromises: in 1987, 12 years after the standards for air
quality set in the 1970 Clean Air Act were meant to come into force, more
than 100m people lived in areas that failed to meet those standards.
Standards that cannot be fairly enforced may suffer from the worst of both
worlds: a lack of credibility with the public, and higher costs for those who
comply than for those who bargain their way into mitigation.

Indeed, because meeting standards is often possible only when a company
or an individual makes a new investment – builds a new office, for instance,

or buys a new car — standards tend to operate disproportionately on new equipment. Yet by driving up the cost of such equipment, they tend to encourage polluters to postpone the very investments that greater greenery requires. One example is the attempt by the American Congress in 1977 to insist on a less polluting design for new coal-fired power stations. Sulphur dioxide was to be scrubbed from exhaust gases until they were as clean as those produced by stations which burnt low-sulphur coal. Because such scrubbers added up to 20% to the capital cost of a new plant, and old generators can be kept running for 40 years or more, replacement of old equipment inevitably slowed down.

While those who find standards expensive to meet do not do so, those who find them relatively cheap have no incentive to go beyond what the law requires. In fact, as the second half of this book shows, companies often do go farther than environmental regulations insist, but only because other incentives, created by the market and the courts, encourage them to do so.

Finally, standards may be much easier to apply to large polluters, such as companies, than to individuals. An inspector may be able to haggle with a hundred companies, but hardly with a thousand households. Yet the least tractable pollution problems, at least in the first world, are increasingly those caused by individual behaviour where setting standards may also have perverse effects. For instance, if governments try to reduce energy consumption by insisting on more fuel-efficient cars, people may find driving so much cheaper that they will make more journeys at higher speed. Or if governments insist on better insulated buildings, people may turn up the thermostat.

Going to market

Bring in the market, and many of these difficulties diminish. Most economic instruments for tackling pollution work by creating incentives for becoming cleaner. When properly designed, they should impose on a polluter the costs that would otherwise be dumped on the environment. Economic instruments, as Figure 9 (page 96) shows, have been embraced with varying enthusiasm in different countries. They have two main advantages over standards. In the short term, they will generally provide any given level of environmental improvement at a lower cost to society than will regulations. This is because, in theory at least, polluters will have an incentive to reduce the muck they produce for as long as it is cheaper to do that than pay more environmental charges, using the technology they judge to be most efficient. Regulations, by contrast, only take account of the costs of cleaning up in a rough and ready way, through applying concepts such as BATNEEC.

Secondly, in the long run, economic instruments offer companies and individuals a continuous argument for going farther than a standard would demand. If companies pay a higher rate for every pound of toxic rubbish they dump, they will have an incentive to use as little toxic material as possible, and to look for new processes that use none at all. If petrol taxes are high,

Figure 9 Number of environmental economic measures, 1987

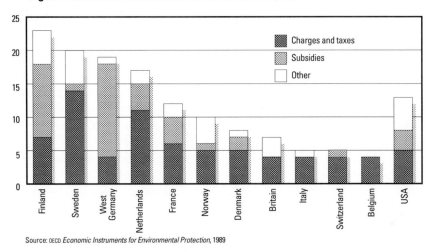

Source: OECD *Economic Instruments for Environmental Protection*, 1989

individuals have to drive frugally all the time, and to replace their car with one that uses less fuel, whatever the standards say. The difference in cost to the community between typical regulation and well-designed economic instruments may be as much as five or ten times, according to some American studies.[1] In reality, the savings are usually much smaller, but still important.

Economic instruments have several other strengths. For example, they can affect the behaviour of millions of people – think of those petrol taxes again – in a way that may be impossible with standards. That effect will become more important, the more governments realise that pollution is the result of millions of decisions by many individuals and small businesses, rather than by a few large and readily regulated companies. To levy taxes, governments require much less information about the costs of curbing pollution: no need to send inspectors to each individual household. A higher tax on leaded petrol will make sure that those whose cars can be cheaply converted will do so; the rest will not. The fact that economic instruments do not require detailed information about the costs facing individual polluters in order to work (any more than value-added tax requires a knowledge of all the taxpayer's circumstances) has another advantage: it means that they are less vulnerable to cosy deals between regulators and regulated.

Economic instruments also provide a positive incentive to buy less polluting technologies, rather than (as with standards) an incentive to postpone change. Such technologies, as the second half of this book argues, play an important role in taking the pain out of greenery; they are also the main way countries can hope to grow richer by growing greener.

Pigou's bright idea

The oldest and most familiar of all such economic instruments are green taxes. Although governments began to show a lively interest in them at the end of the 1980s, they are an elderly idea. In 1920 the Cambridge economist Arthur Pigou proposed the idea of a tax as a way to bridge the gap between private and social cost which is at the root of environmental damage. But old though the concept of green taxation may be, remarkably few countries have put Pigovian insight into practice.

Taxes or charges on polluters have in the past usually been intended to raise the revenue to pay for regulation rather than to deter polluters. They have been levied, mainly in European countries, mostly on dirty water, though occasionally on aircraft noise. They have rarely been used to discourage air pollution or waste dumping. They have almost always been set at levels too low to affect polluters' behaviour. Professor Judith Rees of Hull University looked at the effect on British companies of effluent charges for the waste they put into the sewage system, which varied by region and by quantity and content of the waste. Some of the companies she studied faced a 400% increase in charges over a five-year period. Few did anything to reduce the muck they emitted, let alone move to a cheaper region. Why? Usually the charge was so small that they simply paid. Indeed, a third of the firms did not understand how the charges worked, and so had no idea how to reduce their bill in theory, let alone in practice. Not much hope for green incentives there.

Then at the end of the 1980s, some northern European governments began to discuss carbon taxes levied on the amount of carbon dioxide given off by burning fossil fuels, as part of an attempt to reduce output of greenhouse gases. Sweden and Finland actually introduced such taxes. The EC Commission also became enthusiastic mainly because a carbon tax seemed to offer a new source of environmental revenue to spend on good deeds such as supporting tropical forestry. More modest taxes were also introduced. Italy brought in a tax of 100 lire (10 cents) on plastic bags, which caused an initial fall of 40% in their use. Several American states have wondered about imposing taxes on packaging, but hesitated because of the complexity and the difficulty of raising them to a level high enough to have an impact on corporate behaviour. Denmark brought in a charge on pesticides sold in small containers, since such containers and their toxic contents tend to end up in household rubbish bins. Finland introduced a tax on single-hulled tankers bringing oil into the country's ports since these tankers are often more likely to spill their contents if they run aground. The United States and Norway both imposed a tax on CFCs.

Other green taxes are being discussed. Italy would like to increase substantially its landing charges for noisy aircraft, and tax farms that keep more than 200 pigs but have no waste-treatment facilities. Germany has plans to change the basis of car tax from engine size to exhaust fumes and noise. Denmark has plans for a tenfold increase in the taxation of raw materials and a tripling of the existing tax on rubbish, both measures intended to economise on scarce landfill. Singapore and Oslo both impose tolls on cars entering the city centre. Other cities are thinking hard about road pricing, arguing that it is a more efficient way of sharing out scarce road space than forcing everybody to sit in jams. Britain's Cambridge briefly considered a scheme using electronic measuring equipment to tax motorists more heavily if they travel slowly. The theory, which is sound, was that motorists ought to pay the high costs to others of using their cars at peak hours of congestion. Cambridge dons showed the city that, in practice, a tax on slow driving may have perverse incentives ... .

The environment as revenue-raiser

Green taxes have brought tussles between environment ministries and finance departments. Each wants to claim responsibility. The tussles, though, are not purely about ministerial pique. Environment ministers tend to see green taxes as a way to raise revenue to spend on other green causes. They like the idea of using some of the yield from road pricing to pay for public transport, for instance, or of reinvesting the takings from effluent charges in building sewage works. Finance ministers, on the other hand, sometimes dislike seeing a source of revenue tied to a particular item of state spending. They argue that it is unlikely that the tax will yield exactly the right amount that ought to be spent on whatever good green cause is involved. A carbon tax that reduced carbon output by just the right amount will only by utter fluke yield the sum that should, in an ideal world, be devoted to tropical forestry. It is far more likely to yield more – or less.

Besides, finance ministries see green taxes as a new revenue source. There is a paradox here: if a tax successfully reduces the polluting behaviour on which it is levied, its yield will diminish. Just as governments that tax cigarettes are suspected of wanting to keep many people profitably puffing, so a pollution tax might give government a vested interest in continued dirt. That, of course, is only partly true. While there is no point at which the benefits of cigarette smoking, either to the individual or to society, exceed the costs of the habit, it is possible to reach a point where further reductions in some kinds of pollution would cost more than the value of the benefits that would result. A few gallons a day of raw sewage in the Thames or the Hudson matter not one jot: a few million gallons matter a lot. A wise government could live very happily off the proceeds of taxes that kept pollution at the point where the costs of prevention threatened to exceed the benefits of greater greenery. Because such taxes might often be levied on basic materials – water or energy consumption, for instance – they could yield lots of revenue before they reached the point at which people changed their behaviour.

To raise more revenue from such taxes, and less from taxing income and capital, would be a far-sighted thing for a government to do. Most taxes are levied on things that are good for an economy. Governments get revenue at the expense of some economic welfare. Because income is taxed, people work a bit less hard than they otherwise might do; because capital is taxed, they have an incentive to save and to invest less than they otherwise might. The WRI calculates that these distorting effects of the tax system cost America

4–7% of GNP each year. Rather than taxing good things, why not tax bad ones such as pollution? If taxes make people work less or save less, that is bad; if taxes make people pollute less, that is good.

Indeed, it will become more important to switch taxes away from incomes in the years ahead. Most of the industrial countries are now entering a period when their labour forces will stop expanding. It will be madness to tax the very resource whose supply is most static. Yet that is exactly what the rich countries may be tempted to do. Because capital is mobile, and goods can be moved easily across frontiers, taxes on savings and on spending may well decline. People find it harder to move than do money or goods. So incomes will be easy to tax. Easy, but ultimately expensive.

Not painless

Green taxes, though, have some disadvantages. Some of these explain why they have not been more widely adopted. Sometimes, green taxes are simply not appropriate. They work best when the market works best. Where one dirty company has a monopoly – of electricity generation, say – it may be better to regulate it than to tax: if taxed, it will simply pass the whole bill to the consumer and stay dirty. Green taxes may also be less helpful than regulation when what matters is the concentration of filth: when a river can tolerate a given concentration of effluent through the day, say, but not a sudden flood jammed into a brief half hour. A tax per unit of muck would not discourage sudden discharges. Where what matters most is the capacity of the environment to absorb pollution, regulation may sometimes be the wisest course.

There is a bigger problem. The revenue that green taxes raise represents an increase in costs to the polluter. Splendid, say greens. That is the very way taxes give even cleanish companies a continuing incentive to become cleaner. Politicians may be more doubtful. For companies, the counterpart of that extra revenue is a rise in their costs, which inevitably makes them less competitive against companies (in other countries for example) that bear no such burden. For individuals, the counterpart is also a rise in costs, which is why politicians fret about the inflationary impact of green taxes. Moreover, since such taxes would generally be flat-rate (a couple of pennies on a gallon of water, for instance) they would, like all indirect taxes, tend to hurt the poor proportionately more than the rich. They would be regressive, though in countries where the poor – often women or old people – rarely drive cars, petrol taxes would be a partial exception.

Two points soften this harsh picture. First, standards carry costs, too. From society's point of view, the costs imposed by standards are always higher, though they will be better hidden. Who knows how much national income is lost by raising the standards for building insulation or for the fuel efficiency of cars? For the company or the individual, though, standards will be a cheaper way to clean up. For taxes will be levied on all the pollution a company or individual causes, even if it is as clean as an alternative standard might require. To grasp the point, imagine that a country has a standard for fuel efficiency for cars. Three-quarters of the cars in the country meet the standard. Then the government decides to replace the standard with a petrol tax, set at a level designed to keep the same average level of fuel efficiency. The owners of cars that have already met the standard will now find the cost of driving is higher. That is precisely why they will have an incentive to buy cars that are more efficient still. But it is also why people dislike green taxes.

But – and here comes the second softening point – the revenue that causes these hardships can always be redistributed. The government in the example above could use the proceeds of petrol tax to raise old-age pensions, or to cut income tax. The yield from a tax that hurts corporate competitiveness could be used to cut corporation tax. Such measures do not necessarily hand the gains from green taxation back to the losers. An alternative – though this drives a coach and horses through the "polluter pays principle" is to use the revenue to pay a sort of negative pollution tax. Companies or individuals that improve on a benchmark level of pollution control might get money back, on a sliding scale. In the example in the previous paragraph, those whose cars were of above-average efficiency might get a fuel-tax credit each year. Governments would apply a stick to the dirty and offer a carrot to the clean.

Tradable permits

Green taxes have a further drawback, even in the eyes of green economists. It is almost impossible to set them at the "right" level. That magic point, at which the costs of pollution prevention catch up with the benefits, is hard enough to discover even on paper. To try to hit it by setting taxes at precisely the right level is even more impossible. Most impossible of all is to keep taxes at that right level, year after year. Nothing annoys politicians more than the idea that they may have to change a tax simply because it was set at the wrong level in the first place. Yet nothing is more certain than that most green taxes are set too low to meet their goal.

American economists have developed a different kind of economic instrument which gets round this. Instead of setting a pollution target in terms of price, as a tax does, this sets it in terms of quantity. Such instruments have been known in the past as "marketable pollution rights" or "tradable permits"; American green lobbyists got angry at the thought that anybody might acquire a right to pollute, and so tactful economists now talk of "emission reduction credits". That carries comforting overtones of rewards for good behaviour, rather than profits from bad.

Under such schemes, governments set a standard in terms of, say, tons of sulphur dioxide a year. That total is then shared out among companies or power stations. Each polluter thus has a quota of gas that it can emit. If it introduces new, cleaner technology so that its emissions fall below its permitted level, it can sell its unneeded share to other polluters, or to new companies that may want to set up in the same business. Companies for whom cleaning up is relatively cheap thus have an incentive to be as clean as possible. But the dirty can also stay in business, though carrying the extra cost of buying more pollution credits. One company may also lease its credits to another, if it does not need them but thinks that it may do so in future.

Companies can choose which course is more cost-effective: to clean up and sell, or to stay dirty and buy. Because both high-cost and low-cost polluters do better if they trade, there is an incentive to do so. Because high-cost polluters can save money by buying extra permits rather than cleaning up, pollution will be concentrated among those companies for whom pollution prevention is most expensive. Yet the environment as a whole will be cleaner, because the total number of permits sets a finite limit on allowable pollution.

Such schemes have lots of attractions. They combine the certainty of regulation with the flexibility of the market. They allow governments to stand back and say, "We are simply setting an overall pollution target. It's up to you how you share it out. We are not raising prices: if prices go up, that is the fault of polluters, not government. Our hands are clean." They even make it possible for those who care about the environment to do something constructive, by buying up permits and freezing them. Green lobbyists, who want to see power-station emissions decrease more quickly, could raise the cash to buy up permits and sit on them. Companies get the cash; lobbyists get cleaner air.

An important aspect of tradable permits (to revert to their more tactless name) is the way they are shared out in the first place. One option is to hand them out on the basis of existing patterns of pollution. Dirty companies will get lots; clean companies will get fewer. In America such a process is called "grandfathering". It is a way of recognising that existing polluters have built up a sort of *de facto* right to pollute; if they are deprived of this right they will feel that they have been robbed and make sure every politician knows it. The drawback, of course, is that grandfathering is unfair on those who are already cleaner. Since permits will be traded for hard cash, dirty companies will receive a larger endowment than clean ones.

Another option is to auction off the permits. That way, government ignores all the rights that polluters may feel they have to pollute. Moreover, while grandfathering raises no revenue, auctioning does. In that sense, an auction is similar to a pollution tax. If the government holds an auction, then the counterpart of the revenue it raises will be a loss of income to polluters, just as with a tax; while government can use that revenue to soften the social impacts of its policies, it can no longer claim that its hands are clean.

Meanwhile, in the real world ...

Much though economists love the idea of tradable permits as a device for curbing pollution, they have rarely been tried. (The concept has been frequently applied in other contexts: EC milk quotas in Britain, fishing catches in New Zealand and quotas for textile exports to the United States have all been traded.) There are some circumstances in which they are clearly not appropriate. It would be hard to apply them to the control of toxic gas emissions by companies, for instance: local people would not want to let companies decide whether to meet a minimum safety standard at one plant but not at another. But experience in America has revealed problems even when permits seem the appropriate mechanism.

Easily the most successful experiment with permits was carried out by the Environmental Protection Agency (EPA) in 1985 when it gave oil refineries two years in which to cut the allowable lead content of petrol. Refineries got quotas of lead, which they could then trade with each other. The effect was to let them phase in the cut in lead at their own pace. Half of all the refineries took part in trading.

The lead scheme had three special features that helped to make it work. The amount of lead in petrol could easily be monitored with existing regulatory machinery; the number of firms involved was quite small; and the environmental goals of the programme were clear and widely accepted. The EPA's attempts since 1974 to allow companies to trade air-pollution permits have been less successful. Many cities failed to meet the standards laid down in the 1970 Clear Air Act. Rather than stop new companies moving to such places, the EPA allowed them to buy the right to pollute from established firms which had cut their own emissions, adding other refinements.

Trade in air-pollution permits has undoubtedly kept down the costs of compliance. The effect has been to cut the capital cost of pollution control in the United States cumulatively by an estimated $10 billion, though mainly by letting companies offset increased emissions from one outlet against smaller emissions from another within the same plant. But the amount of trading, particularly between companies rather than within a single firm, has greatly disappointed enthusiasts. One reason has been the complexity of trading rules. Another has been that America's litigious green lobby resented the idea that companies should have a right to pollute, let alone that they should be able to make money by selling it to another firm. They saw the tradable permits scheme as a way to postpone meeting the goals of the Clean Air Act, rather than a way of achieving them more cost-effectively. Moreover, to work well, emissions trading needs better records of emissions than most American states possess. Otherwise, companies will see no reason to pay for what others are illegally taking for nothing.

In 1990 America decided to try again. A new Clean Air Act was passed by Congress. Once again, an important feature of the legislation is tradable permits, but this time enthusiasts think they have designed a more workable package. The act sets a cap on the output of sulphur dioxide and nitrogen oxides from electricity-generating plants. Their output of sulphur dioxide must be cut by 10m tons, and of nitrogen oxides by 2m–4m tons, over the next decade. Whereas the old trading scheme was seen by environmentalists as a way to prop up a law that had failed, the new cap is intended to be a guarantee that, whatever else happens, emissions will fall for good.

The cap was also designed to prevent politicians from arguing about over-all emission totals. Instead, they were able to argue over how that total should be shared out. Dan Dudek of the Environmental Defense Fund (EDF), says gleefully that the cap ensures that politicians would concentrate on the task they were best at: "that of passing out the pork".

The process will be devalued if some polluters cheat. So draconian penalties are a second vital feature. By 1993 power stations must fit pollution-monitoring equipment on all chimneys. Those who emit more than their allowance are fined, at a rising rate and with no appeal, and must then cut by enough to compensate for their past excess.

Bring on the traders

A constant worry about tradable permits is that a proper market may not develop. Only if polluters trade permits will pollution be reduced in the most cost-effective way. If they simply sit on them, then trading will be no better than old-fashioned regulation. Indeed, if those who have been allocated permits buy up more to make sure that new entrants cannot come into the market and compete, the net effect may be even worse than that of standards.

In practice, American experience of tradable permits for air pollution has been that trading is thin. The staunchest advocates of permits blame this on restrictions on trading, and on the opposition permit schemes have met from green lobbyists in the courts, anxious to prevent polluters from making money from selling "rights to pollute". But another part of the story is that large sources of pollution have sometimes sat on their permits and refused to trade, thus effectively keeping out new firms which might one day be rivals.

Permit markets are most likely to thrive, like all markets, where there are plenty of traders. They work best, as do green taxes, where firms cannot simply pass on to consumers the whole extra cost of permits. In Eastern Europe, ingenious schemes to curb air pollution by introducing tradable permits run the risk of being thwarted if companies simply up the price of their power or products. In Britain, where two giant generators dominate the newly privatised electricity industry, it is equally hard to be sure that a proper market in permits could evolve.

To stop existing polluters cornering the market in permits, the American clean-air legislation insists that the government keep back up to 5% of permits and auction them off. That has another advantage. It will provide a public reference price. If a utility asks its regulator for permission to raise its prices to pay for the installation of scrubbers on its smokestacks, the regulator will be able to see at once whether that is a more expensive course than buying some extra emission permits. Anybody in the business of installing pollution-control technology (and, as Chapter 6 in Part II explains, lots of companies are interested) will be able to see how cheap that technology needs to be if it is to be worth installing it rather than buying extra permits.

Just as governments have become increasingly interested in green taxes, so (though politicians find the idea harder to grasp) are they starting to look at other uses for tradable permits. A few American schemes have tried to apply the concept to river pollution. Dutch economists have suggested trying to tackle the Netherlands' appalling difficulties in disposing of manure by setting up a manure bank: only farmers would be charged for their deposits, rather than rewarded for them. Farmers would be able to trade the right to a heap of a certain size with each other. Britain has been considering applying a permit-trading scheme to solve the problem of overcapacity in its fishing fleet. Fisherman would be given a quota of fish that they could catch, which they could sell to each other if they wanted to raise a capital sum and move out of fishing. Such schemes in Canada, Iceland and New Zealand seem to have given fishermen more incentives to conserve stocks.

Opportunities abroad

America is keen to extend the idea of tradable permits into a completely new field: that of international environmental agreements. In particular, it wants an international trading system for greenhouse gases as part of any deal to tackle global warming. Some of the difficulties with that idea are discussed in Chapter 7 of Part I. Though they may be hard to apply internationally, tradable permits might be an ideal way of sharing out environmental obligations among a limited number of countries.

One obvious use might be in the EC. The Community has set targets for air quality, including maximum allowable concentrations of particulates (gritty dust) and sulphur dioxide, that must be met by 1993. Pollution in Britain, and in many other parts of the EC, exceeds these levels. It is not easy to see how Britain can reach these targets, especially for sulphur dioxide, without restricting growth in the offending areas.

One option might be to introduce a system of permit-trading, either within Britain or (better, because the market would be bigger) among EC countries. Such a scheme, suggested by Scott Barrett of the London Business School, would allow new firms moving into an area to buy permits from existing, older firms. Because their technology was newer, they would produce more output from fewer permits. Expansion, instead of being thwarted by pollution controls, would become a mechanism for cleaning up.[2] Britain has already taken a modest step in this direction, by allowing electricity generators to offset reductions made in emissions from one plant against increases from another, to meet the EC directive for large combustion plants. But one generator cannot trade with another.

Within the EC such schemes have plenty of other uses. They might be used to allow the Community to meet the goals of the Large Combustion Plant Directive, adopted in November 1988. It insists on big cuts in sulphur dioxide and nitrogen oxides emitted by large combustion plants. Or they could allow the Community to phase out ozone-gobbling chlorofluorocarbons more cost-effectively (as America phased out lead in petrol).

On deposit

A third kind of economic incentive to clean up may turn out to be the most popular of all, even though – or perhaps because – it raises no revenue for governments. Deposit-refund schemes were originally introduced by companies as a way of retrieving drinks bottles or other containers. As containers became cheaper and labour more expensive, companies abandoned them. Now governments, increasingly worried about the high costs of disposing of rubbish, are exploring deposit schemes with new interest.

As Chapter 5 in Part II describes, easily the most common use of deposit-refund schemes is to ensure the return of drinks bottles. But deposit refunds have been used with a wide range of products. Thus Norway has, since 1978, charged buyers a deposit on new cars. When the car reaches the end of its life, the deposit and something extra is refunded if the car is brought to an approved site. Over 90% of cars are properly disposed of.

Such schemes make good economic sense only if the costs they entail are less than the costs of disposing of waste in other ways that are equally environmentally friendly. The deposits that have to be charged to ensure adequate rates of return may be so large, or the costs of collection may be so high, that other methods of disposal are often more efficient.

Besides, even if consumers scrupulously return all their containers or used tyres to claim their deposits, the waste product does not vanish. It still has to be disposed of. A theme of the second half of this book is that waste will be easy to dispose of in environmentally friendly ways only if thought is given at the start of a product's life to its final destination.

The limits to markets

Different kinds of pollution require different solutions. It will be easiest to apply economic incentives where the causes of pollution are easy to pinpoint: a factory sewage outlet, for instance, rather than a culvert for rain water washed off oily roads. It is easy to charge one factory for its muck; harder to devise a scheme that discourages muck accumulating on roads. It will be easier to use economic measures where a narrow range of readily measurable pollutants is involved. Factories may not mind paying a single charge to cover everything that leaves their chimneys; they will make more fuss if the charge rises steeply as some particular pollutant increases in concentration. The administrative nuisance of measuring the pollutant, hour by hour, may mean that the cost of such finely tuned measures exceeds their benefit.

Devising economic instruments will be hard where what matters is the ability of the environment to absorb a pollutant, rather than the absolute amount emitted. It makes sense to discourage a factory from belching smoke over a crowded city; less sense to discourage one sited downwind or miles from habitation. This is a special problem for water pollution: the total amount of dirt discharged into a river rarely matters as much as the extent to which it is diluted. A company can usually safely discharge much more muck at higher water than when a river is low and sluggish.

Most of these difficulties have to be solved whether pollution is dealt with by "command-and-control", or indeed by cosier systems of regulation, or whether economic instruments are used. Regulations impose costs; they have distributional effects (poor people may not be able to buy a car if higher fuel-efficiency standards make cars dearer); they harm competitiveness.

The greater flexibility sometimes claimed for regulations may be illusory: polluters may insist that all their competitors are treated equally. The more that the process of setting regulations becomes open and public, the more inflexible it is likely to become. This particularly applies in Britain, where there has traditionally been great resistance to setting quantitative standards for environmental quality, and where pollution control has tended to be a matter for quiet negotiating between companies and the pollution inspectorate. That will be changed, partly by the environmental protection legislation of 1990, which aims for a more distant relationship between inspectors and polluted; partly by that act's insistence on more public access to the way standards are set; and partly by the more quantitative approach of the EC Commission. As standards become more rigid, the arguments for economic incentives may appear more attractive.

Any set of standards will be only as good as their enforcement. Any use of the market, whether through taxes, charges or tradable permits, will work only if the market works. Eastern European countries, the dirtiest in Europe, have elaborate arrangements to regulate and penalise polluters; yet the fines are uncollected. In Poland a survey of pollution fees paid by 1,400 manufacturers found that, on average, these amounted to 0.6% of production costs.

Czechoslovakia, Hungary and Poland also have effluent charges for water pollution, and in Poland, serious thought has been given to the use of tradable permits to reduce the country's appalling air pollution. Such schemes need a free market in order to work. It makes no sense to fine a firm when it cannot buy good anti-pollution equipment, because that can only be imported and imports are restricted. Nor does it make much sense to charge an enterprise for pollution when it is a monopoly and can simply pass the entire increase in costs on to its customers. Countries with highly controlled markets will find it harder to use market-based incentives to tackle pollution.

In general, regulations and economic instruments are likely to be employed together, one reinforcing the other. That approach will be most justifiable where markets work worst. A prime example of the need to combine standard-setting with economic instruments is energy efficiency (see Chapter 6 of Part I).

References

[1] Tom Tietenberg, "Economic Instruments for Environmental Regulation", *Oxford Review of Economic Policy*, Vol. 6, No.1, 1990, pages 17–33.

[2] "Environmental Regulation: Market Solutions", unpublished paper.

6

CONSERVING ENERGY

Using energy probably causes more environmental damage, one way and another, than any other human activity (except perhaps reproduction). Nuclear waste, acid rain, ground-level ozone all are ultimately environmental costs imposed in the course of using energy. Most dramatic and irreversible of all, global warming is likely to be the result of the build-up of carbon dioxide, methane and nitrous oxide – all of them gases released when energy is used – in the atmosphere.

No commercially available form of energy comes free of environmental problems. Even hydroelectric schemes, while not releasing carbon dioxide, blight rivers, and were the first source of additional electricity to be banned in austere Sweden. Tidal power, endlessly renewable, mostly clean, involves destroying estuaries. Proposals for tidal barrages in Britain breed fury among bird-lovers. People therefore face a choice. They can decide which environmental threat is most dangerous, and switch to forms of energy least likely to cause it. In the case of global warming, which would head the list for most environmentalists, that would mean switching from burning high-carbon fossil fuels towards lower-carbon kinds: from coal to oil, and from oil to natural gas. Or it means shifting towards "renewables": hydropower, solar power and, inevitably, nuclear power.

Of course, sources of energy that cause fewer environmental problems may well be developed commercially in future. Nuclear-power stations may become smaller and safer. Burning hydrogen produces only air and water (and extremely unpredictable explosions). For the moment, though, the main alternative to using lower-carbon fuels and "renewables" is to try to use less energy.

In practice, all these courses are likely to be necessary. Most projections of world demand for energy foresee a sharp increase, largely in the developing countries, where energy use is still tiny by western standards and where most of the expected doubling of world population will take place. By the end of the next century, people in today's poor countries may use twice (or maybe almost three times) more energy a head than they do today. How much more energy will depend on how much effort has been made to conserve energy.

Yet the scale of savings urged by climatologists is immense. Simply to stop the concentration of carbon dioxide in the atmosphere from increasing further – never mind reducing it – would mean making huge reductions in present use of fossil fuels. Calculations by William Emanuel of Oak Ridge National Laboratory in the United States[1] suggest that today's output of 6 billion tons of carbon dioxide a year (or its equivalent from other greenhouse gases) would have to fall to about 1 billion tons a year, and stay there, to stabilise the quantity of atmospheric greenhouse gases. Only thus might mankind hope eventually to stabilise the rate of increase in the earth's temperature that global warming seems likely to imply.

Doing what comes naturally

How, then, can energy conservation best be encouraged? The first point to realise is that advancing technology tends to bring conservation in its wake. As economies develop, their demand for energy, relative to GNP, tends first to rise rapidly and then to peak, as the basic infrastructure is completed. Basic industries, that convert raw materials into semi-manufactures, are the biggest energy guzzlers: as an economy gobbles less steel, cement, bricks, and so on, it comes to need less energy to produce the same volume of new wealth. It shifts from bulk to bites. An aluminium smelter spends $1.20 on energy for every dollar spent on wages and capital; a computer manufacturer, only 1.5 cents.[2] As Figure 10 shows, the ratio of energy demand to real GDP has been

Figure 10 Primary energy consumption relative to real GDP
(tonnes of oil equivalent per $'000)

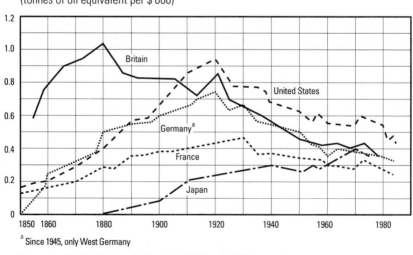

^a Since 1945, only West Germany

Source: Jean-Maria Martin. *Revue de L'Energie.* No. 415. November 1989

falling in Britain since 1880 and since the early years of this century in most other industrial countries. Between 1973 and the end of the 1980s the amount of energy used in the OECD countries to produce a unit of output fell by a fifth.

The continuing savings in industrial countries came from two sources. Some came from changes in industrial structure: steel plants closed down, partly because the domestic growth of steel demand declined, and partly because other, poorer countries built up industries of their own. To some extent, industries moved to other countries, taking their pollution with them. The other, more important reason for the savings, though, was the development of new and more energy-efficient technologies. Making steel by the open-hearth method used roughly twice as much energy as the basic-oxygen conversion process that began to replace it in the 1960s; the fuel consumption of the average German car has dropped by a quarter since the mid-1970s. As almost all technological innovation comes from the OECD countries, such changes gradually influence energy consumption all round the world.

Lots more energy efficiency is clearly possible. One study, by the International Energy Agency in 1987,[3] reckoned that known technologies could economically cut energy demand by at least a quarter by the end of the century, compared with the demand that present levels of efficiency implied. Some are even more optimistic. Amory Lovins (see also page 118) thinks that cost-effective savings of 75% could be achieved in the United States by the complete adoption of the most advanced technologies, including insulating all houses, and by near-perfect maintenance. Improbable: but a study by the WRI[4] suggested that OECD energy consumption could be halved over 30 years. If equally advanced technologies were employed in developing countries, their use of energy might be restrained enough for them to achieve the living standards of present-day Western Europe, while global energy use increased by only 10% above current levels.

Save a kilowatt, save cash
Energy conservation makes economic sense, as well as environmental sense. At the margin, it is almost always cheaper to save an additional kilowatt than to generate one. For no country uses energy in the most efficient way. Investing in conservation almost invariably yields a higher rate of return than building new power stations. Some studies have driven home this point, including one carried out in Canada using 1984 prices, when oil was $22 a barrel. The Canadian study found that it would cost only $13 to save the equivalent of a barrel of oil by cutting average domestic energy use by 30%. To make the same sort of savings by increasing the efficiency of gas furnaces would cost $8–10. To bring on stream the cheapest source of new energy, off-shore oil, would cost $30 a barrel. Clearly a new gas furnace would be a better buy than a nuclear power plant ($60 for the equivalent of a barrel of oil).

Conservation may also make sense from other points of view. It can be undertaken in small chunks, unlike building new generating capacity. The technology is often relatively simple – as simple as mending leaks in gas mains or insulating houses. No tiresome planning permission is needed, no furious residents demonstrate, as when a new power station has to be built in an industrial democracy. And the technology is, generally speaking, safe. Conserving energy never caused a Chernobyl.

The most powerful argument, though, is that of improving economic efficiency. In some countries the evidence of inefficiency is glaring. Capital going into energy production might more fruitfully be steered into other parts of the economy. Thus Mr Lovins points out that if the United States could reach Japanese levels of energy efficiency, which would imply halving the amount of energy it uses to produce each unit of GNP, it would save roughly $300 billion a year, or roughly the equivalent of the 1990 military budget. If the investment used to expand the supply could be shifted from electricity to other industries, what might it not do for America's competitive advantage?

The inefficient poor

Inefficiency is most striking in the third world and in the countries of Eastern Europe, the Soviet Union and China. A study for the World Bank[5] points out that: "It is not unusual to find from one-quarter to one-third of public resources available for investment going solely to electric power. And it is still inadequate." China, easily the biggest energy consumer (and producer) in the third world, also wastes more energy than any other country. In 1982 China used twice as much energy to produce a unit of GNP as the Soviet Union, and four times as much as Japan.[6] Chinese steel mills use anything up to double as much electricity to make a ton of steel as do mills in the OECD countries.

China's energy intensity has been exacerbated by a long-term policy of pegging energy prices well below world market levels. That in turn sprang from an emphasis on developing heavy industry. By 1980 industry accounted for almost two-thirds of all energy use. The same policies, pursued in the Soviet Union and Eastern Europe, have produced similar results. The Soviet Union is (after the United States) the world's second largest energy consumer – but uses that energy to produce far less wealth. In Hungary 70% of energy is used to process raw materials which provide only 15% of GDP.[7] In Poland, which until the start of 1990 priced electricity at a quarter of the world market level, coal production imposes heavy burdens on the economy. It swallows one-fifth of all the steel used in the country for structural supports, and almost a tenth of electricity output. A study by the World Bank[8] pointed out that Poland could turn a prospective coal deficit in 1995 into a surplus by achieving modern European standards of energy efficiency and still enjoy moderate economic growth.

Saving energy would leave all these countries better off, certainly compared with investing in new supplies and sometimes in absolute terms. Why, then, do such investments not take place? A part of the answer lies in energy prices: if they are low, investments in conservation may still look better than investments in bringing new energy supplies on stream, but they may still look unattractive compared with other demands on capital. But another part of the answer lies in the inadequate way the energy market works. Lots of barriers, some institutional, some organisational, prevent countries from investing as much in energy conservation as one might expect.

Pricing properly

A part of the reason that energy is used inefficiently is that the stuff is underpriced. If energy is cheap, people are more likely to use it wastefully than if its price reflects its true cost – to the economy, let alone to the environment.

True, a change in energy prices takes time to influence behaviour. That is not surprising. If people can switch from one activity to another similar one, then prices are likely to have a rapid and important influence. One strong argument for a carbon tax, which would tax energy on its carbon content, is that it would encourage a gradual shift along the spectrum from coal to oil, and oil to natural gas, and natural gas to "renewables". Where energy prices are raised in unison, no such adaptation can take place. Because there is no close substitute for energy, change will be slower and more modest.

This is a common dilemma in environmental policy. Where people can, say, switch from using leaded to using unleaded petrol, pricing policy will work well. Often, though, what is at stake is encouraging people to find ways of economising on a scarce environmental resource: using less water, or throwing away less rubbish. Where substitutes are hard to find, people will change their behaviour more reluctantly, and with more difficulty. The change will be least painful if it is phased in slowly: if people are given clear warnings that prices will rise, and governments then stick to their guns.

Raising energy prices quite clearly hastens investment in efficiency. Consider two bits of evidence. First, the study of the impact of energy subsidies[9] by Mark Kosmo, mentioned in Chapter 4 (Part I), found close links between energy prices and the rate of change in commercial energy efficiency. The relative energy efficiency of American and European industry bears that out. Figures from the International Energy Agency show that energy consumption per dollar of value added in the United States in 1985 was almost three times as high as in Japan, and almost twice as high as in Germany. Energy prices in Japan and Germany have long been well above those paid by American firms. Sometimes, such differences show up in an industry's technology: American cement production is about twice as energy intensive per ton as German production, because the "wet kilning" process typically used in America (but not Germany) involves lavish use of power.

Second, look at the way energy demand in industrial countries responded to the price rises of the mid-1970s. Mark Kosmo draws particular attention to the contrast between the OECD countries and Eastern Europe in the years from 1973 to 1981. In the OECD, real energy prices increased by 82%, while in Eastern Europe they remained virtually constant. As a result, energy efficiency improved in the OECD: in the United States energy efficiency, which had remained almost constant from 1952 to 1972, improved by 32% over the following decade. In Eastern Europe, it hardly altered.

When the oil price collapsed in 1986, investment in energy efficiency declined as well. By the time Saddam Hussein marched into Kuwait in August 1990, real energy prices (see Figure 11) in some countries were at their lowest level ever. Not surprisingly, conservation was no longer a priority either for companies or for individuals. A plateau had been reached. A review of the efficiency of domestic appliances in the main industrial countries by a team from the University of California has found that conservation stagnated in the mid-1980s. Consumers no longer worried about the fuel efficiency of cars or refrigerators (see Figure 12, page 113). Most manufacturers had already built in all the simpler (ie, cheaper) energy-saving devices. More sophisticated technology would take longer to pay for itself. Indeed in Japan where the strong yen caused oil prices to fall particularly dramatically, there was a marked trend towards less efficient cars. In 1988 the average new car in the Japanese fleet did only 27.3 miles per gallon, compared with 30.5 in 1982. New Japanese cars were actually less fuel-efficient than new American cars which, thanks to tough fuel-efficiency standards, managed 28 miles to the gallon in 1990.

To kick-start investment in energy efficiency means higher real energy prices. That means, first, stripping out the many ways in which governments subsidise energy consumption. As Chapter 4 of Part I argued, energy is one of the natural resources most likely to be deliberately underpriced. At the least, each extra unit of energy sold fully reflects the cost of producing it. The industrial countries might ask themselves whether that cost ought properly to include a chunk of the defence budget. The troops in Saudi Arabia were sent (in the nice phrase of Bill Robinson, erstwhile director of the London Institute for Fiscal Studies) to retrieve "an oil well dressed up as a nation".

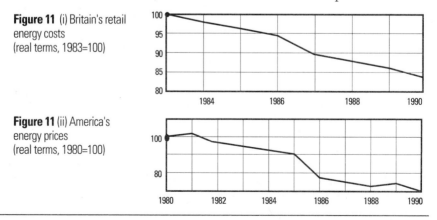

Figure 11 (i) Britain's retail energy costs (real terms, 1983=100)

Figure 11 (ii) America's energy prices (real terms, 1980=100)

Figure 12 Energy intensity[a] and fuel consumption

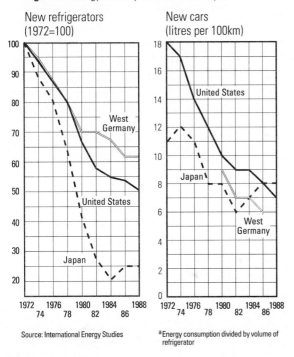

New refrigerators (1972=100)

New cars (litres per 100km)

West Germany

United States

Japan

United States

Japan

West Germany

Source: International Energy Studies

[a] Energy consumption divided by volume of refrigerator

First, tax energy

And beyond that? The arguments for taxing energy more heavily are formidable. Sheer self-interest may help to push governments in that direction. Voters are already used to being taxed on their energy consumption. Now, they may be persuaded that energy taxes are a virtuous way for governments to make money. Besides, energy offers an immense tax base. A tax adding just 1% to the price of coal would raise about $350m a year for the EC, or $2.5 billion if levied globally. Yet its impact on prices would be minute: smaller, indeed than the variations in spot coal prices from week to week.[10] In the United States, where taxes on energy use are tiny in comparison with other industrial countries, a tax on the carbon content of coal, oil and gas would raise enough revenue to wipe out much of the budget deficit and simultaneously restrain energy consumption. Calculations by the Council of Economic Advisers early in 1990 suggested that a tax of roughly $28 per ton of carbon might raise $163 billion over five years, and stabilise America's output of greenhouse gases in the 1990s. Others have argued that that goal would need even higher taxes – and thus yield even more revenue.

Why are governments reluctant? Most of the arguments rehearsed in Chapter 5 (Part I) apply. Energy taxes are seen as inflationary; they are thought to harm the poor more than the rich; they are regarded as harmful to a country's competitive position abroad, especially if they are adopted by one country in isolation. All these arguments assume that an energy tax is not seen as a substitute for some other tax – on spending, payrolls, or corporate profits – whose effects would be even more harmful.

The impact of energy taxes will depend essentially on how the revenue is used. The inflationary impact can be offset by using the revenue to reduce other taxes on spending. It can also be reduced if governments announce, well in advance, plans to make sure that real energy prices go up and stay up. If investors confidently expect real energy prices to be permanently increased, they will bring forward investments to reduce their energy bills. To protect the poor, whose energy bills tend to be lowest in absolute terms but highest in relation to their incomes, some of the yield from energy taxes can be steered into welfare benefits or into a flat-rate energy allowance. And the impact on competition, which in any case will be concentrated on the most energy-intensive industries, can be partly offset if higher government revenues allow lower interest rates or reductions in other corporate taxes.

What of the impact of higher energy taxes on economic growth? Policy makers who recall the 1970s remember not just the improvement in energy efficiency, but the dire recession that followed the oil price rise. Evidence that increased energy prices curb economic activity?

Not necessarily. For one thing, it was the oil exporters, not importing governments, who drove up the oil price. The result was a transfer of income from oil consumers in importing countries to oil producers. But, while oil consumers had tended to spend all but a small fraction of their incomes, oil exporters on the whole did not. The great undeveloped countries of the Middle East, from where most oil exports came, simply stuck most of their hugely increased earnings in the bank. In time, they found ways to spend the money. At first, though, world savings shot up – and a recession ensued.

Moreover, sudden change is always likely to disrupt economic activity. If the oil price rise of the mid-1970s had been announced in advance and phased in over two decades, both consumers and producers would have had time to adapt. The impact on growth would have been negligible. It might even have been positive.

For if it is true that energy is wasted, then policies that encourage it to be properly priced will make economies more efficient. Higher energy taxes would, in time, leave America with more cash to invest in other industries; cut the state borrowing programmes of most third-world countries; and encourage the countries of the old communist block to move out of unprofitable heavy industries and into more promising light manufacturing and services. If higher energy taxes encourage people to invest in technologies that save resources, they will make an economy work more efficiently. Properly designed and carefully applied, they could often have exactly that effect.

A mediocre market

If low energy prices had been the whole of the problem, the solution would clearly have lain in energy taxes. It isn't, and it doesn't. Several barriers seem to prevent the market from making the rational decision to invest more in conserving energy than in developing new supplies. These barriers are not a reason for avoiding imposed increases in energy prices. But the more the barriers can be knocked down, the smaller will be the price increases needed to achieve any given level of energy saving.

The existence of these barriers is encapsulated in the fact that energy users seem to need to earn much higher rates of return to induce them to make their investments in conservation than do producers of energy to encourage them to invest in supply. If the market worked perfectly, then both would seek the same return. Companies would step in and look for ways to arbitrage between them, until their rates of return moved into line. If a country's energy-producing capacity were fully used, then users would gain as much from cutting their demands as producers would gain from increasing supply. But this does not happen.

Big investments in new energy supplies – opening a mine, for instance, or building a power station – typically need to show a real return of 5–10%. By contrast, companies tend to look for paybacks on energy-saving investments of 1–3 years, implying a much higher 30% internal rate of return. Work at Britain's Science Policy Research Unit found that in the early 1980s, companies grappling with recession sought payback periods that were shorter still.

Obsessed with rapid returns, many companies are reluctant to make even obvious investments. Under a British scheme to coax firms to save energy in the early 1980s, the average age of boilers replaced was 41 years. Several were more than 70 years old. When the scheme began, the average payback period was expected to be 3.7 years. Rising fuel prices cut the actual payback to two years. By any standards, that is a remarkably good return.

Private individuals also apply high discount rates to investment in energy efficiency. One American review of the market for space and water heaters, refrigerators and freezers, found that people were willing to pay more for energy efficiency only if the extra cost were covered by savings within less than three years. Some expected paybacks within a few months, implying a nonsensical discount rate of up to 800%.

Hidden sense

Consumers are not being wholly irrational. The true costs of investing in energy efficiency, for both companies and individuals, may be higher than they seem. Simply finding out how best to save energy is a cost in its own right, and often a high one. It may be difficult (impossible in Britain where labelling is sparse) to find out which domestic appliance is most energy efficient, or what is the likely return on insulating a loft or replacing a boiler. In the case of transport and domestic uses of energy, a few basic solutions, widely applied, are sufficient to improve efficiency. The answers for industry may need to be developed case by case. That uses up scarce managerial time.

When fuel bills are a relatively small part of total costs, managers may simply not bother. They may prefer to concentrate on developing new markets and products, rather than retrenching in such a complicated and demanding way.

Companies and individuals alike may hesitate to replace old equipment with new simply because the new will save energy. The new equipment may have lower running costs over its lifetime than the old, but its initial cost may be higher (though, maddeningly for energy conservation, much less than the cost of providing new power supplies). An individual may regard the replacement of a boiler or air-conditioning system in a similar light. The individuals who stand to gain most from energy conservation are often the poorest. They are precisely the people least able to afford the capital cost of a new refrigerator or better insulation. A study[11] by Jerry Hausman in 1979 found that Americans on incomes of $6,000 a year had implied discount rates of 89% on purchases of energy-efficient durable goods, while those on $50,000 a year had discount rates of only 5%.

Many other barriers may skew the market. For instance, insulating a commercial building is a cost that falls on the landlord; the returns, in the form of a lower electricity bill, accrue to the tenant. Not surprisingly, private individuals are more likely to pay for energy efficiency if they own their own homes than if they rent them. Even though the tenant may enjoy a lower fuel bill, some of the value of insulation will eventually go to the landlord. Within the public sector, any cuts in spending on current budget that a school or hospital achieves by cutting its fuel bills will have their counterpart in a rise in its capital spending. But while spending more on capital account may force it to cut back on other investments, the benefit to the current account may be taken by the government.

Tariff structures may also hide the gains from energy saving, from producers as well as consumers. Companies may be charged less, the more power they buy. Individuals may pay a standing charge and a variable tariff to cover operating costs. If they reduce consumption, they still pay the same standing charge, even if the effect is to reduce peak demand and so the need for extra investment in power supplies. For example, Britain's regional electricity companies, privatised in 1991, make their main profits from selling extra units of electricity; that gives them no incentive whatever to reduce their customers' consumption. Worse, the cost of building new power stations, to supply the extra demand they generate, will fall first on the separately privatised generating companies.

Finally, the business of supplying power is normally carried out by entities which are either state-owned or at least state-backed. Their investments may therefore appear to be risk-free. In any case, they are likely to have access to much cheaper capital than consumers of power. That will artificially raise the rate of return they can earn by building new power stations, relative to the return that the consumer can expect on investments in energy efficiency.

Aligning the costs

To make the energy market work better means finding ways to remove as many of these barriers as possible. Probably the easiest to dismantle is the information barrier. Information is cheap and easy for governments to provide; difficult for companies to acquire. Thanks to green consumerism, more companies may see it as in their interest to provide better information voluntarily. In America and Britain some home builders are taking part in schemes to certify that a new house meets a certain minimum level of energy efficiency. That gives an incentive to buyers to purchase, and to builders to construct, more energy-efficient homes.

The imperfections of the market are also often taken as a reason for going further and setting standards: for the fuel efficiency of cars, for the insulation of new buildings, for the energy consumption of new domestic appliances. Some Californian cities have recently tackled the problem of applying higher standards to existing products by insisting that second-hand dwellings and commercial buildings must be insulated to certain minimum standards before the title can be transferred. The weakness of standards was set out in Chapter 5: they may, by raising the price of new products, actually discourage investment in new and more efficient technologies; and they may dictate solutions, rather than leaving companies to develop them for themselves.

One way to make standards work more flexibly, suggested by the Environmental Defense Fund (EDF), might be to give companies tradable efficiency credits. A manufacturer whose average refrigerator was more energy-efficient than an official benchmark, set in terms of energy use over the lifetime of an average machine, would get credits, while a manufacturer whose average was below the benchmark would have to buy them. That would leave an individual manufacturer free to make some refrigerators of below-average efficiency and others of a higher standard.

Another ingenious option, suggested by Michael Grubb,[12] would be to tax less energy-efficient products and to use the revenue to pay a subsidy on more efficient ones. The size of the transfer between less efficient and more efficient products would be calculated partly to reflect the difference in the payback requirements of energy producers and consumers. The effect of the scheme would be to cut the price of products that were expensive to buy and cheap to run, and increase the prices of those that were cheap to buy but used lots of energy.

Some proposals also draw on the idea of penalising the energy-extravagant to benefit the energy-efficient. A scheme proposed in (but not passed by) the Massachusetts legislature in 1990 would have set revenue-neutral "feebates" for commercial buildings of 50,000 square ft or more. Buildings that are designed to use less electricity than average would get a rebate, while those which tend to use more than average would pay a stiff fee for their electricity connection. Such a scheme could potentially make a huge profit for builders of efficient buildings.

Other schemes, adopted mainly in the United States, try to bridge the gap between the payback periods demanded by consumers and producers by influencing the behaviour of energy producers. The 1979 Public Utilities Regulation and Pricing Act (known as PURPA) laid down that utilities could not automatically pass on the costs of building new power plants. They had to demonstrate to their local regulatory commission that this was the "least-cost" option for meeting peak demand. Some regulators have decided that options for reducing peak electricity demand must be considered side by side with options for increasing supply.

The effects of PURPA have been reinforced by the difficulties of building new power stations in the United States. When a utility is operating at full capacity, it may indeed make better sense to look for ways to shave the peak off demand, rather than going to the endless trouble and expense of building a new plant. As a result, American utilities have become interested in finding ways to persuade their customers to use less electricity. More than 60 utilities, serving almost half of all Americans, now have programmes to encourages sales of devices for saving electricity, such as energy-efficient light bulbs. Most pay rebates to buyers, but some give a subsidy to dealers, to encourage sales.

Paying more for less

To be truly attractive, such schemes need to find ways to pay utilities more, the more they reduce demand for their product. That perverse idea can be achieved only by increasing the rate paid by those customers who do not invest in energy conservation, another example of taxing the polluters to subsidise the virtuous. To make it possible, state regulators have had to change their rules, allowing the profits of utilities to be uncoupled from their sales. That made it possible for utilities to be compensated for the revenue they would otherwise get from selling electricity, and for them to keep part of the savings enjoyed by their customers, too.

One such programme is described in Part II, Chapter 7. It allows the New England Electric System to add the cost of conservation into its rate base in the year in which it spends the money, and raise prices to consumers accordingly. Another scheme will allow Niagara Mohawk Power Corporation of New York to add into its rate base the $30m cost of its efficiency programmes, and to make an additional $1m of profit, if it achieves the state's goal of saving 240m kilowatt-hours a year. Prices per kilowatt hour will rise by 1.4%, but those customers who take part in the programme will have lower bills.

As such conservation programmes blossom, utilities may see energy saving as a marketable concept, just as electricity or gas are marketable. This is the ideal of Mr Lovins (see also page 109), who has invented the concept of the "negawatt", meaning electricity savings. "One can think of a 14-watt replacement for a 75-watt lamp, for example, as a 61-negawatt power plant."[13] Mr

Lovins views with excitement the emergence of a market in negawatts. In at least eight American states utilities that want a certain number of negawatts put them out to bid, and see what customers are willing to provide or save at what price.

One man who has turned this into a business is Angus King. In 1988 he worked for a firm building small generating stations and selling electricity to utilities. Declining power prices made this increasingly unprofitable. "For 9 cents a kilowatt hour, you can build a hydro-station," he discovered. "For 5 cents you can't build much of anything, but you can change light fixtures." So in 1989 his company, Northeast Energy Management, sold 48m kilowatt hours of electricity to the Central Maine Power company, about a third of the growth in that utility's industrial and commercial load for the year. But Mr King did so by contracting to get the power company's customers to cut their electricity use, rather than by building new power stations. His company goes to an industrial user and offers to pay about two-thirds of the cost of installing more efficient equipment. The user meets the rest of the cost, and keeps all the resulting savings on its electricity bill. For the user, the payback period on energy-saving investments is thus cut from about five years to 18 months. Mr King gets paid by the power company the same rate per kilowatt that he would get for generating new electricity.

Wanted, more arbitrageurs

The pressure on power companies to find ways to conserve energy will increase, as the costs and difficulties of building new power stations increase. Third-world countries will find it harder to borrow the money, as international aid organisations start to worry about the environmental effects of ever greater energy supplies. First-world utilities will find themselves faced with increasing hostility to building new plants. Local people, anxious not to have a potential polluter as a neighbour, will gang up with greens to insist that there are cheaper ways to meet demands for power. Already, that lobby has helped to mothball Britain's programme for building nuclear power stations.

For governments, and for many in the power industry, the shift of attitude will be painful. It has been easy to think of energy consumption, like GNP, as a mark of wealth, a measure of development. Third-world countries need only look at Poland to see where that philosophy leads. It will be important to think in terms of producing energy services, rather than raw energy: warmed homes, working machinery and mobile cars. Watts and gallons give no indication of warmth or mileage, but it is the latter that matters to consumers.

Conservation is more complicated than supplying new power. It involves many small investments, rather than a few giant ones. That is why it is ultimately important to find ways to release the force of the market. Higher prices alone will not achieve that, although low prices will make sure the market stays asleep. Promoting energy conservation, though, is essentially an organisational problem. It needs organisational ingenuity to give men like

Mr King a useful role. More can be done to encourage conservation in the design of a utility's tariff structure than in the design of car engines or boilers.

References

[1] Quoted in William Fulkerson, Roddie R. Judkins and Manoj K. Sanghri, "Energy from Fossil Fuels", *Scientific American*, September 1990, page 85.

[2] Marc H. Ross and Daniel Steinmeyer, "Energy for Industry", *Scientific American*, September 1990, page 49.

[3] IEA/OECD, *Energy Conservation in IEA Countries*, Paris, 1987

[4] J. Goldemberg, J.B. Johannsen, A.K. Reddy, R.H. Williams, *Energy for a Sustainable World,* Washington DC, 1987.

[5] *Financing of the Energy Sector in Developing Countries,* April 1989.

[6] Yu Joe Huang, "Potentials for and Barriers to Building Energy Conservation in China", *Contemporary Policy Issues,* California State University, July 1990.

[7] William Chandler (Ed.), *Carbon Emission Control Strategies*, WWF, 1990.

[8] IBRD internal document, "Poland and the Environment", June 1989.

[9] Mark Kosmo, *op.cit.,* Chapter 4, note 1.

[10] M.J. Grubb, *The Greenhouse Effect: Negotiating Targets,* Royal Institute of International Affairs, London, 1989.

[11] Jerry A. Hausman, "Individual discount rates and the purchase and utilisation of energy-using durables", *Bell Journal of Economics,* Vol. 10, 1979, pages 33–54.

[12] M.J. Grubb, *Energy Policies and the Greenhouse Effect*, Royal Institute of International Affairs, London, 1990, page 132.

[13] "Four Revolutions in Electricity Efficiency", *Contemporary Policy Issues*, July 1990.

7

FOREIGN AFFAIRS

At one time environment ministers and their officials stayed at home and worried about dirty rivers and smoky air. No longer. These days they jet from city to city, haggling far into the night over clauses and sub-clauses, just like defence experts or trade ministers. The environment has become the new stuff of international diplomacy, as important and intractable as disarmament or tariff barriers.

What has changed? Environmental policy is not new. Every government now accepts that it has some responsibility for the environment of the country it rules, even if some take the obligation lightly. But the issues that increasingly dominate environmental policy are not national but international. The most difficult questions involve environmental damage inflicted by one country, or by a group of countries, on other countries, or on the planet.

The reason these problems are so difficult to resolve is that they require the flimsy machinery of international agreement to take on the role that national governments perform at home. If a company is tipping sewage into a river, imposing on other users of the river costs that it incurs but does not pay, government can step in and oblige the company to shoulder those costs, by cleaning up its effluent. Without a world government or any prospect of one, no institution exists to ensure that countries do not inflict on the planet environmental costs that they are not willing to carry. No organisation can compel Brazil to stop destroying the rain forest, or force China to stop spewing sulphur dioxide from its power stations to fall as acid rain on Japan, or punish the United States if it refuses to curb its output of carbon dioxide.

The international aspects of environmental policy are the ones to which the most interesting new thought is being given by economists and political scientists. They are also resulting in a rising number of international agreements. In the past, countries made agreements to prevent a valuable species

Table 14 Multilateral environmental treaties entering into force in USA

Category	1930–39	1940–49	1950–59	1960–69	1970–79	1980–89
1. Fur and feathers	1	–	–	–	3	1
2. Whaling	1	1	1	–	–	–
3. Fishing	–	–	–	2	–	2
4. Marine pollution	–	–	–	1	2	3
5. Air pollution	–	–	–	–	–	4
6. Miscellaneous	–	–	–	2	–	1
Totals	2	1	1	5	5	11

Source: Robert Hahn and Kenneth Richards, "The Internationalisation of Environmental Regulation", Carnegie Mellon University, February 1989

being hunted or fished to extinction. Between 1930 and 1959 the United States put into force only a handful of such treaties, mainly on whaling. In the 1960s and 1970s the number rose to five per decade, as marine pollution and endangered species became prominent issues. In the 1980s the total was 11, of which four dealt with air and three with marine pollution (see Table 14).

Free riding

International environmental problems take many forms.[1] Sometimes one or two countries do something which they may see as in their interest, but which may harm most other countries. An example would be Brazil's destruction of the Amazon rain forest, or Britain's reluctance in the early 1980s to do anything to stop the sulphur dioxide emitted by its coal-fired power stations from falling as acid rain on the countries downwind of it in Scandinavia. Such examples are the international equivalent of the timber company that logs out a hillside, making a large profit but inflicting floods on the farmers living downstream.

Sometimes those who perpetrate environmental damage and those who suffer it are the same countries. The extent to which different countries cause and suffer damage may differ, but all or most participate. One example would be global warming. Every country burns the fossil fuels that fill the atmosphere with world-warming carbon dioxide; and every country will suffer some loss if the world's climate changes dramatically. Another example is the hole in the ozone layer caused by CFCs. These instances are more akin at a national level to the congestion of urban roads: almost all drivers help to cause traffic jams, and all fume in them.

A national government could ban the timber company and tax the traffic. But how does one persuade sovereign governments to accept self-restraint? Countries will usually do only what they regard as in their own self-interest. By reaching an international agreement to follow wise environmental policies, countries are likely to do better than if they pursue such policies alone. If one country bribes Brazil not to destroy the rain forest, it will have far less effect than if all countries do so together. Norway could, for instance, spend a large chunk of its smallish GNP writing off Brazil's debts, and get little in exchange. But if everybody handed over a smaller chunk of national wealth to a fund to give Brazil green aid in exchange for conservation, then Brazil might indeed be persuaded to keep its forest intact. The gains from cooperation are greater, relative to the costs, than the returns from going it alone.

Conversely, if most countries agree to be sensible, then an individual country can generally do better still by dropping out of the agreement. It can thus enjoy the rewards of what economists call, in a vividly expressive phrase, "free riding". If bus passengers are on their honour to pay their fares, they will do better if everybody is honourable than if only one or two pay up. But the few passengers who cheat do best of all. In the same way, if every country but one contributed to a world fund to conserve the Brazilian Amazon area, that one country would still enjoy all the benefits that accrued to the rest. It could still relish the idea that half the world's species were being protected, and would be protected from the harm that rain forest destruction probably does to the world's climate.

This is the central paradox of world environmental agreements. All countries do better if the nations of the world cooperate than if they do not; and yet individual countries face a strong incentive not to cooperate.

Welcome aboard

Countries, like people, are more likely to free-ride, the greater the benefits of doing so relative to the cost. That is partly a function of numbers. If three countries all border on a lake, and reach an agreement to stop discharging sewage into it, then all are more likely to stick to their side of the bargain than they would be if 20 countries were involve. The gains each individually enjoys as a result of an entirely unpolluted lake will be much larger than if the lake is only two-thirds clean. The incentive will be smaller if the choice is between a clean lake and an almost clean one.

People who cheat on buses run the risk of a large fine when an inspector comes aboard. Countries that welch on international agreements face no such threats. The ways that countries can impose their wills on each other are limited and uncertain. Take, for evidence, Iraq's invasion of Kuwait in 1990. The only threats available to the world's countries, unusually united and determined, were trade sanctions and military attack. It is hard to imagine the destruction of rain forests or the ozone layer or even global warming leading to military action against the villains (though a dispute over fishing in the North Sea between Britain and Iceland in the first half of the 1970s brought in the British navy) much less convincing global trade sanctions. It is highly likely, as Chapter 7 of Part II predicts, that there will be an increase in the use of environmental trade restrictions of one sort or another; but these are unlikely to persuade countries to change their policies unless either the country is small and poor, or the costs of change are insignificant.

The only other threat of much use in bolstering international environmental agreements is that of public opinion. Countries dislike being cast as international pariahs. Brazil bitterly resented the international abuse heaped on it at the height of the Amazon fires in 1988–89, but it reacted by reducing the tax incentives to cattle ranchers and trying to attach tougher green conditions to new electricity schemes. Britain finally accepted the need to reduce sulphur-dioxide output from power stations, and to stop the dumping of sewage sludge in the North Sea, not because it saw any advantage for its own citizens, but because of the political costs of being dubbed "the dirty man of Europe".

Countries may also agree to adopt environmental policies that are not obviously in their interest in the hope of cementing relations in a broader way with other countries. America in 1973 spent a large sum cleaning up the Colorado River, in response to Mexican complaints that the water had become increasingly saline. Why? Probably because America wanted to build a friendship with its Latin American neighbours, and especially with Mexico.

When victims pay

The deal on the Colorado River and Britain's decision to stop dumping sewage sludge are examples in international environmental policy of the polluter-pays principle at work. Probably, such examples will become rarer with time. International agreements will increasingly embody what has been dubbed (by Karl-Göran Mäler, in the *Oxford Review of Economic Policy*, see note 1) the "victim-pays principle".

Countries will often see a clear interest in bribing those who pollute to stop doing so. That will be particularly true when one country harms another, or many others, but is itself little damaged. It is also more likely to be the case when the polluter is poor: bribes will be worth more to it, and the costs of taking action will seem more of a burden. A good example of this is in Eastern Europe where it is unlikely that there will be much investment in preventing water and air pollution when there are other, even more pressing calls on scarce capital. The countries of Western Europe, which suffer from heavy metals dumped in the Baltic and waves of sulphur dioxide wafting into their forests, can buy much more pollution prevention by spending money in Eastern Europe than by spending yet more on their own sewage treatment and factory chimneys. Sweden already helps Poland with technology to curb acid rain. For every $5 western Germany spends on cleaning acid from its atmosphere, it can achieve the same effect by spending $1 in eastern Germany. In 1982, when Germany was still divided, West Germany agreed to pay East Germany the equivalent of $36m to help build a water treatment plant on the Spree River which flows from eastern Germany into west Berlin.[2]

If third-world countries are clever, they will see the victim-pays principle as a way to trade on the green consciences of first-world countries. Debt-for-nature agreements, under which first-world green organisations or governments redeem third-world debt to channel the cash into conservation, are a sort of victim payment; so is the $5m America has pledged to spend on elephant conservation under the African Elephant Conservation Act. Looked at from another angle, of course, such payments reflect the value that the rest of the world puts on conserving species, of the sort described in Chapter 3.

In accepting green aid, developing countries strike a bargain. Their side of the bargain will be conservation. To complain about "eco-colonialism" will be to miss the point. When a third-world country accepts green aid, it will be accepting, too, that the rest of the world has an interest in what a country does with its wildlife or its forests, and can realise that interest by making a payment. To complain about loss of sovereignty is not relevant: those who make such bargains accept some restriction of sovereignty as part of the deal.

When neighbours agree

Until recently, most international environmental agreements covered countries in a single region. Many agreements like this exist, such as the 1976 Barcelona Convention for the protection of the Mediterranean, or the 1975 Geneva convention on long-range trans-boundary air pollution. The waters of a river such as the Rhine, or an enclosed sea such as the Baltic or Caribbean, have been the most fruitful objects of conventions on water pollution. More recently, neighbouring countries have increasingly signed up agreements on air pollution.

The countries of Europe, huddled together on a small continent, have not surprisingly been the most frequent instigators of such agreements. They have two other advantages: a fairly common set of greenish values (more common than, say, those of Indonesia and Australia); and, in the EC Commission, a body to which a dozen of them have transferred supra-national authority.

Under such agreements, the balance of costs and benefits facing each country is often different. Rivers flow in one direction; winds tend to blow more in one direction than another. The agreements quite often reflect this by setting different targets for different countries. For instance, under the 1976 Bonn convention to protect the Rhine from chloride pollution the four countries that share its banks – the Netherlands, Germany, France and Switzerland – have agreed to split the costs of abatement in the ratio of 34:30:30:6.[3] The EC's 1988 directive to limit emissions from large combustion plants sets target cuts in sulphur dioxide output of 70% by 2003 for Belgium, the Netherlands and Germany, of 67% for Denmark, 63% for Italy, and 60% for Luxembourg and Britain. Greece, Ireland and Portugal are temporarily allowed to increase their output of sulphur dioxide as they develop their poorer economies.

Going global

Now the world has begun to move from regional agreements towards global ones. First, the damage caused to the ozone layer by CFCs, and now the threat to the climate from global warming, have led to attempts to reach agreements that are without precedent. Every country releases some CFCs into the atmosphere; every country is threatened by the hole in the ozone layer, which shields the earth from harmful ultra-violet radiation. An increase in the amount of such radiation reaching the earth's surface could cause an increased rate of skin cancer and cataracts in human beings as well as other biological damage. With global warming, caused by the accumulation in the atmosphere of gases which trap the sun's returning rays, it is even more true that every country bears some share of the blame, and every country's climate is at risk. Every country on earth therefore has an interest in seeing that an agreement is reached about both kinds of pollution; but similarly, every country needs to make costly adjustments if an agreement is to be completely effective.

In the second half of the 1980s a majority of the world's countries reached two agreements to curb the use of CFCs: first, the Vienna Convention, a broad and unspecific treaty, pledging governments to think more about the issue and discuss future action signed in 1985; and then the Montreal Protocol, a specific agreement attached to the convention in September 1987, committing signatories to reduce their consumption of five CFC compounds by half by 1998. In June 1990 that was extended to include more chemicals, and tightened to pledge an end to CFC use by the end of the century.

This agreement, which had 67 signatories in early 1991, was a spectacular and unprecedented achievement. Many politicians hope that it points the way to a convention on global climate change, on which talks began in Washington DC in February 1991. In fact, there are important differences between the Montreal negotiations and those on global warming which will make the latter infinitely more difficult. But there are also some lessons that can be drawn from past experience in designing treaties and environmental policies, which might lead to a better treaty on global warming.

From ozone to greenhouse

Like the negotiations over CFCs, talks on climate change begin with a large measure of scientific uncertainty about the problem they face. When negotiations on the Vienna convention began, scientists believed that CFCs were harming the ozone layer, and indeed the United States had banned the nonessential use of CFCs as aerosol propellants in 1978. Canada, Sweden, Norway and Denmark had all followed suit. But it was the discovery in 1984–85 by a team of British scientists of the hole in the ozone layer over Antarctica that gave negotiations the fillip they needed. In the following years more scientific observations of depletion helped to refine understanding. In 1986 Swiss scientists found an ozone hole over the Arctic.

Once the damage done by CFCs was no longer scientific speculation, but visible on satellite photographs, it became easier to give talks a sense of urgency. A common characteristic of international environmental agreements is that they often require countries to accept economic costs on the basis of a fair amount of scientific uncertainty. But reducing uncertainty makes agreement much easier. West Germany held out for years against cuts in emissions of sulphur dioxide from its power stations. Only in 1982, when its forests began to die, did West Germany change its stance.

The uncertainties about global warming are much greater than they were about CFCs. The theory is sound enough: few scientists argue that the accumulation of carbon dioxide, methane, nitrous oxide and CFCs in the atmosphere has been increasing, and that this will help to prevent the heat of the sun from bouncing back into space. Beyond that, though, there are great areas of uncertainty. Scientists are unsure how far the greenhouse effect may be offset. As more water evaporates, the sky may be cloudier, and clouds will shelter the earth from some sunshine. The increase in carbon dioxide may cause plants to grow more vigorously, taking up carbon dioxide as they do. On the other hand, the greenhouse effect may be reinforced: the warmer sea may absorb less carbon dioxide than it currently buries, and melting polar ice may release great bubbles of trapped methane.

As a result, although most scientists agree that the world will warm, they are unsure about the speed with which warming will occur. Yet speed is crucial. The faster warming takes place, the less time species will have to adapt to higher temperatures and the more creatures and plants are likely to die out as a result. Nor are scientists sure what the effect of warming will be on the planet. Expanding oceans and, perhaps, melting polar ice will increase sea level, though it is just possible that increased evaporation may reduce it. Probably, storms will become more frequent. Perhaps the increased heat will cause deserts to spread; though if rainfall rises and plants thrive on their richer diet of carbon dioxide, perhaps deserts will shrink and crops will flourish. Scientists find it impossible to predict which regions will gain and which will lose. Some think there will be no winners; others are less pessimistic.

It would help climate negotiations if there were clear evidence that global warming is taking place. The six warmest years on record fell in the 1980s, although 1990 topped them all. The drought in mid-western America in 1988 was what finally turned global warming into an important political issue in the United States. But most scientists are not yet confident that this is incontrovertible evidence that global warming is under way. For the moment, and probably until at least the early years of the next century, the evidence for global warming will continue to rest on what computer-based models of the climate suggest, and on evidence of carbon-dioxide bubbles trapped in Arctic ice.

Who emits what?

Not only is the evidence for global warming still speculative; it is not clear where all greenhouse gases come from. CFCs are greenhouse gases as well as ozone destroyers; they are entirely manmade, and so easy to track down.

Carbon dioxide comes partly from deforestation, which accounts for 10–30% of mankind's annual output of that gas. Most of the rest comes from burning fossil fuels: coal, oil and gas. Two other greenhouse gases, methane and nitrogen oxide, are harder to trace though both, molecule for molecule, are much more effective trappers of reflected heat than carbon dioxide. Methane comes from rotting waste, flatulent animals, leaking natural-gas pipelines, fermenting rice paddy-fields; nitrogen oxide, partly from the engines of cars and the chimneys of coal-fired power stations, but also from fertilisers and land-clearing. Both gases are likely to be far harder to curb, for both technical and economic reasons, than emissions of carbon dioxide.

One reason for the successful negotiation of the Montreal agreement was the evidence that ozone depletion was dangerous to health. Global warming does not yet enjoy this perverse advantage. It may, if crops more frequently fail, result in more starvation; it may, if the sea level rises, make homeless the one-third or so of mankind that lives within 40 miles of the sea. But CFCs had a greater advantage in terms of scare value. In 1986 the American National Aeronautics and Space Administration estimated that a 3% annual increase in CFC emissions could deplete the ozone layer by 10% by the middle of the next century, and the Environmental Protection Agency predicted that a 10% depletion could cause nearly 2 million extra cases of non-melanoma skin cancers in the United States alone. If only scientists could establish a link between the greenhouse effect and the American cancer rate, a successful climate convention would be virtually guaranteed.

Perhaps the most important difference of all between negotiations on CFCs and those on climate change is one of technology. In the case of CFCs, one relatively simple group of products is involved, made by few companies in few countries (Du Pont alone accounts for a quarter of world output). For the biggest uses of CFCs – as refrigerants, aerosol propellants and bubbles in insulating foam – there are possible substitutes. By 2000 Du Pont reckons that substitutes of various kinds might replace some 70% of current CFC use with two new families of chemicals, collectively known as hydrofluoroalkanes

Figure 13 How CFCs might be replaced by the year 2000

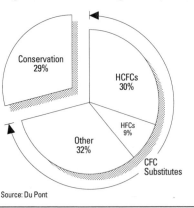

Source: Du Pont

(HFAs), accounting for some 40% of that total; a final 30% of current use could be met (see Figure 13, page 128) through conservation.

None of this is true of fossil fuels. Their use touches almost every aspect of human life. They are produced, not by a handful of large companies, but by a great many countries, some of which rely on exports of fossil fuels for the main part of their foreign-exchange earnings. Above all, there are no conven-ient substitutes. The choices that face the world with present technology are stark: it can switch from carbon-rich to carbon-poor fossil fuels, it can build many more nuclear power stations, or it can invest far more in energy conser-vation. In practice, all will be needed, but each is much more complicated than substituting one chemical for another in the air conditioner of a car.

The biggest manufacturers of CFCs are the very companies that have taken the lead in developing these substitutes. As Scott Barrett has pointed out,[4] manufacturers played an essential part in achieving a ban. A year after the Montreal protocol set its target of cutting CFC consumption by half, Du Pont announced that it would support a ban on production by the year 2000. This preceded and greatly encouraged the decision by the United States and the EC to phase out all CFC use by the end of the century. Part of the reason for Du Pont's decision may have been its strong sense of environmental responsibil-ity. Part may have been a fear of being sued at some future date by people with skin cancer. A third factor was probably the immense sum ($1 billion in the 1990s) that Du Pont intended to invest to develop and produce CFC-sub-stitutes. The world market for CFCs is worth only $4 billion–5 billion a year. So a government-supported ban was essential to protect the market for sub-stitutes. As Chapter 7 of Part II argues, this was an interesting example of congruent interests between companies and environmentalists.

No similar alliance is likely to emerge with fossil fuels. The only two groups with a powerful interest in a climate convention are the nuclear power industry and the manufacturers of equipment for energy conservation. Britain's Association for the Conservation of Energy, the trade body repre-senting the latter group, has lobbied hard for a tough approach to energy use. But the nuclear power lobby is an awkward ally for environmentalists and (as Chapter 6, Part I, pointed out) the energy-conservation industry is highly fragmented. The oil companies, by contrast, are huge and highly skilled political operators. While the CFC manufacturers have come to international conferences on CFCs to stiffen the resolve of governments to phase out their own product, an oil company representative at the Second World Conference on Climate Change in Geneva in November 1990 acted as go-between for the Saudi Arabian and American governments, two of the main opponents of tar-gets to reduce carbon-dioxide output.

Costs and benefits

International agreements on the environment are, as Mr Barrett has shrewdly noticed, rather like producer cartels. Countries or companies join cartels because the gains from acting together are greater than those from going it alone. But if cooperation from time to time demands large sacrifices, some will cheat and the cartel will eventually collapse. OPEC pushed up the oil price on the back of strong demand; once demand fell and big production cuts became necessary to prop up prices, some producers preferred to free-ride.

The gains to countries from cooperating over CFCs were clearly greater than those from acting alone. And the benefits of avoiding ozone depletion are both reasonably well defined and well distributed: no one country or group of countries stands to gain much more than others. Nor are the costs of cutting CFCs vast: witness the many countries that had acted on their own even before the Montreal protocol, and the large number that had signed it by the end of 1990.

Few of these points hold true for global warming. If the doomsters are right, the gains from international action would indeed be huge, far larger than any one country could achieve on its own behalf. But they are uncertain and far off; while the costs are easier to guess at, and certainly enormous. As scientists become clearer about the effects of global warming on different countries, the balance of costs and benefits to each country will become clearer. That may not make an agreement easier. While Bangladesh or little Kiribatu may vanish under the sea, some of the biggest emitters of carbon dioxide (America or the Soviet Union, for instance) may find that they can grow grain where grain never grew before.

Unpopular arithmetic

Nothing infuriates environmentalists as much as the suggestion that the costs of tackling global warming may vastly exceed the benefits. Yet that arithmetic is an essential starting point for any negotiations. Scientists approach from a different direction. They pose the question: "What rate of warming is ecologically manageable?" One set of answers emerges from a study conducted by a team of climatologists and energy experts for the Dutch Ministry of Environment.[5] The team concludes that the maximum rate of warming the planet can tolerate is 0.1° Celsius a decade, with an absolute limit of 2° Celsius above current levels. An international agreement to protect the climate could therefore establish a global budget setting out how much carbon dioxide can be spewed into the atmosphere by 2100. The study reckoned that the world could afford 55 more years of carbon-dioxide releases at current rates between 1985 and 2100, and that the central issue was to find fair ways of sharing out that limit.

The scientific assessment undertaken by the International Panel on Climate Change in 1990 took a similar line. This body was set up to prepare the ground for negotiations on a climate convention. Its scientific study concluded that the output of long-lived gases building up in the earth's atmosphere – carbon dioxide, nitrous oxide and CFCs – would have to be reduced by over 60% at once in order to stabilise concentrations at today's levels. If no action is taken, global mean temperature will rise by about 0.3° a decade, and a total of perhaps 3° by the end of the next century.

But what the planet can tolerate may be less than what humanity will willingly pay. With greenhouse gases, as with other kinds of pollution, there will be a point at which the benefits of preventing an extra ounce of carbon dioxide from escaping into the atmosphere are overtaken by the costs. At that point humanity would be wiser to spend its scarce capital on preventing other kinds of environmental damage.

But how to find that magic point? Economists have mainly totted up the costs of curbs. A few, notably Professor Nordhaus (see pages 132–133), have tried to attach some numbers to the benefits. Trying to quantify the costs is controversial enough. It is hampered by scientific uncertainty (about how fast the world will warm and where the warming will occur) and by economic uncertainty (about what will happen to world energy demand, economic growth and population over the next century).

One attempt, by Alan Manne of Stanford University and Richard Richels of the Electric Power Research Institute,[6] argues that the cost to the United States of stabilising carbon-dioxide output at its 1990 level by the end of this century and then cutting it by one-fifth would be roughly 3% of annual GDP by 2030. The costs would be lower for other OECD countries, with more nuclear power and greater reserves of oil and gas (both fuels give off less carbon dioxide than coal when they burn). For developing countries, for example China, even limiting carbon-dioxide output to double its 1990 level would cost 5–10% GDP.

A case for caution

Such immense numbers have to be treated gingerly. A tiny change in the assumptions behind a projection that runs a century into the future can have a huge cumulative effect. Robert Williams of the Centre for Energy and Environmental Studies at Princeton University has drawn attention[7] to how much the study by Messrs Manne and Richels depends on getting the right number for the underlying trend towards great energy efficiency. This inherent trend (described in Chapter 6 of Part I) has led to a steady decline in the ratio of energy demand to GDP in most developed countries for most of this century (in Britain, since 1880). It seems reasonable to assume that the trend will continue during the next century. But if Messrs Manne and Richels have underestimated the future pace of that trend by one single percentage point a year, energy demand by the end of the twenty-first century would be only one-third of the amount they assume. If so, the cost of curbing carbon-dioxide output may also be much lower.

Manne and Richels also assume that there is no underlying trend towards energy efficiency in developing countries. That may be true today, but not for long. The sheer impossibility of financing new power supplies fast enough to match economic growth will increasingly force developing countries to pay more attention to energy efficiency. At least one Indian utility has begun to explore the concept of least-cost supplies discussed in Chapter 6.

Calculations of the costs of curbing carbon dioxide may be difficult, but they are easy compared with the task of estimating the benefits. Here language can be muddling: a benefit of curbing greenhouse gases may take the form of avoiding some of the costs of adapting to a hotter world. Thus, while building sea walls is a cost of adapting to the rise in sea levels that global warming may bring, avoiding the need for the expense of building sea walls appears in the arithmetic as a benefit.

Estimating benefits calls for wild leaps of imagination. Professor Nordhaus has leapt in a series of papers (including an essay in *The Economist* of July 7th 1990),[8] and believes that the measurable gains may be small. Only 13% of America's national output, he points out, comes from parts of the economy even mildly sensitive to climate change. If sea levels rise, land may be lost and sea walls will have to be built, but over 75 years the cost would be 0.1% of cumulative private investment. In the third world some farmland may be lost, to sea level rises and higher temperatures. But the fertilising effect of more carbon dioxide may lift food output. Overall, he insists, there is "no strong presumption of substantial net economic damage".

While the benefits of preventing global warming are easily overestimated, according to Professor Nordhaus, the costs of curbing greenhouse gases will rise sharply as more are eliminated. He believes that perhaps one-sixth of greenhouse gas output could be prevented relatively cheaply. That would include the elimination of CFCs, which are cheap to scrap partly because they have substitutes, and partly because they harm the ozone layer as well as the climate. It would also include an end to uneconomic deforestation, of the kind described in Chapter 4, Part I. Beyond that point, further reductions may need taxes or regulations of the carbon content of fuels. The costs will then rise rapidly. To halve greenhouse gas output , if it is done gradually, might cost about \$200 billion a year, or about 1% of global output. If done quickly, it could cost much more.

Greens view such a conclusion with horrified disbelief. Certainly, Professor Nordhaus has deliberately left a number of things out of the equation. He makes no allowance for the irreversible loss of species that will not be able to adjust to increased temperatures. Some of those species might be unmourned beetles; others might have commercial value, actual or (more probably) unexplored and unknown. The values that humanity ascribes to the other creatures which share the planet (described in Chapters 1 and 3 of Part I), play no part in Professor Nordhaus's equations.

Nor does he put in a number for the possibility of catastrophe. What if warming suddenly causes polar ice caps to melt, or the warming Gulf Stream to shift many miles south, or an unprecedented drought? Each of these disasters has its band of scientific adherents; each might be worth paying an insurance premium to prevent. Curbing carbon-dioxide output is such a premium.

Nor, again, do Professor Nordhaus's numbers take account of the double benefit from some carbon-curbing measures. Using less fossil fuel will simultaneously reduce acid rain, oil spills, urban smog, traffic jams. Nor yet – and this could be most important of all – do his calculations peer into the really distant future, and consider the impact on the planet of a trebling, or a quadrupling, of greenhouse gases in the atmosphere.

Even so, it is right to ask the question about costs and benefits. Without it, governments are unlikely to think clearly about designing a climate agreement that sticks. For if countries find that the costs imposed on them by such an agreement greatly exceed the benefits they expect, they will cheat and the agreement will collapse.

The trials of targetry

Three questions will dominate all discussion of a climate convention. How far should the world aim to go in curbing greenhouse gases? How should the curbs be shared among countries? And how should potential free-riders be persuaded to pay their fares?

Although the first question is logically the one to begin with, its answer is more likely to emerge as the sum of replies to the second two. Finding a way to share out the curbs will be an argument disguised in long wrangling over other points. Ought there to be a single target for stabilisation (such as holding carbon-dioxide output at 1990 levels in the year 2000, as a clutch of industrial countries have promised)? If so, ought the target to be for carbon dioxide alone (that makes life easier for France, with its plentiful nuclear power) and if so, should it take account only of carbon dioxide released by burning fossil fuels, or should it cover deforestation too? Brazil, with its burning forests, sends up carbon dioxide on a first-world scale. Alternatively, should the target be for all greenhouse gases? America wants to talk about all greenhouse gases, and will press for some allowance for the cuts it has already made in CFCs by voluntarily banning CFCs in aerosols long before most European countries.

But if all greenhouse gases are to be counted, ought there to be some mechanism for taking account of their different power to trap the sun's returning rays? Methane is about 21 times more effective, molecule for molecule, as carbon dioxide; and CFCs about 12,000 times more effective. If "radiative forcing" is thus taken into account, so should the lifetime of gases in the atmosphere. Methane does its damaging work for ten years; nitrogen oxide for 150. Allow for that, and what ought one to do about the wildly varying estimates of the durability of carbon dioxide at anything from 50 to 200 years?

Carbon dioxide accounts for roughly half the climate-changing impact of greenhouse gases, though its share is declining. So setting goals in terms of carbon dioxide alone makes little sense. Yet measuring the output of other gases is fraught with difficulties. The amount of CFCs and of carbon dioxide released from burning fossil fuels may be relatively easy to calculate. Not so the carbon dioxide given off by deforestation, let alone each country's output of methane and nitrogen oxide. And if output of gases is to be measured, what about the creation of new stinks? Clearly, some allowance should be built in for reforestation, as growing trees will lock up carbon dioxide.

The choice of gases will give advantages to some countries, handicaps to others. So will the basis against which cuts or growth is measured. Japan has offered to stabilise its output of carbon dioxide per head at 1990 levels by the end of the century, but the number of Japanese heads is predicted to grow by 6% in that time. As Japan's population will start to decline in the next century, the world may not mind if Japan chooses such a basis, so long as it sticks to it. But what about third-world countries, whose populations will double or treble as the century advances?

Third-world countries, for their part, point out that almost all the man-made greenhouse gases now concentrated in the atmosphere have been put there by the activities of the rich world. As third-world GDPs grow, so will their outputs of warming gases. But why should they be forced to rein in, and perhaps restrict their future growth, just to accommodate the past misdeeds of the rich? The average person in a developing country annually uses the equivalent of one or two barrels of oil in the form of fuel bought on the market. In Europe and Japan that number jumps to 10–30 barrels, and in America to more than 40. So third-world countries will want to tie targets to population and the growth of GNP. Rich countries will insist that targets be "grandfathered", at least in the first instance: that each country's target comes near to matching its present output of greenhouse gases.

Whatever is the basis for targets, how ought they to be adjusted? Should they aim for parity in percentage reductions, or in absolute cuts? As energy-efficient Japan points out, a percentage cut would cost gas-guzzling America far less than its own frugal citizens.

Figure 14 Carbon-dioxide emissions, 1987

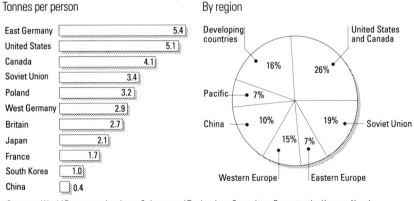

Sources: World Resources Institute; Science and Technology Committee Report to the House of Lords

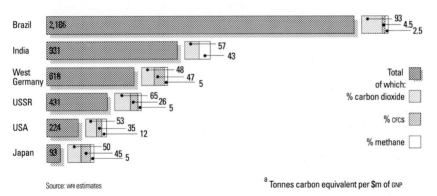

Figure 15 Net greenhouse-gas emissions per unit of GNP, 1987 [a]

Source: WRI estimates

[a] Tonnes carbon equivalent per $m of GNP

Time is money

Finally, plenty of arguments will rage over the pace at which gases should be curbed. Already, the level of output commits the world to a warmer climate in future even if not a kilowatt of fossil fuel was burnt from tomorrow on, the planet's temperature would still rise. Greenhouse gases will linger longer in the atmosphere. At present levels, each year of burning raises total concentration, and so the commitment to future warming. So stabilisation merely means that in future temperatures may rise more slowly than they will do if output of greenhouse gases continues relentlessly to increase.

Rapid adjustments will be expensive; gradual adjustments will invariably cost less. (Of course, no adjustment at all may eventually force panic-stricken nations to rush through even larger cuts, from a much higher base, than may be necessary if they start to change their habits soon.) Whatever target governments set themselves, its absolute level will matter more than the date on which it is first met. To aim for, say, a 20% cut in a country's carbon-dioxide output by 2025 will be far cheaper than to try to reach the same target by 2010. Yet thanks to the power of compound interest, it will be more important come the year 2100 to have achieved a cut of 20% on 1990 levels around the beginning of the twenty-first century than to have levelled off 5% below 1990 levels in 2005.

To make a treaty work, targets may have to be flexible. At the least, developing countries will need room for some growth in energy consumption. Other environmental treaties have allowed poorer countries to aim for easier goals. Indeed, the Montreal protocol set third-world countries a deadline for CFC reductions ten years later than it gave rich nations. By encouraging countries to do what is in their own economic interest (such as ending energy subsidies) a treaty is likely to bring more reluctant participants aboard and – equally important – keep them there.

When money changes hands

To capture potential free-riders, a treaty will have to keep down the costs to them of joining. There are two main ways to do that. One is to set them easy targets; the other is for other countries to bribe them to join. Logical recalcitrants will trade off the cost of complying against the benefit of bribery. The tougher the targets they are set, the higher the bribes will need to be.

But the need to pay bribes will drive up the cost of an agreement to other countries. They will then have to carry not only the costs of their own adjustment, but a share of the cost of bribery, too. The more they need to spend on bribes, the weaker the targets they may want. Weaker targets will reduce not just the cost of an agreement to their own citizens but the number of potential free-riders, too.

The Montreal protocol set a precedent, by promising third-world countries cash to help them meet environmental goals. The money to help third-world countries pay for the technology to live without CFCs will be doled out from a special new global environment fund which will be partly managed by the World Bank. The CFC fund was set up only after a long battle with the Americans who initially refused to contribute to it, mainly on the grounds that it risked being a huge new demand for aid cash. As the Americans foresaw, the money needed to bring countries into a global-warming treaty will be far greater. And that will not be the last time the participation of some third-world countries has to be bought. Governments are already hoping to draw up a treaty on biological diversity, setting goals for species conservation. The possibilities for abuse are obvious. Most species are in a handful of developing countries. Yes, they will promise, we will be green – but only at a price.

The question of technology transfer will be even more complicated. Third-world countries will want assurances, before they start haggling, that they will have access to first-world technology to cut their output of greenhouse gases. This has proved one of the hardest problems to resolve under the Montreal protocol. At the London conference in June 1990 Maneka Gandhi, India's current environment minister and widow of Sanjay, insisted that her country be given not only cash but the technology to make CFC-substitutes. When William Reilly, head of America's Environmental Protection Agency, pointed out that the technology was owned by companies and not by the government, she retorted: "Well then, *you* develop it and then *you* give it to us."

Mrs Gandhi was mollified by an executive from Du Pont, who offered to explore a joint venture in making alternatives to CFCs as long as Du Pont kept control of the technology and safety standards and was in some way paid for its involvement. But he pointed out that India might be wiser not to manufacture the entire expensive range of substitute gases for its tiny market, but to invest in the technology to apply them: redesigned air conditioners, refrigerators, and so on. This suggests plenty of future arguments about the precise mechanics of compensation. If India has to pay extra to buy the gases to be used in place of CFCs, that will clearly be a claim on the fund. But what if India decides to build its own plant to make the substitute gases? Ought the fund to pay for that, however uneconomic?

Carbon taxes or greenhouse permits

Complicated and expensive though such questions will be for CFCs, they will be infinitely more difficult for greenhouse gases. That is one of the reasons for considering, as part and parcel of any agreement on climate change, some machinery that would simultaneously discourage countries from producing greenhouse gases and transfer cash from those who might be willing to pay to those who might need to be bribed. Already schemes have been devised by academics for an international tax on the carbon dioxide produced by each country, with the proceeds to be spent to help poorer countries adapt; and for internationally traded permits to produce greenhouse gases, whose distribution would be designed to penalise some countries and bribe others.

Economic instruments have two important uses in international treaties. First, they offer a mechanism to transfer resources from the virtuous to the potentially wicked. Second, they hold down the cost of regulating global pollutants. As Chapter 5 of Part I argued, such measures will almost invariably deliver any given environmental benefit at a lower cost to society than will straight regulation. Simply setting each country a target for cutting its output of CFCs, carbon dioxide and other harmful gases will be a more expensive – perhaps far more expensive – approach than using a mechanism that takes account of the costs of curbing.

This is doubly important for global pollutants such as greenhouse gases. What matters environmentally is not how much gas each individual country produces, but the overall world total. For the planet, therefore, the most efficient approach will be to allow some countries to curb less, and others more, than whatever global target the agreement lays down. To set a constant target for each country – say, stabilisation at 1990 levels by the end of the century – may appear fair, but will really be deeply inefficient. Just as the costs of switching to lead-free petrol are far higher for an ancient Ford than a nearly new BMW, so the costs of implementing an identical target will be far higher for, say, energy-efficient Japan than wasteful Poland.

But there is a further point. With regulation alone, companies will have a powerful incentive to move from participating countries to those that refuse to sign any agreement, or that cheat. Because economic instruments reduce the costs of complying, they also reduce the incentive to move in order to break the agreement. Efficiency alone, in other words, offers some hope of keeping a grip on potential free-riders.

Taxes and tradable permits each have their advocates. Most of the advocates of an international carbon tax are politicians, including Carlo Ripa di Meana, the EC Commissioner for the Environment. He is keen on a tax levied by the Commission on each member country, based on the amount of carbon-dioxide it produces. The revenue would go into a fund that the Commission could spend on environmental good works. Most schemes for global carbon taxes envisage one levied by a world agency on each country, according to the amount of gases it produced. The tax would be set at the same level for each country, but the revenues would be handed back on some formula designed to bribe non-cooperators. Those might be the developing countries or large energy producers.

Scott Barrett is one of the few academics who have argued for a tax. He points out that, if an international agreement laid down the total quantity of greenhouse gases that could safely be emitted and then shared out tradable permits among nations, the world would (in theory, at least) know with some certainty the total amount of gases that could be produced. It would not know the price at which such permits would change hands. That price would reflect the cost of curbing greenhouse gases (since no permit would be bought if its price was higher than the cost of suppressing an equivalent amount of greenhouse gas).

With a tax, on the other hand, humanity could be sure about the cost of reducing greenhouse gases, but not of the quantity that would be abated. It might be safer to be sure about the cost than about the quantity. For suppose the cost of reducing greenhouse gas output rose steeply after the first 20% or so had been cut (and Professor Nordhaus thinks that it would). In that case, a tough limit to quantity might mean that the costs of getting rid of extra greenhouse gases soared. Rather than buy expensive permits, lots of countries would simply cheat.

A greenhouse tax might be imposed separately by individual countries. Indeed that may well happen on a regional scale: by the end of 1990, the EC Commission's environment directorate was drawing up plans for EC-wide carbon taxes. But some proponents of greenhouse taxes envisage a vast international agency to collect and recycle the revenue. The sheer sums of cash such an agency would have at its disposal make that vision unworldly. Professor David Pearce points out[9] that a global carbon tax designed eventually to halve carbon-dioxide output could result in tax revenues of some $600 billion, of which $480 billion would be paid back to developing countries. To put that figure in perspective, $600 billion is six times as much as all aid disbursements to third-world countries in 1989. "It is scarcely credible", argues Professor Pearce, "that any single international agency would have the capability to manage such resource transfers."

The alternative might be a mechanism to allow countries to trade permits to produce greenhouse gases. Under such a system Japan (which would find it expensive to reduce its output of gases) might buy permits from Poland (which would find it cheap, as long as it had the cash that a permit sale would bring in). Or Britain's National Power might reforest a stretch of Brazil with trees that would mop up carbon dioxide in exchange for being able to build another coal-fired power station.

Best of all, a company in America making refrigerators might set up a subsidiary in India to make refrigerators there too. If its refrigerators were much more efficient than average for new machines in India, it could earn permits there, which it could then use to make models in America that were less effi-

Table 15 Shares of global carbon-dioxide emissions and shares of global GDP (%, rounded)

	Share of world carbon-dioxide (fossil fuels only [a])	Share of world GDP
USA	24	27
USSR	19	8
China	9	2
Japan	5	14
Germany (FRG)	4	7
UK	3	3.5
Poland	2	0.5
Other	34	
Regional groupings		
W. Europe	15	
E. Europe, incl. USSR	26	
LDCs	16	

[a] Excludes gas flaring, cement and bunkers.
Source: David Pearce, "International Greenhouse Gas Agreements: Part 1 – International Tradable Permits", Department of Economics, University College London, mimeo, 1990

cient than the American average. Or it could simply make money by selling its permits on the world market. Thus a system of tradable permits could, in theory, give companies with energy-efficient technologies a big incentive to transfer their technologies to less efficient countries in the third world and Eastern Europe.

Elegant though this idea may sound, it brings problems of its own. First, if the scheme covered (as it logically should) all greenhouse gases rather than just carbon dioxide, there would be plenty of room for argument about how to trade one off against another. All those scientific uncertainties about the sources and durability of different gases would bubble to the surface. Secondly, even if the agreement covered only carbon-dioxide, the price of permits would be strongly influenced by the behaviour of the three biggest producers of the gas: the United States, the Soviet Union and the European Community.

Third, there would be the question of what to do if a country exceeded its permits. That raises all the awkward questions of penalising cheats. But without a credible arrangement for punishing the uncooperative, nobody would have an incentive to pay for a permit. That American refrigerator manufacturer would end up with worthless pieces of paper. This is simply another version of the free-rider problem described earlier in this chapter.

Finally and most difficult of all, how should permits be shared out? They cannot, as Table 15 clearly shows, be based on relative wealth: China and the Soviet Union would never agree. Ought they to be distributed, as Dr Grubb has argued,[10] on the basis of the number of adults in each country (which would disproportionately reward the third world, but recognise the moral principle that every adult has an equal right to the atmosphere? Or, as is more realistic, ought the initial share-out to reflect fairly closely existing output of gases, with perhaps some provision for changing the formula over time?

For and against hope

A convention on climate change will almost certainly be signed by the middle of 1992. If so, it will be a remarkable achievement. Together with the Montreal protocol, it marks an extraordinary willingness to talk seriously about the global environment in a way that was unimaginable as recently as 1980. Even more extraordinary is the fact that this will be an agreement based largely on the testimony of scientists: indeed, on scientific speculation rather than observable fact. Bear in mind that most politicians heard of the greenhouse effect for the first time in 1988. It will have taken four years to move from first fears to promises of policy change.

But what will those promises be worth? The Montreal protocol involves a commitment to self-sacrifice by a handful of companies mainly in rich countries. Most of those companies agreed partly because they could see the prospect of a profitable alternative: the manufacture of CFC substitutes. A climate change convention, by contrast, threatens to deprive energy producers of their livelihood with no promise of alternative gain. It is hardly surprising that, at the Second World Climate Conference in Geneva in November 1990, Saudi Arabia agreed to start negotiations on a climate change convention but objected to every mention of carbon-dioxide. It had some support from the United States.

To the extent that energy-consuming countries do indeed reduce their demands on fossil fuels, the price of those fuels will decline. It will probably fall, anyway, in the mid-1990s recession. That will give a huge inducement to some countries to increase their use of fuels, moving into the most energy-intensive industries such as metals manufacture, cement production, heavy engineering. In more scrupulous countries, those industries will howl for special exemptions or tax concessions.

It may well be that the countries who need to be bribed to co-operate in a climate-change agreement are not, for the most part, those of the third world. Most third-world countries, living close to subsistence level and dependent on the whims of climate to feed their burgeoning populations, probably have more to gain from a successful treaty than the better insulated developed countries. For the rich, the costs of adapting to climate change may seem much lower – and easier to share out – than the costs of trying to prevent it. Better, they may think, to build a few sea walls than to raise taxes on petrol.

It will be the big energy producers whose support most needs to be bought. Saudi Arabia and Iran, the Soviet Union and China, perhaps even the United States, will all face large losses of income from a successful climate treaty. The Soviet Union, the world's largest energy producer, will hate the idea of signing an agreement which potentially deprives it of its most promising source of hard-currency earnings. Saudi Arabia, which dominates the world market for oil, has nothing else to sell.

For some energy producers there may perhaps be partial compensations. The Soviet Union might gain if Europe bought its low-carbon natural gas for hard currency, even if it could sell less of its huge reserves of coal. Sitting on 40% of the world's natural gas reserves, the Soviet Union will be in a powerful position to dictate that fuel's world price. China has calculated that climate change could reduce its agricultural output, kill off four of its six main timber species and wreak havoc with its water resources. It may therefore agree to try to cut the growth in its output of carbon-dioxide even if that means it has to mine less of its coal stocks. It is hard to see such offsetting gains for the United States, producing almost a quarter of all the carbon-dioxide made by burning fossil fuels. As the world's second largest energy producer, it will lose revenue from exports; and may be expected to compensate other, poorer energy producers, too. Small wonder that the United States has been so unenthusiastic about negotiating a climate convention.

Probably the best that can be hoped for between now and the end of the century is an agreement to reduce those sources of greenhouse gases that cause other kinds of environmental harm, too, or that cost least to prevent. Making the Montreal protocol work well should be one priority; finding better ways to advance energy conservation, especially in the third world, Eastern Europe and the Soviet Union, should be another. Without firm evidence of the warming impact of greenhouse gases – perhaps, without some climatic catastrophe – it will probably be impossible to go further.

Only if technological advance really reduces the costs of curbing greenhouse gases will that prediction turn out to be wrong. Just as the development of CFC-substitutes made possible the Montreal protocol, so the development of substitutes for fossil fuels would give the best hope to a climate-change treaty – especially if the substitutes were no more expensive than the originals. Such magic matter may be unattainable; but if it is, only industry can invent it. In that sense, environmental progress depends crucially on giving the right incentives to industry. That is the theme of the second half of this book.

References

[1] This chapter draws extensively on the *Oxford Review of Economic Policy*, Vol. 6, No. 1, Spring 1990, and especially on articles by Partha Dasgupta, Scott Barrett and Karl-Göran Mäler.

[2] Scott Barrett, "Ozone Holes, Greenhouse Gases and Economic Policy", London Business School, July 1989.

[3] Peter H. Sand, *Lessons Learned in Global Governance,* WRI, Washington DC, 1990.

[4] *Op.cit.,* note 2 above.

[5] Florentin Krause, Wilfrid Bach and Jon Cooney, *Energy Policy in the Greenhouse: from Warming Fate to Warming Limit,* Earthscan Publications, London, 1990.

[6] "Global CO_2 Emission Reductions – The Impacts of Raising Energy Costs", forthcoming in *The Energy Journal*.

[7] "Will Containing Fossil Fuel Carbon-Dioxide Emissions Really Cost So Much?", forthcoming in *The Energy Journal*.

[8] And also in "To Slow or Not to Slow: The Economics of the Greenhouse Effect", Yale University Department of Economics, February 1990, mimeo.

[9] "Economics and the Global Environmental Challenge", *Millennium Journal of International Relations,* December 1990.

[10] *The Greenhouse Effect: Negotiating Targets, op.cit.*; see Chapter 6, note 11.

PART II

THE CHALLENGE TO COMPANIES

INTRODUCTION

For most companies the outbreak of green fever that began in the late 1980s is either a threat or an irrelevance. The managers who have been packing into conferences on environmental law, pollution technology and green auditing have been driven more by anxiety about the costs of getting an environmental decision wrong – an expensive law suit, a planning application refused, angry customers or worried workers – than the opportunities from getting it right. Only in marketing departments has the advent of the green consumer caused a quiver of excitement.

Beyond a doubt the new greenery will impose costs on companies. Many of them are discussed in the following chapters. Yet it also represents an extraordinary opportunity, perhaps the biggest opportunity for enterprise and invention the industrial world has ever seen. Those who spot how to make the most of this will flourish.

The impact will be immense within companies. The demand for cleaner products and processes will change the way they think about innovation. Prodded by green consumers, companies will start asking their suppliers quite new questions about the origins of their raw materials and the way they are handled; cornered by regulations, companies will give growing attention to ways of disposing of waste. When a new product is conceived, an early question will be, "But what happens at the end of its life?"

The costs of green policies will be an extra burden on industry. Often, indeed, governments will load on to industry costs that they feel unwilling to impose directly on voters. Companies investing in reducing emissions will have less cash to spend on developing new products; management time spent monitoring environmental performance is time not available for corporate growth. To that extent, industry can becoming greener only by growing more slowly.

But that is an inadequate and dispiriting account of what is likely to happen. At a conference on sustainable development in Bergen in May 1990 Björn Stigson, head of AB Fläkt, a Swedish engineering firm, produced an intriguing analogy. "We treat nature like we treated workers a hundred years ago," he said. "We included then no cost for the health and social security of workers in our calculations, and today we include no cost for the health and security of nature." Environmental protection may be to the next 50 years what the rise of the welfare state has been to the past 50: a drag on growth, true, and a large burden on corporate costs; but also a huge hard-to-quantify source of increased human well-being.

It will also be the source of a radical shift in consumer tastes. Developing products that use nature most frugally at both ends of their lives will call forth whole new generations of technology. The change will be more pervasive than those that followed the invention of the steam engine or of the computer. Fortunes await those who devise cheaper ways to dispose of plastics or to clean up contaminated soil. The great engineering projects of the next century will not be the civil engineering of dams or bridges, but the bio-engineering of sewage works and waste tips. Industry has before it that most precious of prospects: a spur to innovate.

An enemy, and yet a friend

The world will not grow cleaner without the co-operation of industry; for only through industry can technologies be developed that will satisfy human needs while at the same time making fewer demands on the environment. The challenge for government and for environmentalists is to spot ways of creating the right incentives, so that industry finds it profitable to be clean and unprofitable to be dirty.

Many environmentalists wince at the very mention of industry. As they rightly see it, industrial activity is the immediate cause of most environmental damage. It is industry that spews gases into the atmosphere, dumps poison in rivers, builds factories on open fields and digs mines in rain forests. It is industry, too, that makes the products that pollute: the packaging and plastics, the cars and the disposables. Much environmentalism is a new version of the old hatred of business by the utopian left. Many of the policies promoted by radical greens are more concerned to stop companies from doing whatever makes money than to make the world a cleaner, greener place.

Such utopianism is foolish. Perhaps, back in the middle ages, there was a time when human activity had little lasting impact on nature's balance. That day is gone for good. Today, 5.6 billion people live on the earth; within a century that number will climb past 10 billion, perhaps to 15 billion. Even in the poorest countries, where the lives of millions are barely touched by industry as the developed world knows it, the impact on the environment is already immense. Sheer numbers will inevitably make that impact greater still. And that even without the universal desire for the fruits of development. Bringing water supplies and electricity to villages are sure ways of increasing the demands third-world countries make on the environment; yet they save third-world women hours of walking to fetch water and find wood. Those saved hours mean healthier mothers, better nourished children and improved hygiene.

It is utopian, too, to think that the fairly poor will not want the trappings of western wealth. Top of the shopping list of every liberated East European is a family car. A senior official of Britain's Friends of the Earth recalls with pain the hostile reception he got when he delivered his standard green lecture on the environmental damage done by cars to an audience of trade-union officials. Many of the products that harm the environment have made life easier for people who can still remember that life was less pleasant before. Washing machines use more water than hand washing but mean less work; plastic packaging preserves food longer and means fewer shopping trips; chemical herbicides kill bugs more quickly than endless hoeing.

Above all, disposable products – be they nappies, plastic cups or hospital gowns – have frequently brought huge increases in convenience, at the cost of extra pressure on the environment. Disposables save labour, and labour is a resource that will be increasingly scarce in rich countries if population growth does not revive. As labour costs go up, so disposable products of all kinds will become more attractive. However much the greenest greens may bemoan the "throw-away" society, powerful economic forces will continue to encourage it.

How technology helps

It is important for environmentalists to understand these forces. Rather than yearning for a world that can never be recreated, they need to help develop incentives for industry to supply human needs in the least polluting way. The

Table 16 Estimated lifetimes of global resources (years)

	Current consumption rates		2030 rates[a]	
	Reserves[b]	Resources[c]	Reserves[b]	Resources[c]
Aluminium	256	805	124	407
Coal	206	3,226	29	457
Cobalt	109	429	10	40
Copper	41	277	4	26
Molybdenum	67	256	8	33
Nickel	66	163	7	16
Platinum group	225	413	21	29
Petroleum	35	83	3	7

Source: Robert A. Frosch and Nicholas E. Galloupoulos, "Strategies for Manufacturing", *Scientific American*, September 1989, page 96

[a] Assuming population of 10 billion will consume at current US rates.

[b] Quantities that can be profitably extracted with current technology.

[c] Total quantities thought to exist.

best hope for the environment lies in accepting what Paul Gray, former president of the Massachusetts Institute of Technology, has called "the paradox of technological development".[1] The industrial economy causes environmental damage; but it also offers the main way to repair that damage.

Since time began, technology has enabled mankind to use the earth's resources more frugally. The wheel needs less energy to shift a heavy weight than does the sledge. The closed stove delivers the same amount of heat as the open fire for far less fuel. Domesticated grain produces more protein from an acre of land than do wild grasses.

Technology can still perform such ancient conjuring tricks. Indeed, the ability of technology to find ways of squeezing more and more output from the same volume of input, especially if given the right price signals, helps to explain why previous pessimists, who prophesied environmental catastrophe through the exhaustion of some vital raw material, have so frequently turned out to be wrong. Consider, for instance, this speech by President Theodore Roosevelt, delivered in 1905 when America's railways were gobbling wood for sleepers: "Unless the vast forests of the United States can be made ready to meet the vast demands which this [economic] growth will inevitably bring, commercial disaster, that means disaster to the whole country, is inevitable. The railroads must have ties. If the present rate of forest destruction is allowed to continue with nothing to offset it, a timber famine in the future is inevitable."[2]

Within a matter of years, the voracious demand for wooden sleepers from American railways had been slowed by the development of techniques for treating wood with creosote, and then by the replacement of wooden ties with concrete.

President Roosevelt was not uniquely alarmist. Forty years before he spoke a British economist, W.S. Jevons, had published a book called *The Coal Question* in which he expressed deep fears for the future for British industry:[3]

> I draw the conclusion that I think anyone else would draw, that we cannot long maintain our present rate of consumption; that we can

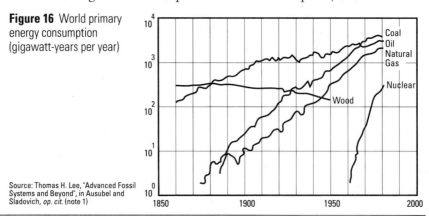

Figure 16 World primary energy consumption (gigawatt-years per year)

Source: Thomas H. Lee, "Advanced Fossil Systems and Beyond", in Ausubel and Sladovich, *op. cit.* (note 1)

never advance to the higher amounts of consumption supposed ... the check to our progress must become perceptible considerably within a century from the present time; that the cost of fuel must rise, perhaps within a lifetime, to a rate threatening our commercial and manufacturing supremacy; and the conclusion is inevitable; that our happy progressive condition is a thing of limited duration.

That was in 1865, only five years after oil, now the world's largest single source of primary energy, was discovered by drilling. Calculations for 1968[3] reckoned that at current annual rates of demand, enough fossil fuels (coal, oil and gas) remained for the next 2,500 years.

Such erroneous pessimism as that of Roosevelt and Jevons ought to be a reminder to those who now forecast environmental catastrophe. It is, of course, extremely hard to guess correctly the course of technology. (Professor Partha Dasgupta[3] defends economists from charges of unique myopia by citing the proceedings of a gathering of British scientists in 1876: "Although we cannot say what remains to be invented, we can say that there seems no reason to believe that electricity will be used as a practical mode of power.") But here is also a reminder that technologies have cycles, and that public alarm at their side-effects may frequently coincide with the arrival of a new technology, which does not have those side-effects but may well have others. Technology, as this chapter discusses, tends to solve one environmental problem by creating another. But it retains the ability to deliver unexpected solutions to apparently insoluble dilemmas.

The old magic still works
The past century has seen two particularly remarkable examples of the ability of technology to make more from less (see Figure 17). The first is energy. Between 1900 and the 1960s, the quantity of coal needed to generate a kilowatt hour of electricity fell from nearly 7lb to less than 1lb. More striking still, the entire world's per head demand for commercial energy in the ten years to 1987, a period of fast population growth, did not change, while wealth per head rose by 12% in real terms.

A glance at car technology suggests there could be plenty more efficiency ahead, always given the right price signals. Renault has already built a prototype of a car that can do 100 km on 3 litres of petrol in towns, 2.2 litres on the open road; Toyota is developing one which will do the same distance on 2.6 litres of diesel in the city, 2.1 litres on the open road. At present, the sales-weighted fuel economy of new cars in America is 8.4 litres per 100km. Remember that those prototypes were being developed at a time when oil prices in real terms were declining worldwide. Calculations by General Motors suggest that the fuel price in America per vehicle mile, in 1989 prices, fell from 4 cents at the start of the 1980s to 2 cents by the end.

The increased ability of the world to feed itself has been even more strik-

Figure 17 Primary energy consumption relative to GNP

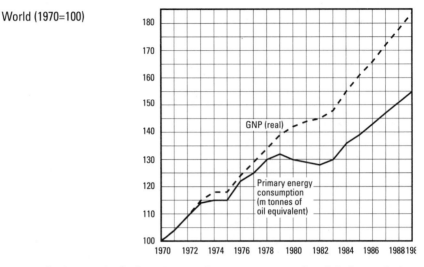

World (1970=100)

GNP (real)

Primary energy
consumption
(m tonnes of
oil equivalent)

ing. Anybody who looked at the terrifying projections for global population growth in the early 1960s found it unimaginable that the world could escape a devastating famine in the next three decades. There have indeed been some famines, although most, like that in Ethiopia in the mid-1980s, have been partly linked to political disorder. But the appalling catastrophes that might have taken place have not. Instead, food output more than doubled in the world's poor countries between 1965 and 1988, well ahead of their soaring populations. The world's two most populous countries, China and India, have become self-sufficient in grain. The proportion of the world's people suffering from malnutrition has fallen (although the absolute number has increased). To a large extent, this transformation has been the accomplishment of the "green revolution", the breeding of new high-yielding strains of cereals, and especially of rice. One reason for Africa's growing hunger is that there has been no green revolution in its staple food crops of cassava, millet and maize.

The message of such examples is clear, and often repeated throughout history. It is that technology can often be environmentally helpful, finding substitutes for scarce natural resources, or allowing existing resources to be stretched farther. The task for government is to encourage industry to develop such technologies. One of the main difficulties with that simple precept is the law of unintended consequences. Time and again, an apparently benign technology has turned out to have a sting in its tail.

Unintended consequences

Nothing sums up this point more poignantly than the life of Thomas Midgeley. A self-taught chemist on the research staff of General Motors, Mr Midgeley and his team solved the problem of engine knock by discovering tetraethyl lead in 1921. This breakthrough led to the development of high-octane petrol, which in turn made feasible more fuel-efficient high-compression petrol engines.

Then in the late 1920s, Midgeley was given the task of finding a non-toxic, non-flammable substitute for the refrigerants in commercial use at the time. These were ammonia, methyl chloride and sulphur dioxide whose unpleasant characteristics made them unsuitable for use in the home. Mr Midgeley came up with a compound called dichlorofluoromethane (freon 12). He demonstrated its safety to a meeting of the American Chemical Society in 1930 by inhaling a lungful of the gas, and then using it to blow out a lighted candle. The product ensured the success of the Frigidaire division of General Motors, and became invaluable in the second world war as an aerosol propellant for insecticides such as DDT.

The life of the man who put lead into petrol and chlorofluorocarbons into the ozone layer came to an end in 1944. In 1940 he had been crippled by an attack of polio. He developed a pulley and harness contraption to help himself in and out of bed, but strangled himself with the harness. It was a peculiarly appropriate demonstration of the unintended and malign consequence of even the most benign technological innovation.

Once a substance proves malign, moreover, it may be extremely difficult to get it out of the system. A side-effect of the green revolution has been a large increase in world use of chemical pesticides and fertilisers. Yet the world cannot easily afford to return to old varieties of grain that needed less of both, or at least not without the development of new genetically engineered varieties that may turn out to have other drawbacks. Even when industry agrees to get rid of a harmful product, the alternative may be much less convenient. Manufacturers of vacuum pumps voluntarily agreed to get rid of polychlorinated benzyls (PCBs), used in vacuum-pump oil, in 1971. Yet nothing as good for the task has yet been devised. A small quantity of mercurials in emulsion paint provided excellent protection against mould. The alternative has been to use several different compounds in much higher concentrations, without being entirely sure about the ways in which those compounds may react on each other.

Often, one environmental gain may be possible only if accompanied by a loss. Put a catalytic converter on a car and its fuel efficiency declines: the engine emits less nitrous oxide and sulphur dioxide, but more global-warming carbon dioxide. Ban CFCs, and it becomes harder to insulate refrigerators and buildings. The ozone layer is protected, but at the expense of higher greenhouse-gas emissions. Biotechnology will pose many more questions of the same sort, such as, is it better to have genetically engineered crops that need no pesticides, or may the environmental costs ultimately exceed the benefits?

Think of impact, not product
Yet with all these reservations, the fact remains that industry has the ability

Figure 18 Single factor productivity: United States electricity industry (1970=100)

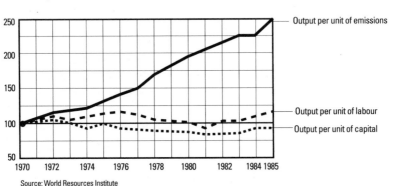

Source: World Resources Institute

to squeeze more output from natural resources. Inventive industry can find new ways to achieve the same impact on its market: to sell people warmth, for instance, it may be more sensible to sell them better home insulation than more electricity. Increasingly, value is added by design, information, quality; people spend more on attributes of a product that have nothing to do with the quantity of material put into its manufacture, and everything to do with the application of human ingenuity.

As manufacturing processes become better controlled, waste is reduced. As products from Coke cans to calculators become lighter, it takes less material and energy to make them. The important task for government is to find ways to encourage industry to use raw materials frugally. Such frugality brings double benefits. For every pound of raw material used is ultimately a pound of waste: use less water, and there will be less dirty water; use less packaging, and landfills will not fill up with discarded paper and plastic.

The best way to try to make sure that industry applies technology to solving environmental problems, rather than creating new ones, is to give the right price signals. Only if prices are set to reflect the true cost of using environmental resources will companies start to value them as they value labour and capital, and aim to improve their productivity in the use of the environment as they strive for higher productivity of labour and capital.

A study by Robert Repetto[4] of the WRI developed a measure of productivity for the American electricity industry that tries to take account of environmental productivity. Making assumptions about the damage caused by power-station emissions, he reckons that the cost of these unpriced outputs from the electricity industry in the mid-1980s was almost as large as the value of labour or the fuel the industry used. If the electricity industry had accounted for its success in cutting emissions, especially in the 1970s, when measuring its overall productivity, its performance would have been between two and three times as good as it appears from conventional estimates (see Figure 18).

A common green interest

Setting price signals, devising regulations or standards is government's job. The green revolution is underpinned by governmental intervention. But industry and government have a common interest in making sure that such intervention leads to the greatest possible increase in the quality of the environment at the lowest possible cost. Companies are concerned to try to make sure that environmental standards are set at levels that they can reach but their competitors cannot; governments want to make sure that companies put cash and inventive energy into devising environmentally benign technologies. Once one company comes up with a green technology that allows it to meet a higher environmental standard than its competitors, government can insist that the higher standard becomes universal.

This is not what has happened in the past. Those managers at environmental conferences are there because they have been trained to think of government regulation as a nuisance, not an opportunity. Yet when government intervenes, through regulation or through setting price signals, it creates new markets. Suddenly, electric cars become profitable; waste-management shares boom; desulphurisation plants are in demand.

It is important for both industry and government to realise how far the market for environmental technology will be created and sustained by governmental intervention. Consumers' taste for green products will boom and fade, though always returning to a higher level of environmental consciousness from every trough. In the recession years of the mid-1990s the green consumer will be replaced, at least at mass market level, by the penny-pincher. Only the wealthier, trend-setting shoppers will still pay a premium for green goods.

But a market for environmentally friendlier products will remain. It will be sustained by a number of things: by the rising legal penalties for polluting accidents, by the difficulty of persuading local communities to accept new factories which may be polluting, and above all by ever tighter regulations about waste disposal. Governments, harried by voters, will continue to press for tighter standards for waste water, for dirty air, and above all for solid rubbish, both hazardous and harmless. As these pressures will fall directly on companies (and on waste-disposal authorities), they will be largely hidden from voters, who will assume that they are being offered a free ride to greenery.

In fact, government regulations will raise the returns on all kinds of environmentally friendly investments. A water-treatment plant, uneconomic in the early 1980s, will look a much better buy once the costs of sewage discharges goes up and the insurance premiums for an accidental spill become astronomical. A precipitator in the smokestack, once ridiculed by the finance director, will seem a bargain when the alternative is an entire new plant.

For governments the trick will be to devise controls that foster green technology. That will be difficult. The temptation will be to regulate pollution by double-guessing companies: laying down the technologies they must use, instead of setting targets for their output of dirt and leaving corporate ingenuity to come up with answers. If governments seek the cooperation of the greenest companies, they will have to avoid protecting their particular technological solution to any given environmental problem.

There are dangers, of course, in relying on a confluence of interest between government and industry to raise environmental standards. Companies will always be tempted to press government to set standards in terms of a technology that they have devised, rather than its impact; and for government it will often be easier to do things that way. Large companies with lots of political clout will see the alternative to, say, CFCs in terms of another chemical; or the alternative to cars running on leaded petrol as cars running on lead-free.

But standards set in terms of specific technologies discourage innovation. That often comes not from the politically weighty giants, but from the minnows, since environmental innovation, like many other kinds, tends to come from "outsiders", like small companies, suppliers and foreign firms.

These are the companies for whom the environment presents the greatest opportunity. The new technologies that they invent are the world's best hope of enjoying a continued rise in living standards without putting ever greater pressure on the environment. The cleanest countries will be those whose environmental rules make it easiest for such companies to flourish. The most successful companies will be those that best turn such green rules to their own advantage.

References

[1] Jesse H. Ausubel and Hedy E. Sladovich (Eds), *Technology and Environment*, National Academy Press, Washington DC, 1989.

[2] *Ibid.*

[3] Quoted in Partha Dasgupta, "Exhaustible Resources", in Laurie Friday and Ronald Laskey (Eds), *The Fragile Environment,* Cambridge University Press, 1989.

[4] "The Concept and Measurement of Environmental Productivity: An Exploratory Study of the Electric Power Industry", paper for Towards 2000: Environment, Technology and the New Century, Conference sponsored by WRI and OECD, Annapolis, 1990.

1

THE CONSUMER, GREEN BUT FICKLE

What a fright the green consumer gave companies in the late 1980s. Retailers and manufacturers were knocked sideways by the most dramatic change in customers' tastes that they had ever experienced. The shoppers' revolt broke out in Europe, but when it spread across the Atlantic, it found customers who were already used to throwing their purses behind every health scare at a moment's notice.

The companies that green consumers touched, which were mainly retailers and manufacturers of consumer goods, have felt a lasting and traumatic impact. They have learnt that greenery can be profitable. Managers who had long regarded environmentalists as a nuisance, pressing for product changes without appreciating their expense, suddenly discovered that ordinary people were willing to pay a premium for a product that they perceived as better for the environment than a rival brand. Once green was upmarket, it was worth worrying about.

The sheer speed with which green consumerism erupted in some countries will also leave its mark. A whole generation of managers will remember for the rest of their working lives how quickly British customers stopped buying aerosols containing CFCS, or Americans suddenly panicked over Alar in apples. That will make companies more interested in the contents of their products, and more alert to the first whiff of a new green alarm.

Yet the tide of green consumerism had probably reached high-water mark by the middle of 1990 and begun to ebb. Important though it has been, it is not the main force that will drive the greening of business through the 1990s. There are more durable pressures. That will come as a disappointment to those who hoped that greenery might not need much more government intervention, and who were encouraged by the sight of people voting with their wallets. If consumers could be left to decide what was green and what was not, then governments could leave them to it. Dirty firms would be punished by the market. Ungreen products would languish unsold. Companies would realise that the market would reward them for caring about their impact on the environment.

That first naïve hope has quickly died. It is clear that the environment is much too complex to be saved by shoppers. To be effectively green, shoppers need guidance. Giving them guidance is in the interests of government and companies alike. If, for instance, shopping power is to back energy conservation, people need reliable information on which domestic appliances use energy most frugally. Unguided people are a menace to companies, since they may listen credulously to every green guru who has a particular axe to grind.

Deciding which products and processes are truly green is immensely complicated. That difficulty has beset another kind of green consumer: the green investor. There are investors who like the idea of buying into a fund that invests in "green"companies. But such funds will find it almost as difficult as the ordinary shopper to pick the truly virtuous. They will have to decide whether to prefer the dirty company in the plastics recycling business to the petrochemicals company earnestly trying to reduce the danger of oil spills.

Decisions are problematical and may seem like a trade-off between apples and pears. Governments, aided by good research, are the best placed to set green goals. For the sake of the environment, that is just as well. For the green consumer alone is too fickle a creature to supplant government action.

If consumers are to be truly effective, governments need to provide more than just information. They need to make sure that the market sets the right signals. An attraction of green products to producers is that they can be sold at a premium to dirty ones. That is the reverse of the polluter-pays principle. How much better if the burden of taxes and regulation on dirty products were to make *them* the expensive ones. Yet only with a few goods – such as lead-free petrol, or cars with catalytic converters – have some governments used taxation to tilt prices, in order to give consumers the right message. Many more such incentives are needed, if the power of the green shopper is to be harnessed properly.

A revolution at the check-out

Green consumerism has differed from country to country and shoppers have concentrated on different products in different places. In America customers fretted about packaging but were not much interested in the contents of mercury batteries; in Britain "green" batteries sold wonderfully, but customers continued to accept plastic bags from supermarkets; and Germans worried about the plastics used to make drinks bottles.

The change in consumers' tastes was most dramatic in Britain, whose absence of green consciousness among voters and shoppers alike had long astonished other northern European countries. Companies found that product markets collapsed or erupted in what sometimes seemed an arbitrary way. It was a hair-raising experience. "At least with regulations," said Ron McLean,

Table 17 Green activists and green consumers

	Green activists[a]		Green consumers[b]	
	1988	1990	1988	1990
	%	%	%	%
USA	33[c]	...	45	...
Australia	14	33	27	64
Great Britain	14	25	19	50
West Germany	13	...	52	...

[a] Green activists: those who had undertaken 5 or more "green" activities, such as donating to environmental charities.

[b] Green consumers: those who had selected one product over another for environmental reasons.

[c] Figures give percentage of sample.

Source: MORI

who runs environmental management for Arthur D Little, a consultancy in Europe, "you know what's coming for six months before, and can lobby." Managers in some companies have been left scarred, in just the way that American managers have been scarred by the experience of Superfund (described in Part II, Chapter 2). They vow never to be caught out again. That alone is likely to ensure that some companies remain warily green even if the immediate pressure from the consumer fades.

Within a few months, people learnt to ask for aerosols that contained no CFCs, washing powders free of phosphates and beef that had not been grazed on cleared rain forest. The public, long squeamish about using toilet paper made partly from recycled fibre, suddenly clamoured for it. A poll by MORI, a market-research group, found that between November 1988 and May 1989 the proportion of respondents who said they had chosen a product because of its environmental friendliness soared from 19% to 42%.

The structure of British retailing, dominated by a few powerful chains which dictate to manufacturers, also helps to explain what happened. Most of the supermarket chains reacted swiftly to the revolution in shoppers' tastes, forcing manufacturers to follow with equal speed. In other parts of Europe, where retailers also have strong market power, they have also picked up and amplified the change in shoppers' attitudes. But in northern Europe green consumerism is old hat. Germans and Scandinavians have been buying phosphate-free detergent for years. The change has therefore been less traumatic. Surveys by market researchers tend to show that German consumers are in advance not just of Britain, but even of the verdant Dutch, and that environmental awareness is the norm rather than the exception. Dutch and German consumers are much more active than those in Britain or America. More are willing to recycle old newspapers, to take glass containers to bottle banks (91% of the Dutch, according to a 1989 poll) and to dispose of old batteries separately from other household rubbish, a practice unknown in Britain. In 1990 German shoppers showed a new sort of assertiveness, ripping surplus packaging from products before they left a shop. Supermarkets hurriedly installed in-store recycling bins.

In the United States people were worrying back in the early 1970s about issues, such as chlorine bleach in paper, that only dawned on the British in the late 1980s. The late 1980s saw a rise in green consciousness among consumers in America, just as in Europe. A survey of Americans by Michael Peters (MPG), a British product-development consultancy, in the summer of 1989 found that 53% of those questioned had declined to buy a product during the previous year because they were worried about the effects the product or its packaging might have on the environment. Three-quarters of those surveyed said they would buy a product with biodegradable or recyclable packaging, and roughly as many were willing to pay a little more for such goods. A parallel survey the firm conducted in Canada found the public's greenery was just behind America's. Two-thirds of those questioned said they would be more likely to buy a product with recyclable or biodegradable packaging, and about 60% said they would be willing to pay more for such products. But in America, the relative weakness of retailers *vis-à-vis* manufacturers has meant that supermarkets have mainly followed, not led. Manufacturers of consumer goods, such as Procter & Gamble and Coca-Cola, and some companies in other service industries, such as McDonald's, have been the leaders.

For deep greens the green consumer is the ultimate oxymoron. Consumers are the problem, not the solution: consuming uses up the earth's capacity to produce materials and absorb waste. When, in September 1989, SustainAbility, a British environmental consultancy, ran a Green Shopping Day, Friends of the Earth threatened to run a rival No Shopping Day. Beyond a doubt, the truly green should consume less, not differently. But until such a miraculous change in human nature comes about, it is surely good that customers should ask for greener products.

How it happened

Greenery in the shops grew mainly from the same roots as greenery at the polls. Several events seem to have contributed. The atmosphere was ripe: in the summer of 1988 the press was full of stories of burning rain forests and vanishing ozone. In September two British authors, John Elkington and Julia Hailes, published *The Green Consumer Guide*.[1] Within four weeks it had shot to the top of the bestseller list. It has since appeared in ten other countries, with similar impact. Lots of imitators have appeared, especially in the United States. While other "green" guides, both before and since, have concentrated on general instructions to use bottlebanks and insulate houses, this guide offered a star rating for companies and products. It listed refrigerators by energy efficiency, dishwashers by water efficiency and petrol companies by the number of sites selling lead-free petrol. Most influential of all, it gave grocery chains stars for greenery, and listed a range of criteria on which they had been judged.

PART II

In Britain, a sign that consumers were ready for guidance of thi. the success of Friends of the Earth in persuading most supermarke within a matter of months to introduce non-CFC propellants into own aerosols. Several supermarkets followed this with programmes to remove from their commercial refrigerators and from packaging. The impact of t campaign quickly fed back up the product chain. Soon the rest of the aerosc industry had agreed to withdraw CFCs from most products by the end of 1989. As aerosols were Britain's main use for CFCs, that in turn hit demand for the gases from ICI, and encouraged that company's search for alternatives. Other companies that had been selling aerosols set to work to develop propellant-free products as fast as possible.

Companies reacted to this sudden shift in tastes in different ways. Many buried their heads and hoped the whole upheaval would disappear. Others, more rationally, argued that environmental considerations would always influence consumers less than quality and price. This was effectively the reaction of Marks and Spencer, awarded only one star in the *Green Consumer Guide* compared with four apiece for Safeway and Sainsbury, two other big chains. But others again decided that greenery was now regarded by some customers as an aspect of quality.

An important revelation was the fact that shoppers were willing to pay a premium for products they regarded as green. This was particularly true in Britain and North America. The first quantitative study of Britain's green consumers was completed by Mintel, a market-research firm, in June 1989. It excited boardrooms with its finding that some shoppers were willing to pay a premium of 25% or more for organically grown food and environmentally friendly products. The MPG work in America and Canada suggested this was also true there (though to a lesser extent – only 29% of American shoppers said they would be willing to pay as much as a 5% premium), but not true, or no longer true, in Germany, where customers tend to assume that companies will be green, rather than seeing it as a distinction.

Companies in continental Europe have for some time seen greenery as a way to move upmarket. For instance, Germany's AEG, a producer of white goods, recovered from near-bankruptcy in the early 1980s by building a washing machine that used less detergent, energy and water than its rivals. Tengelmann, a large German retailer, began a campaign to attract green customers in 1984, when the German retail market was in the doldrums. In Britain, that example was seized on by Tesco, a chain trying to rebuild its shabby image. It too saw green consumerism as a wonderful opportunity to move upmarket and took greenery well beyond the supermarket shelves. By the end of 1989 it had become the first British retailer to install bottlebanks at most of the stores with room for them, and the first to offer facilities for customers to recycle plastics.

The link between greenery and the top of the market emerges from several pieces of market research. In America a study by Cambridge Reports/

Research International found that green consumers (defined by people's interest in green issues, rather than spending patterns) were almost twice as likely as the non-green sort to earn over $50,000 a year and to be college graduates. The Mintel study found that a quarter of British adults could be described as "strong green". Although they exist across all social divisions, they were most common among the young, better off and better educated, and in the economically buoyant south. One possible moral: greenery is chic.

Looking at life cycles

A company that sets off down the green path quickly finds it to be a long and tortuous road. Companies have begun to accept that if they are to boast of their greenery, they need to think not just about the impact of their product in the hands of the consumer, but about the process by which that product is made and sold. So the supermarket that starts by getting rid of aerosols using CFCs goes on to replace its refrigerators with those using another coolant; the company that boasts its drinks bottles can be recycled goes on to provide a bottle bank; the detergent manufacturer that begins by removing phosphates may end up analysing the impact of a washing powder on the environment right through its life cycle.

Some companies have found that their initial response to the green consumer carried them farther than they might ever have expected at the outset. For instance Gateway, a British supermarket chain, is now committed to developing new shops in town centres and avoiding green-field sites wherever possible. Coca-Cola, which has already cut the amount of raw materials used in its drinks packaging, launched a joint venture with Hoechst Celanese early in 1991 to make bottles for soft drinks out of recycled plastics, thus closing the loop between initial product and eventual scrap.

Migros, Switzerland's biggest retailer, has a computer programme to check the "eco-balance" of its packaging: which kinds take most resources to make and to dispose of. Prodded partly by their customers, a growing number of companies on both sides of the Atlantic have become interested in studying the "eco-balance" or life-cycle impact of products. They try to take account of the effect on the environment not just of the materials used to make a product and its packaging, but of the energy involved from raw-material extraction through to transport to the customer, and of the amount of a product a customer needs to use to produce a given effect. There may be no point in making a green detergent if customers need to use three times as much to clean their clothes; or in producing a refillable container if it uses much more material and customers do not make the return trip.

As a retailer's greenery grows, so the pressure passes back up the chain to suppliers. When customers first turned green, supermarkets generally found that their conventional suppliers could not switch track fast enough. Instead, they looked abroad, to countries that had gone green earlier. So three of the companies to benefit most in Britain's green boom were West German or

Belgian: Varta, a German manufacturer of batteries, whose mercury-free and cadmium-free batteries increased their market share of sales through groceries from 7% to 17% in the space of six months in early 1989; AEG, a West German white-goods manufacturer, whose sales rose by 30% in the year to May 1989, at a time when it was claiming to be "caring for the environment through technology"; and Ecover, a Belgian manufacturer of phosphate-free washing powders, whose admittedly small sales increased from $1m in autumn 1988 to $5m just over a year later.

Similarly when Loblaw, a Canadian grocery chain, decided deliberately to take a leaf out of Tesco's book and use greenery to move its image upmarket, it found it hard to find suppliers in North America. Many of the 100 green products it put on its shelves in 1989 were imported from Europe, including Ecover. Not for the first time, it paid to have gone green early.

Once retailers found that their customers cared about greenery, they began to pass the message up the line to their suppliers. Loblaw's president, David Nichol, recalls the many years the Canadian government spent trying to persuade Procter & Gamble to introduce a phosphate-free detergent. "When we started selling a phosphate-free detergent, they got one on the market within six months."

Lean on the suppliers

In a more radical departure, companies have begun to ask searching questions of their suppliers. America's three leading tuna canners, with 70% of the market, decided in April 1990 to ensure that their fish was caught only in "dolphin-friendly ways". As the Brazilian rain forest blazed in 1989, Marks and Spencer sent a team to find out whether their beef grazed on deforested pasture. McDonald's hamburger chain was attacked in the *Green Consumer Guide* for encouraging deforestation by their beef-buying policy and rebutted the criticism only after close scrutiny of its suppliers all over the world. British do-it-yourself chains have begun to cross-question suppliers about their policies: one, B&Q, looked at the peat bogs they use and eliminated one it thought was badly managed. Another, Do-It-All, wrote to its suppliers, asking them to ensure that CFCs had been removed from all products and packaging. Tengelmann wrote to suppliers in 1989 telling them that all products and packaging containing cellulose must be chlorine-free.

The process does not stop there. In countries where retailers call the tune, they are demanding that suppliers set themselves the same green standards as they try to adopt. Retailers that once set rules for standards of hygiene and freshness now also specify green rules. For instance, Gateway wrote to all its suppliers with a string of qualities it "wished" to find in its products, from energy efficiency and manufacture from local materials where possible, to keeping down transport costs. In exchange, it promised to price environmentally friendly products fairly, to reflect true production costs.

On the billboards

The rise of the green consumer has been accompanied by the rise of the green advertisement. Casting around for green things to say about their companies, lots of marketing departments begin by taking what a company is already doing and describing it as "environmentally friendly". Is the lorry fleet using lead-free petrol? Has the office just been insulated to save electricity? Are the paper towels already using a fair proportion of recycled material? Splendid. Call in the copywriters and think of a slogan. Or simply put a picture of a bunny rabbit or a tree on the packet, and guess that some customers will read the message that was never there.

Others, more reasonably, have gone for "cause-related marketing", an idea piloted in the early 1980s by American Express to raise money to repair the Statue of Liberty. Businesses such as banks or computer companies whose own activities do not impinge on the environment in ways that are obvious to consumers have offered to give some of their turnover to a green charity. The beneficiaries have tended to be mainly the safer, middle-of-the-road charities, rather than aggressive ones like Greenpeace. Even so, such schemes have caused much soul-searching among some recipients. The Worldwide Fund for Nature (WWF), long skilled in raising cash from companies in exchange for the right to use its logo, suddenly found that lots of newly greened companies saw the familiar cuddly panda as the most distinctive of all environmental symbols. That brought benefits, as fund-raising grew easier. But with the money came qualms: suddenly, WWF's supporters wanted to know whether the logo was going to companies whose greenery was impeccable, or simply to those willing to bid for it.

So green marketing has rapidly turned out to be a morass. Several British companies have had their knuckles rapped by the Advertising Standards Association, the industry's watchdog. Initially, some were told off for calling their product "environmentally friendly" or "green", rather as food firms were once scolded for calling their cottage cheeses and crispbreads "slimming". Most have now switched to "environmentally friendlier". Some companies cheerfully boasted that their cleaning products contained "no phosphate", without mentioning that neither their product nor those of their competitors had ever contained it.

Boasts about a product's destructibility have repeatedly caused difficulties with environmental claims in America. Nothing is gained by claiming that a drinks can is "recyclable" if there are no facilities to recycle it. And it is meaningless to call a plastic bag "biodegradable" if American landfills are so airtight that it will take several centuries to rot. A heavily advertised American line of "biodegradable" plastic bags did not rot even when exposed to the air, and left small plastic pellets behind when they did. That enraged consumer lobbyists as well as greens.

Some advertising suggested that copywriters were more ignorant about the environment than the average consumer. A British ad for a new Rover car claimed it was "as ozone friendly as it is economical" because it used lead-free petrol, disregarding the fact that petrol, lead-free or not, has no direct effect on the ozone layer. BP Oil, falling into a similar trap, advertised its unleaded "Supergreen" petrol by saying it caused "no pollution of the environment".

Such silliness is only the fringe of the affair. The fact that a product environmentally friendlier in one respect may not be in others is far more difficult for companies. Procter & Gamble and Wal-Mart, America's third largest retailer, earned some derision for putting a green label on a brand of paper towels made from chlorine-bleached unrecycled paper packaged in plastic, simply because the inner tube was made of recycled material. ICI launched a range of household cleaners early in 1990 with a claim that they were "environmentally friendly". Friends of the Earth promptly rang the press to point out that, while the impact of the cleaners might be fairly benign when they were washed down the kitchen sink, their manufacturing process was a significant cause of water pollution, and needed lots of energy.

How green is green?

More fundamentally, it may genuinely not be clear whether a process really meets the green claims made for it. Or – and this will increasingly be the case – it may be truly impossible to tell whether one product or process is greener than another.

An example of the first sort ended up in the French courts. Rhône-Poulenc, the world's third largest phosphates producer, quarrelled with Henkel, a German chemicals manufacturer, over the impact on river life of phosphates in detergents. Phosphate-free detergents account for 90% of the market in Germany, where more cleaning preparations are used than elsewhere in Europe. In ungreen France, their share was only 6% until Henkel launched a product called Le Chat in 1989. Then sales tripled. Rhône-Poulenc retaliated with studies which, it claimed, proved that phosphate-free detergents were more harmful than the old kind, and ran posters of dying fish supposedly killed by phosphate-free suds. Henkel took the company to court, and succeeded in getting the campaign stopped.

It is not clear that detergents are an important source of phosphates in water supplies (though that has not stopped the phosphate-free share of the world detergent market climbing from 6% in the early 1970s to 60% by 1988). Nor is it clear that mercury in batteries that are thrown away is a source of water contamination. That has not stopped battery manufacturers from eliminating mercury in zinc carbon and zinc chloride batteries, and doing handsomely from it, like first in the field German Varta (see page 159).

Mercury-free and cadmium-free batteries still contain lead and harmful acids. Green advertising often tends to emphasise the nasty things taken out of a product, without saying much about other nasty substances still there, or put in as substitutes. As Procter & Gamble put it, "Too many environmental claims are currently based on the absence of particular ingredients. Users of such claims are thus able, in one phrase, to imply the safety of the ingredients they do use, and impugn the safety of those they do not use, without substantiation in either case. At the extreme, some such claims are based on the absence of ingredients which are not used in any product in the category."

Green but muddling

Sometimes a company finds that the green bandwagon becomes a treadmill. As the debate over green claims became more sophisticated in Britain in 1990, one paper producer, Scott, tried to beat the environmentalists at their own game by claiming that it pursued a "holistic" approach to the environment. It argued that "the forests which supply its worldwide fibre needs use up more carbon dioxide than is produced by burning fossil fuels in 30 power stations". This claim was promptly challenged in *ENDS*, Britain's best environmental newsletter, which argued that planting rotations of trees did not store continuously increasing quantities of carbon; replacement trees eventually mop up carbon at the same rate as the trees that grew there before them.

The argument over nappies has been even more muddling for the poor consumer. A fight broke out in Britain between two manufacturers, Peaudouce and Procter & Gamble, whose pulp is supplied by Stora, a Swedish firm. Peaudouce breached the guidelines for British advertisers, which lay down that any claim to do better than a rival product "should be expressed in terms which accurately reflect the extent and nature of the evidence available to substantiate them". Peaudouce bragged that "a nappy can't hope to be environmentally friendly unless its pulp is 100% non-chlorine bleached. Many leading nappy brands don't achieve this standard." Stora retaliated by arguing that the effluent from the pulp-making process it used, which did include chlorine, was environmentally superior in other ways to the Peaudouce process. No parent without a degree in chemistry could have hoped to disentangle the debate.

In America the debate has become still more complex. Procter & Gamble commissioned work on the relative environmental impacts of disposable and cloth nappies. Add in the chemicals to soak them, the hot water to wash them and the petrol for the vans which run American nappy services, and Procter & Gamble was able to mount a vigorous case for the environmental friendliness of the disposable. Green parents who want to swaddle their babies in cloth have begun to worry about the pesticides used to grow the cotton, so Seventh Generation, a American mail-order company specialising in products for green consumers, is doing a booming business in "green" cotton.

The proliferation of such debates has had two effects. First, it has encouraged the drawing up of advertising codes of conduct to try to set out what green benefits can and cannot be touted. In America, states have begun to legislate on definitions of "biodegradable" and "recyclable". The Federal Trade Commission and the Environmental Protection Agency have been working to develop uniform national guidelines for environmental marketing claims. In Britain the Department of Trade and Industry has been considering bringing green advertising claims under the legal controls operated through the Trade Descriptions Act of 1968. The act might be changed to make it possible for firms making green claims to be asked to produce their evidence. The Advertising Standards Authority has urged companies to produce documentary evidence to support broad claims. And the Independent Broadcasting Authority has drawn up a special code of conduct. Its own scientific advisers are being used to make rigorous assessments of green claims.

At the same time, consumers have become more sceptical about green claims. A survey of British consumers by advertising agency Ogilvy & Mather found that between August 1989 and February 1990 the proportion of shoppers changing to a "greener" brand or switching to a different outlet to buy a greener product had stopped rising, and was static at 23% and 14% respectively. The agency also reported that the most "active" consumers, who had been most likely to make green purchases, were becoming disillusioned and making fewer green purchases.

Some shops find that people are reluctant to buy green products if they do not work as well as conventional alternatives. The chemicals that make a product "ungreen" – optical brighteners in washing powders, mercury in long-life batteries – may be impossible to replace with something that does the job equally well. Never before (except perhaps in wartime) have manufacturers tried asking their consumers to accept lower performance for the sake of some greater good.

Fad or forever?

The question companies most want answered is whether green consumerism is a passing fad, or here to stay. In the same way as it arrived at a different pace in different countries, so experience will not be the same everywhere. Some survey evidence[2] suggests that German consumers, who have been green for longer than any others, also have a longer environmental memory than the more recently greened Dutch or the British.

Indeed, the longevity and effectiveness of green consumerism in Germany suggests a lesson for other countries. The media hype will fade – as it did in Britain in 1990 – but an underlay of consumer sensitivity will remain, and may re-emerge. Consumers will come to take it for granted that retailers and their suppliers care about the environment. Criticism from one of the green lobbying organisations who are the self-appointed policemen of the environment will cost sales. But good green behaviour may simply become one of a bundle of indicators of quality that customers look for when they shop.

Advertising is an important medium of consumer education. Because so much has been spent by companies in the late 1980s on advertising their greener products, consumers have been taught to think in new ways. For example, Procter & Gamble, one of America's biggest buyers of advertising space, has worked hard to teach consumers about greener packaging, and to promote the idea of a bottle refilled with concentrated washing liquid from a plastic pouch. A generation of shoppers will have had their perception of packaging permanently altered by such campaigns.

Wanted: informed consumers

Even those companies which have benefited from green consumers bewail their ignorance. If only, they sigh, it were possible to point out the slender links between phosphates and eutrophication, or lay before them the finer points of the arguments over bleach and water pollution. Then, perhaps, consumers might understand why one washing powder is wrong to claim that it is greener than its rivals, and stop switching their shopping habits with such maddening unpredictability.

Plenty of shoppers are undoubtedly ill-informed. Research by Gerstman and Meyers, an American firm of packaging designers, found that 43% of those surveyed did not understand that a plastic ketchup bottle is not biodegradable and is unlikely to be recycled. In the early days of British green consumerism, in 1988, the market-research firm of Gould Mattinson Associates found that "respondents were frequently unable to explain why products were harmful [but] there seemed to be an instinctive suspicion of clingfilm, burger boxes and pesticides". More dramatically, a survey, carried out in the summer of 1989 when furious Americans were punishing Exxon for the *Exxon Valdez* oil spill by cutting up their account cards, found that British respondents rated Esso one of the greenest companies in the country.

Shoppers need to be well informed about environmental cause and effect in order to be effectively green. Hence the attraction of "eco-labelling". Many supermarkets now have their own schemes, often with sketchy criteria. So do some industries. Ten British paper merchants have agreed on a labelling scheme to explain the contents of recycled paper. In western America in 1990 four big grocery chains hired a consultant to review environmental claims by their suppliers. Products that met green criteria were to be awarded a "Green Cross" seal of approval. A rival body based on the east coast, "Green Seal", also proposed to vet products. It had plans to look at a restricted range of products, including household paint, face tissues and light bulbs, and assess their impact on the environment from every conceivable viewpoint. For instance, it planned to look at the amount of electricity needed to run light bulbs, the impact of mining the metals to make them and the consequences of disposal. Such private schemes are inevitably second-best and muddle shoppers.

Now governments are beginning to run eco-labelling schemes. Norway, Sweden, Canada and Japan all established programmes in the course of 1989. The prototype is Germany's Blue Angel: in operation since 1977, it is now run by the federal environment ministry, and covers everything from quiet lawnmowers to recycled wallpaper. At one point the Blue Angel logo was recognised by four out of five German consumers, more than recognised their own president. Several European countries, including Britain, France and the Netherlands, are considering schemes of their own. America has moved more slowly: federal definitions of what "organic" means were introduced in the 1990 Farm Bill and there is a move to bring in a federal eco-seal to be awarded by the Environmental Protection Agency. But most of the initiative has been at state level: California has considered a state-wide scheme, and a group of north-eastern states have been talking about common regulations on labelling. The European Commission, fearful that the rival schemes of member states could make free trade more difficult, is planning a scheme. The Nordic countries have similarly agreed on a common scheme, with common standards administered by national governments.

Read the small print

All face problems, some of which crystallise the difficulties facing even the most earnest green consumer. For instance, ought the label to be awarded simply on the way a product affects the environment when it is used, or should the manufacturing process and its disposability also be considered? The Blue Angel award is generally made on one particular criterion: for instance, anti-corrosive coatings may qualify for the award if they have a low lead and chromium content; and burners for central-heating systems may be included if they have high energy efficiency and low emissions of soot, sulphur dioxide and nitrogen oxide. A label gives the particular reason for the award. But the schemes now being drawn up are taking a cradle-to-grave approach. That, as so many companies have already discovered, is infinitely more complicated than simply labelling an aerosol as CFC-free or giving the energy consumption of a refrigerator.

Then there is the question of making sure that the process which gets the coveted label really is the most environmentally friendly. The board devising Canada's eco-labelling scheme tried to decide which was the most environmentally friendly kind of drinks container: glass bottles, cardboard cartons, recycled plastic containers, or what? One research paper suggested that each was best, for different reasons.

As eco-labelling schemes become more widespread, environmentally conscious companies may welcome them. But when the British government began to consider such a scheme, the Confederation of British Industry attacked the idea. Procter & Gamble, by contrast, argued that it would help to protect firms which are scrupulous about their product claims against those which are not. It would also help with "the difficult problems of communicating environmental information, which is often complex and technical, in a way which consumers will understand".

Should such schemes be restrictive or wide-ranging? Ought the label to be available only to detergents and paper products, or to dog food and – why not? – bank accounts? Ought they to reward "best" technology, or simply "better"? Companies worry that, if some of their products receive accolades, the others will be thought ungreen. They complain that schemes may give more recognition to products that are already green than to those which are made in greener ways than before. The Confederation of British Industry has asked for a right of appeal for rejected firms. And companies fear that the more information they have to provide on a product's greenness, the more a label will effectively cost them.

Other firms pray that they will also lead to uniform standards. *Managing the Environment*,[3] a study of the greening of European companies, quotes the lament of a manager from Perrier, a French soft-drinks manufacturer which has half its turnover outside France. "The rules change every day. Italy is changing its bottling rules; worse than that, some cities have different rules on plastic bottles. The Germans are taxing plastic bottles. The Swiss have outlawed metal containers and are ahead in preferring carton boxes."

The same consideration persuaded Germany to drop its opposition to an EC labelling scheme. The Germans had feared that this scheme would devalue their own Blue Angel – either the EC label would be harder to get, in which case nobody would want the Blue Angel, or it would be easier, in which case (perversely) people might think both labels were worthless. Then German companies decided that an EC scheme might make it easier to sell products developed for their own long greened consumers, and hostility diminished.

Eco-labelling will encourage governments to think through their priorities by bringing out the complexity of environmental choices. Is it more important to save paper by encouraging mothers to use cloth nappies, or to save hot water and the energy that heats it by encouraging disposables? Is it better that food and medicines should be swathed in layers of tamper-proof packaging, or sold with as few wrappings as possible? Such questions are too complicated to be left to even the most enthusiastic individual.

When shoppers move on

Though better information for shoppers is an admirable aim, nobody should trust consumers always to be a force for change. Fashion is fickle: even though shoppers in most countries will almost certainly remain more swayed by environmental concerns than they were before the advent of the green consumer boom, the first force of that boom is probably spent. Their impact anyway is on a limited range of products: few consumers think green when buying, say, a video-recorder or a pair of shoes. Yet the processes by which they are manufactured may also have considerable impact on the environment. Moreover, many companies sell not to consumers but to other companies, which are unlikely to change their buying patterns as whimsically as high-street shoppers. The farther back up the production chain a company is, the more it is insulated either from green shoppers or from a scrutiny of suppliers by environmentally conscious supermarkets.

Ultimately, the wary instinct of the deep greens has some basis: the consumer may indeed be the enemy of the environment, and not the friend. For

the protection of the environment may require people to accept less convenient ways of doing things: to buy fewer throwaways, for instance, reversing
the trend to replace individual labour with waste-creating disposables. In
time, ingenious technology will make such choices less painful. But companies will be more likely to invest in such technology the more the government
sets the ground rules.

Money talks

"Goodness is the only investment that never fails," said Thoreau. Not a
maxim financiers often preach, but the success of the green consumer in turning managers into environmentalists has inspired others to bring greenery to
the stock exchange. The demand for green investments from individual
investors on both sides of the Atlantic grew in line with the demand for green
products at the supermarket check-out. Indeed when Eagle Star, a large
British financial group, surveyed some of its unit-trust holders in 1989, it
found that 72% rated the ecological stance of a fund manager as important,
while only 46% gave such weight to the manager's ideological views.
Predictable result: a rush of new environmental funds, offering punters the
hope of doing well by doing good. Some are run by idealists, hoping to use
shareholders' votes to lean on companies. Others are more hard-nosed, and
hope to match a new environmentally conscious kind of shareholder with the
companies that are doing best from greenery.

The concept of "ethical" or "social" investment was originally developed in
America, spurred by the desire of institutions such as churches and universities not to put money into companies doing business in South Africa. Since
1981 such investors and the institutions that advise them have had their own
club, the Social Investment Forum (SIF). Most of its members apply at least
one ethical criterion in selecting their investments, generally connected with
South Africa; but some also screen out companies involved in defence, nuclear
power, tobacco, alcohol and gambling, and those with bad employment and
environmental records.

Partly to cater for such customers, a growing number of mutual funds offer
ethically screened investments. Biggest is the Calvert Group, with assets at
the end of 1990 of $500m. By that date such funds in America had assets of
$1 billion. The portfolios of such groups include the shares of companies that
do not profit from environmental activities – banks, say or computer manufacturers – but whose approach to green issues is regarded as virtuous. A different kind of "environmental" fund started to appear in America in the
summer of 1989, investing in one of 100 or so securities that seemed likely to
benefit from the boom in cleaning up pollution. These vary greatly in greenness. Typically they are run by one of the large securities houses, such as
Merrill Lynch (see page 169). Some $600m had flowed into such funds by the
end of 1990. An older, purer version of this type of fund is New Alternatives,
a small fund set up in Long Island in 1982. It invests mainly in companies

developing alternative energy and pollution-control technology.

In Britain the complexities of trust law make it harder for institutions to worry about the morality of their investments, rather than just the rate of return. So the demand for ethical investment has come less from churches and universities (nowhere near as well-heeled as their transatlantic counterparts) and more from virtuous private individuals. The first screened unit trust in Britain was launched in 1984 by Friends Provident (a company, as its name suggests, with Quaker roots). Friends' Stewardship Unit Trust is still by far the biggest social fund in Britain.

The Merlin Ecology Fund is the greenest of the British funds, launched in April 1989 by a group now known as Jupiter Tarbutt Merlin. This fund now has a companion, Merlin International Investment Trust. Both initially steered clear of investments in businesses which they deem intrinsically polluting (such as oil), even if a firm is working hard at reducing the environmental damage it did. That austere attitude has now softened. The group looks for the most environmentally responsible companies within each sector, including, for example, Echo Bay Mines, a North American gold-mining company with a good green record.

All told, ethically screened unit trusts, pension funds and investment trusts in Britain had assets of around £260m in mid-1990, although the total of institutional investment with some ethical screening was several times larger. As investors moved out of unit trusts at the end of 1990, ethical and green funds seemed to be holding on to their cash better than the less virtuous.

Such funds are now starting to spring up outside Britain and America. Norway's leading investment company, Investa, has launched one. The Artus fund, launched in Cologne, Germany, in 1989, puts most of its cash into Merlin and New Alternatives. The idea spread to banking in Germany: the Okobank of Frankfurt was founded in May 1988 to lend money on green projects.

By and large, green funds aim to give their investors a return at least as good as they would earn on less virtuous investments. That is important for lawyers who, on both sides of the Atlantic, are likely to take the pragmatic view that, as long as an ethically screened investment does better than the market average, then the use of the screen is unlikely to be challenged in the courts. Research on the performance of screened funds is sketchy, and is mainly conducted by true believers. But one study by Peter Kinder, a member of the SIF, of 400 stocks screened for a broad range of constraints, including South African operations and green virtue, found they did marginally better than the Standard and Poor's 500 index over five years from the start of 1984. In Britain, the Ethical Investment Research Service has constructed eight hypothetical portfolios of British shares over five years from October 1983, screened mainly for South Africa, nuclear weapons and tobacco (though not greenery). Only two had yields worse – by a whisker – than the FTA all-share index.

Both the true believers and the bandwaggoners think the market for envir-

1 THE CONSUMER, GREEN BUT FICKLE

onmental goods and services, from waste management to air pollution control, will continue to expand rapidly. When, early in 1990, Touche Remnant, a British investment-management group, got together with ECOTEC, an environmental consultancy, to launch a new investment fund to attract industrial and institutional investment into European companies in environmental protection and waste management, ECOTEC argued that the European market for these services was already worth about £20 billion a year and was likely to double within five years.

Looking for good to do

Even so, such investors have sometimes found it easier to weed out baddies from their portfolios than to find cast-iron goodies. Okobank, for instance, took in DM73m ($46m) of deposits in its first two years, but could find borrowers for only DM25m. In its case, lack of a branch network made it hard to find suitable customers. But a more general problem is the one also faced by green consumers and green labellers: how green is green enough?

In America a divide has opened between the attitude taken by funds set up by conventional financial institutions, some of which see the environment mainly as an area of vigorous new growth, and more austere greens. New funds set up in 1990 by, among others, Merrill Lynch, John Hancock and Fidelity Investment rapidly attracted greenbacks: Merrill Lynch sold out its initial $50m offering within three days, and $83m more poured in before brokers were told to stop selling. But greener greens point out that all three funds put money into companies such as Waste Management, the biggest waste disposal firm, which has been involved in such ungreen activities as incinerating toxic waste at sea and dumping recyclables in ordinary landfills. "Just because Waste Management picks up garbage does not make them a contributor to our environment," wrote one indignant investor in the Freedom Environment Fund, a subsidary of John Hancock; on the contrary, retorted Dave Beckwith, the fund's manager, such companies "are socially positive by definition. They contribute to a clean environment by what they do."

Even the more verdant funds can find themselves tied in knots over such issues. Calvert invested in Hawaii Electric, which wants to build a 500-megawatt geothermal power plant on Hawaii's Big Island. Geothermal power seems good green stuff, except that the plant will be built in a rain forest, and is vigorously opposed by the Sierra Club, one of America's main green campaigning bodies. Calvert eventually sold the stock, but for economic rather than environmental reasons.

A different approach is taken by Global Environment Fund (GEF), a California-based fund launched in 1990. It is unusual in a number of ways. First, it is the brainchild of two environmentalists, Jeffrey Leonard and John Earhart, senior staff of the Worldwide Fund for Nature and the Conservation Foundation. Second, its aim is to invest in smallish companies with technologies that can be made to work in the United States but which might eventually solve environmental problems in Eastern Europe or the third world. Some of the companies that pass for "green", Mr Leonard argues, are beneficiaries of quirks of regulation: they might, for instance, have bought waste space that now comes in handy for dumping, or be willing to dispose of toxic waste that larger firms do not want. Meanwhile, small firms that are genuinely trying to develop greener technologies often struggle to find capital. GEF is seeking out such companies, concentrating on those that are privately owned, aiming to invest long-term where possible.

GEF raises its cash from wealthy individuals and worthy institutional investors. When not helping the small and needy, GEF has started from the assumption that, as Mr Leonard puts it, "there are no pure plays". For example, most environmental investment funds would put near the top of their lists Wellman, a New Jersey company that is the world's largest recycler of bottles made of PET plastics. The company keeps plastic bottles from cluttering landfills by recycling them into products such as plastic resins and nylon fibres. But Mr Leonard claims that even Wellman is not pure green: the company, in which GEF holds shares, has some of the same problems with groundwater pollution as any other plastics manufacturer. He argues that green investors should look not at whether a company is in a "clean" business, such as making computers, but at how hard it is trying to be cleaner.

For green activists it is a short step from investing in greenish companies to trying to use shareholder muscle to make others greener. As has ever been the way with the debate on investor ethics, some argue for a quiet word with the chairman, others for selling the shares and making a fuss. The Norwich Union, a large British insurance company, argues for judicious leaning on corporate managers. A more assertive line was taken by Pensions and Investment Research Consultancy (PIRC), a body that mainly advises British local-authority pension funds, to draw attention to the destruction of peat bogs to supply garden compost. With Friends of the Earth, PIRC wrote to the 40 largest shareholders of Fisons, Britain's biggest producer of peat, shortly before the company's annual meeting in 1990, urging them to question Fisons's policy on alternative fertilisers and pointing out that green activists were planning a boycott of companies selling peat-based products. PIRC also raised the issue at the annual meeting. It expects to repeat this strategy with other companies.

Energetic green shareholders are more likely to pester managements with awkward questions. Merlin has set up a research department, the first of its kind in Britain, to improve the information available to environmental investors. Mr Leonard uses his Fund's shareholding to send long questionnaires to chief executives of companies such as Wellman, saying, "Our intentio is to maintain and provide for our investors a compendium of environmental information that we believe is important in assessing potential investments and monitoring the economic performance of our portfolio companies." If the company also changes its behaviour as a result of the inquisition, so much the better.

A broader attempt to mobilise shareholder power in this way was launched in the autumn of 1989 by America's SIF. It brought together a number of environmentalists and investors to draw up a set of principles which they hoped to persuade companies to sign called the Valdez Principles (a name hardly calculated to endear them to companies), which are broadly modelled on the Sullivan Principles, which laid down guidelines for firms operating in South Africa. The first six set out various rather woolly good intentions: to use natural resources sustainably and energy wisely, for instance, and to min-imise waste creation. Many American companies already have environmental policies with tougher versions of these. But the final four made corporate lawyers gulp. They committed signatories to make compensation for envi-ronmental damage; to disclose incidents of such damage; to have at least one environmentalist on the board; and annually to carry out and publish an inde-pendent environmental audit.

The sponsors wanted to provide a rating of corporate green intent, with high marks for firms that were trying hard, and low for the unrepentantly grubby. The institutions backing the Valdez exercise, including the con-trollers of New York City and of the state of California, hoped to use that as a handy guide to greenery. But of the 3,000 American companies approached, only 17 (mainly tiddlers) had signed by the end of 1990. The disclosure clause caused the greatest anguish: some companies felt that they might lose more by owning up to every polluting accident than by keeping mum. But the cleaner companies objected to being told to volunteer to be scrutinised by outsiders who might not assess them with understanding; while the dirtier had nothing to gain by participating. SIF therefore decided to try a different tack: in spring 1991, 66 American companies faced shareholder resolutions to adopt the Valdez principles. Some might just get through: at the annual meeting of Amoco in 1990, Valdez supporters won 12% of the vote.

Neither green consumers nor green investors are substitutes for govern-ment intervention. Their influence is too random, too poorly informed, to provide consistent pressure on companies to take the most cost-effective steps to be cleaner. Yet by changing the climate in which companies operate, both groups have altered the perception of many chief executives. As Chapter 3 argues, some pollution prevention pays for itself. But as long as companies give it a low priority, they are unlikely to undertake it. Green consumers and investors have changed that. Companies now know that, just as it is not done to exploit their workers, it is not done to be dirty. A change in social attitudes does not instantly turn sinners into saints. But it raises the penalties for being caught *in flagrante*, and the rewards of being seen to be good.

References

[1] Gollancz, 1988.

[2] "Green, Greener, Greenest? The Green Consumer in the UK, the Netherlands and Germany", survey by Brand New Product Development Ltd and Diagnostics Market Research Ltd, London, September 1989.

[3] Published by Business International, 1990.

2

HERE TO STAY

In the recession years of the mid-1990s green consumers will worry more about saving money than saving the planet, and green investors will care more about returns now than returns in the twenty-first century. So will companies be able to stop worrying about the environment? Some may, but others will find themselves driven by potent forces more durable than shoppers' whims. These forces are the subject of this chapter.

One will be the growing desire of ordinary voters not to live next to an environmental eyesore. Call them NIMBYs – Not In My Back Yard – and recognise them as exemplars of environmental property rights. Voters think they own the rights to quiet streets, clean air, safe water. Plonk an airport or an incinerator or a chemical plant in their home town, and you diminish the value of those rights. Another force will be the cost of making mistakes, both in terms of lost reputation and hard cash. A third pressure will be that of regulation. Voters will continue to want tougher green regulations on companies, especially as their costs will be largely hidden. They will be encouraged by the bureaucrats who staff environmental agencies around the world. Like bureaucrats everywhere, they will see it as part of their job to expand the amount of work they have to do. Put together NIMBYs, risk of mistakes and rules and yet another pressure appears: the need to reduce the growth of rubbish. Rubbish will preoccupy companies in the 1990s as much as other kinds of pollutants did in the 1980s.

This catalogue ignores one more influence which is harder to gauge than the rest: the price of energy. As the first half of this book explained, energy use plays a part in many kinds of environmental damage. The need to tackle the greenhouse effect has already encouraged governments to threaten to increase energy prices. But even without carbon taxes, environmental regulations will continue to push up the price of energy. Low-sulphur coal is generally dearer than high-sulphur, and scrubbers are a large investment; so preventing acid rain will mean dearer electricity. Oil tankers will carry huge insurance premiums to protect them against the costs of cleaning up after oil spills, and they will increasingly have to be double-hulled. Cars fitted with catalytic converters will use more petrol; so the cost of motoring will rise. But to some extent all these influences depend on whether the recession leads to lower energy prices. While the underlying trend of energy prices will be driven upwards by environmental considerations, the short-term prospect is probably for a decline.

Greening the back yard

Where companies are located (and roads, and airports, and many other noisome modern nuisances) will more and more be determined by the power of local NIMBYs. "The siting problem" is what the Americans call it. Who wants a chemical plant across the road from their house? Or a landfill half a mile from their children's school? Who wants an incinerator as a neighbour, or an oil rig? Nothing will drive the greening of world industry faster than the growing hostility of people to installations that they consider to be polluting. Mention the possibility that the pollution may be carcinogenic, and the backyard gates slam shut for good.

NIMBYs are often rich: they can afford to put calm before jobs. They are also frequently women: all those professional mothers who take time at home to raise their children make ferocious adversaries for companies whose activities might conceivably harm children's health. And they are the old, or at least the retired middle classes, who no longer have much reason to care about local employment and have plenty of time to lobby their younger friends in government and the media. NIMBYs will help to redistribute wealth, as exasperated companies site new plants in poorer regions, where jobs still matter most, or in poorer countries. But they will also force those companies that have no choice to work hard at their green image. And they will hugely raise the costs of getting rid of waste. Through these two routes, they will raise the costs of dirty processes and the rewards of being clean.

NIMBY squeamishness imposes real costs on companies that are thought of as potential polluters. When they want to build a new plant or to expand an existing one, they have less choice of sites than other firms. Their managers have to spend more time searching for solutions, and winning planning permission. Such costs are higher in America than almost anywhere else. Frank Blake, an American lawyer specialising in environmental law, sums up the result.

"Companies can't do much without getting a permit, which is given mainly on environmental grounds," he says. "So industries that want to get permits need to have a good green reputation. For many of my clients, my advice is simply, 'Forget it'. The larger companies can afford to negotiate through the very expensive and time-consuming process, but not the small. Companies tend to rebuild on existing sites, rather than trying to find new ones. And they don't go to places where getting permits is hardest, like the north-east." Do frustrated companies go abroad? "I'm sure it happens all the time."

The costs of getting it wrong

Nothing will do more damage to a company that hopes to cultivate a reputation for greenery than a polluting accident. But an accident may cost a company more than its reputation. It also may mean an immense bill. For other companies in the same line of business, it will mean a rise in insurance premiums, and another click in the ratchet of environmental regulations. Like the siting problem, fear of accidents will be a constant pressure on companies to become greener.

Accidents can often transform a company's attitude – or a country's, or an industry's – to environmental safety. Seveso led the EC to tighten rules to prevent industrial accidents; Bhopal taught chemical companies to set high standards in the third world; a fire at a warehouse belonging to Sandoz, a Swiss chemical company, transformed that company's environmental policies.

Accidents also carry financial penalties, especially in the United States, where courts impose ferocious punishments. Exxon spent over $2 billion cleaning up the Alaskan oil spill. As a result many American shipowners raised their liability insurance from $100m–150m to $750m or so. The difficulty of finding insurers to cover pollution risks of over $1 billion led Shell to announce that it would no longer ship oil to many American ports. In Europe the size of compensatory settlements of all kinds is converging, although it still tends to be only a fifth of those awarded in American courts.

Regulators everywhere are tending to take a tougher line on polluting accidents. When, in August 1989, Shell UK accidentally allowed 156 tonnes of crude oil to escape into the river Mersey, Britain's new National Rivers Authority promptly took the company to court where it was fined £1m, many times the biggest fine previously awarded against a polluting company in the British courts. Shell had already spent £1.4m cleaning up the mess. Ominously, the judge said that he had weighed Shell's good environmental record against its large resources. Oil companies will have spotted two morals: large companies are more likely to be hit hard by the courts *pour encourager les autres*; and time and money spent on conservation before an accident gives some protection against even heavier punishments when one occurs.

The legal liabilities that frighten American companies most, though, are not for dramatic accidents. American environmental statutes generally provide for criminal as well as civil penalties. As a result, managers now quite often go to prison for breaking environmental laws, such as failing to get a permit for some activity or to fulfil its terms. In one notorious American case, a Hungarian entrepreneur, a former freedom fighter, was imprisoned for failing to get a permit to dump used tyres in a bog beside a motorway. Penalties are getting heavier. In the 1988/89 fiscal year the Environmental Protection Agency (EPA) imposed some $37m in fines for environmental crimes. That was a quarter of the entire amount levied in environmental fines by the agency since 1974. As well, 50 people were fined and given prison sentences of eight years each.

Many of these prison sentences are for offences under the Superfund legislation. In 1980, in the wake of a public outcry over a toxic-waste dump at Love Canal, in New York state, Congress passed the Comprehensive Environmental Response, Compensation and Liability Act (CERCLA) to compel the clean-up of thousands of abandoned and uncontrolled hazardous waste sites. To pay for this, the law set up a trust fund financed by taxes on the oil and chemical industries, to clean up toxic waste sites. This "Superfund" has become a behemoth, towering over American environmental policy, gobbling vast quantities of public and private cash and management time. The EPA aggressively chases companies held potentially responsible for the presence of waste on sites, to recoup from them the costs of cleaning up.

Superfolly

Under Superfund legislation (expanded in 1986 under the Superfund Amendments and Reauthorization Act) and subsequent court decisions, liability for these costs is extraordinarily wide. It may fall on almost anybody who has ever had anything to do with a toxic-waste dump: the operator; the companies who transported the waste; the current owner of the site; the owner of the site at the time the contamination occurred; and indeed any company whose waste was ever dumped on the site, even if the dumping was perfectly legal at the time.

But the net spreads wider. A lender who forecloses on a company and thereby assumes ownership for any contaminated properties acquires liability as part of the package. A 1990 court judgment frightened bankers by appearing to make a company's bankers liable even if they have not foreclosed, if they might have influenced their client's treatment of toxic waste. However, one effect of America's 1990 savings and loan crisis may be to change this: as the Federal government has become the reluctant owner of a huge number of bankrupt thrifts, it has also acquired their exposure to Superfund claims.

The liability is both strict, regardless of fault or negligence, and joint and several: clean-up costs can be assessed on the basis of a company's ability to pay, rather than on the volume or toxicity of the waste it has dumped. The only shred of protection goes to companies that investigated a site before they acquired it and found no Superfund liability, a provision that does much to explain the rise of the environmental audit (described in Chapter 6 of Part II).

Chasing companies through the courts for their share of clean-up costs has now become one of the main activities of the EPA. The biggest settlement so far, in May 1989, was for $66m for a site in California, but the potential bills have soared into the *Exxon Valdez* category. Shell has been wrangling with the

EPA since 1983 over a $1.9 billion bill for damage at a site in Colorado, in a case in which only the lawyers have cleaned up. The average cost of restoring the sites so far identified by the EPA is $25m a site, with some running up to $100m. Several companies have been forced to shut down as a result.

No other country has anything as stringent as the Superfund legislation. But the idea may well spread. Once governments decide to clean up old waste dumps, they face an inevitable choice: do taxpapers foot the bill, or does the government try to find private companies to pick up the bill?

Draconian though the retrospective liability under Superfund may seem, it has a certain contagious logic. Plenty of European greens argue that, if the polluter pays principle means what it says, then polluters must be liable for polluting incidents for which they were responsible, even unintentionally, in the past. The alternative is to make the taxpayer responsible for cleaning up such pollution, and that is unfair. The implications of such a view are hair-raising: many polluting activities, from dumping nuclear waste to ploughing grassland (which releases nitrates into water courses), may take years to manifest themselves.

Germany has already been considering plans that would make it easier to force companies to pay for cleaning waste sites. The EC is considering introducing civil liability for waste, although it is unlikely to come into effect before 1992 at the earliest. Under a draft directive issued by the European Commission in autumn 1989, companies that produce waste would carry strict civil liability for damage caused by their wastes to persons and property, and for injury to the environment, until the wastes are handed over to a properly licensed disposal firm. An individual plaintiff would be able to take a company to court to stop the damaging activity, and to force the polluter to pay the costs of cleaning up the mess. In its draft form the directive provides for joint and several liability to make banks or receivers liable if they acquire polluted land when a lender defaults. The directive also allows claims to be made for 30 years after polluting waste has been dumped, although that is being strongly contested by the insurance industry. American companies in Europe are taking no chances since some American states, led by New Jersey, have begun to impose even tighter laws on toxic dumps, forbidding the sale of a property which has not already been cleaned.

Some companies even take seriously the prospect of such legislation in the third world. As Jill Shankleman of Environmental Resources, a British consultancy, puts it: "American managers say, 'Superfund has cost us millions of dollars. Upgrading our plants worldwide will cost us 10% of that. It's good insurance.'" Cornelius Smith, in charge of environmental policy at Union Carbide, takes the view that: "It doesn't take a rocket scientist to figure that they'll have Superfund in five, ten, fifteen years."

Pick it up, don't put it down
The need to avoid taking environmental risks has had a powerful effect on

those companies in the riskiest businesses. But even without the threat of the courts, the costs of polluting have been rising. Rules on air pollution have become tighter; charges for dirty water are increasing; and above all, the cost of dumping waste has gone up. Governments in the rich countries have worked for up to a century to clean the air, and for a generation to clean the water. Now, prodded by NIMBYs, they are turning their attention to the third kind of muck: the stuff dumped on land.

Of all the industries that NIMBYs hate, few are as loathed as waste disposal. Getting rid of toxic waste is already expensive and likely to be more so; getting rid of ordinary rubbish will rapidly become more of a problem in the course of the 1990s. Finding places to put landfills or incinerators is becoming harder in every industrial country. Disposing of hazardous waste is obviously the most difficult, but the costs of getting rid of ordinary rubbish are rising. Think of the space to get rid of waste as an exhaustible resource, just like oil and copper, and it is clear what will happen. As the resource is used up, its price will go up rapidly. That will encourage people to economise in their use of it, or use technology to come up with other options.

But while the scarcity of oil and copper will cause price rises in the products that use them, the same may not be true for rubbish. Neither those whose products end up in landfills, nor those who buy the products, carry the costs to society and the environment of their disposal. Companies have faced rising bills for getting rid of toxic waste, and that has altered their behaviour. It will be much harder to make sure that those who create ordinary domestic rubbish carry the costs of their actions – and so change their behaviour.

In practice, the exhaustion of space is not so much geographical – in theory, lots of land still remains for waste dumps – but regulatory. Governments, prodded by their voters, are steadily reducing the number of options for disposing of waste, and raising the costs of using those options that remain. This problem is worst for toxic waste. Exporting it was once the easiest way to avoid thinking about it. The greenest countries in Europe were the ones most likely to pay somebody else to get rid of the muck. West Germany in 1985 exported nearly 15% of its hazardous and special waste (definitions and ter-

Table 18 Toxic trade: hazardous and special waste
('000 tonnes)

	Production	Imports	Exports
USA 1985	265,000	40	150
W. Germany 1985	5,000	75	700
UK 1986	3,900	83	–
Canada 1980	3,290	120	40
France 1987	2,000	250	25
Netherlands 1986	1,500	–	155
Sweden 1980	500	–	15

Source: OECD, *Environmental Data 1989*, Paris

minology vary from country to country, making it hard to measure what is happening), lots of it to Eastern Europe. The Swiss, who hold referendums to decide where to put new incinerators, not surprisingly end up exporting more than half their hazardous waste. The British have been a rarity in the past, dealing with all their hazardous waste at home but importing waste from elsewhere (mainly Ireland and the Netherlands) to incinerate or dump (sometimes at sea).

Travelling muck

Most exports of hazardous waste from industrial countries have ended up either in Eastern Europe or in the third world. Either way, the technology to handle it is much less sophisticated than in the west. Perestroika will stop most dumping in ex-Communist Europe. Cleaning the third world will be tougher. Third-world countries resent becoming dirt dumps, but may find it hard to enforce their own environmental regulations to prevent it. But under a convention drawn up by the United Nations Environment Programme and agreed at Basle early in 1989, signatory governments will agree that waste should not be moved across borders unless: the recipient country has agreed to accept it; and, more important, the exporting country is satisfied that proper arrangements have been made for its final disposal.

In the words of Carlo Ripa di Meana, the EC environment commissioner, "1992 must not turn into a tourist visa for wastes", so EC countries are preparing for the barrier-free market by working towards an agreement to become self-sufficient in the disposal of toxic waste. Shipments across borders between EC countries would not necessarily be prevented: it may sometimes be more economic for one country to dispose of the waste of another, such as Ireland, which generates too little to justify large investment in treatment plants. Strict national self-sufficiency would also increase shipments of waste around Europe, as countries lugged the stuff not to the nearest treatment site, but to the nearest national one, which might be much farther away.

European electors are becoming more hostile to treating another country's waste, even at a good profit. In 1989 a poll by MORI, a market-research firm, found only 44% of the British saw toxic waste as one of the most important environmental issues, compared with 66% for nuclear waste. But three-quarters of those polled thought that Britain should not accept imports of toxic waste from other EC countries under any circumstances. There is a similar hostility to disposing of other people's muck in the United States. South Carolina and Alabama which, like third-world countries, see themselves treated as dirt dumps for the prosperous north, have both tried to ban waste shipments from some other states.

Rules on the disposal of hazardous waste within countries have been growing tighter. Several European countries, including Germany, France, Belgium and Britain, have traditionally burned some of their waste on ships in the North Sea. A conference in March 1990 agreed to stop that practice by the end of 1991. The same conference tightened the rules on dumping dangerous substances into the North Sea, which are to be cut by at least a half in the decade to 1995.

With the sea closed off, the rules governing waste disposal on land have also become tougher. While national governments have been ratcheting standards upwards, the EC Commission has been doing the same. It sees an urgent need to adopt common standards for the disposal of waste of all kinds. Otherwise, waste will tend to seep towards the country with the lowest (ie, cheapest) standards. The Commission has already produced two directives raising the standards for municipal incinerators, and in autumn 1990 it was drawing up a draft directive to set stricter rules for all incinerators, including those which used waste as fuel.

Dearer rubbish too

The costs of getting rid of toxic waste are already high; those for ordinary rubbish are just beginning to rise. Ordinary rubbish can still be exported – usually. The incident that crystallised the rubbish problem in the minds of American voters was that of the wandering garbage barge from the New York suburb of Islip. Ports as far away as Belize turned back the ship, loaded with 3,000 tons of London Island muck, in the spring of 1987. That incident has had less dramatic parallels in other parts of America and in Europe.

Land dumps, both for hazardous and non-hazardous waste, are also becoming harder to find in all developed countries. America's EPA reckons that 80% of existing landfills will shut by 2010. Some 13 states, mainly on the east coast, will run out of landfill capacity by the mid-1990s unless (improbably) they can open new ones. Japan will run out by 2005. The Netherlands has, in effect, run out already. In Los Angeles furious citizens have campaigned to close the last remaining dump owned by the city at Lopez Canyon and a project to build a new incinerator collapsed in the face of bitter local opposition. The Californian state legislature shut down almost one-third of its 623 landfills in 1989. West Germans, who in 1988 exported 2.1m tons of rubbish to East Germany, have lost that helpful outlet since reunification.

The squeeze on landfills in most countries is simply a consequence of NIMBYism at work. But regulations reinforce the effect of the NIMBYs' actions. Standards for siting and running landfills are being driven up. The EC Commission, determined to set common standards for waste-disposal facilities to discourage trans-frontier dumping, has drawn up a directive that will turn landfill sites from cheap holes in the ground into expensive bits of civil engineering. It will also raise the costs of monitoring them after they are filled, and increase the amount of paperwork to keep track of what is dumped where.

That will have a dramatic effect on waste-disposal costs in some EC countries, including Britain. A study by two landfill specialists from Harwell Laboratory, presented at their annual waste-management symposium in May

1990, makes horrifying reading.[1] Of 100 landfills studied, 62% had no measures to stop surface water from seeping in; 54% did not monitor leaching into groundwater in the surrounding area; 63% had no boreholes to monitor the potential build-up of dangerous gas; and 80% made no attempt to control their smell. Britain's local authorities, which operated almost three-quarters of the landfills surveyed, are clearly in for some nasty surprises, one of which will be a steep rise in the costs of getting rid of rubbish.

In America landfill costs for hazardous waste went from around $80 a tonne at the start of the 1980s to around $255 a tonne by the end, with the main increase being in costs of treatment rather than dumping. OECD figures for Western Europe show that the costs of landfill for asbestos in October 1989 ranged from $41 a tonne to $338. That was perhaps ten times higher than a decade earlier. Incineration costs have probably risen still faster, though they vary less widely: from around $1,145 a tonne for some of the nastier, high chlorine wastes in West Germany up to $2,300–2,595 a tonne in Britain, with a European average of around $1,825 a tonne.

One effect has been to make landfills an investment as attractive as a goldmine for any company willing to weave its way through the maze of Superfund legislation. The American arm of Hambro, a British merchant bank, has been buying up family-owned landfills, finding them high-quality management and preparing them for flotation on the New York stock exchange. Those landfills that are not run by municipalities or by one of a handful of big waste-management companies are generally run by families. They are often immigrants (because a waste dump was once a cheap and easy business to start in): Armenian families tend to dominate southern California, the Dutch Chicago and the Mafia New York. "It's a farmer mentality," says Fred Iseman of Hambro America. "They rarely think in terms of marketing, and may not have enough capital to develop the site. They tend to think of the site as a plot of land that brings in a steady income." With good management and access to private capital, Mr Iseman reckons that the profitability of such sites may quintuple in a couple of years. In autumn 1990 he was looking at similar opportunities in Britain.

For the companies whose rubbish must be disposed of, the sheer size of the bill they will increasingly face will have a powerful effect, direct and indirect. Directly, it will raise the costs of being dirty, and encourage them to seek out production processes that leave less muck. Indirectly, it will lead consumers to demand products that are cleaner, which is a harder idea to turn into reality. Chapters 3 and 4 (Part II) look at the ways in which companies are grappling with the need for cleaner processes and cleaner products.

Carrots, as well as sticks

Wise companies can see that all environmental regulations are likely to grow tighter. To wait for the regulations and then try to act may be more expensive than to try to anticipate them and build them into new investments. A company that takes environmental responsibility more seriously than it. may find it can introduce new technology at its own pace, rather than ha to do it quickly and therefore expensively. "Our job is to do it our way, befc we have a sword hanging over our heads," says Richard Mahoney, chie executive of Monsanto, a large chemical company. In the long run it may be cheaper not to build dirty plants in the first place, rather than clean up the mess.

Governments, realising that companies would prefer to clean up in their own way, rather than be compelled to do so, will increasingly hold out legislation as a threat. The German government (see Chapter 4 of Part II) has persuaded companies to set up an elaborate recycling scheme by brandishing the threat of new laws; the EC Commission is trying the same strategy on plastics manufacturers. The threat of laws to curb toxic emissions has driven the larger American chemical companies to set themselves rigorous targets.

While companies could easily regard all these pressures as negative, the clever ones can see positive gains as well. One will be in recruitment. The links between employee care and environmental care will become more important as the number of new workers stops growing. "The two top corporate priorities for the 1990s are the environment and recruitment," points out Tom Burke, director of Britain's Green Alliance, an environmental lobbying group. "I tell firms that they are linked. Good people don't like working for a company with a bad environmental image."

Take two small surveys by KPH Marketing carried out in the summer of 1990. In one the respondents were 117 graduates and 27 post-graduates at the University of Surrey, mainly in engineering and science disciplines. When asked what factors they would take into account in choosing future employers, the students put connections with oppressive regimes top of the list. Second-equal came companies' environmental policies and their record on personnel. More than half the students described their concern about green issues as either "strong" or "very strong". The firms thought to have the worst environmental records included Exxon (34%), British Nuclear Fuels (28%), Shell and Union Carbide (both 12%) and McDonald's (11%). All these companies have been making strenuous efforts to improve the greenery of their image.

In the other, 101 marketing, personnel and administration managers selected at random from Britain's biggest 25,000 businesses, were questioned. Almost a quarter of the sample said they would take a drop in salary to work for a more environmentally responsible company. While the managers regarded salaries, working conditions and career prospects as the main consideration when choosing an employer, 76% thought a socially responsible image was important. Asked what that meant, they put environmental policy third, after personnel and marketing policies.

Companies that succeed in convincing clever young managers that they are genuinely interested in their impact on the environment will find it easier to recruit. Even in those industries that the bright young regard as grubbiest – chemicals, petrochemicals, heavy industry – companies that work hardest at being green may do better than rivals in the same business.

What companies want most, though, is to hear that greenery is profitable. That will be true, though not without some qualifications. Companies that make technology for cleaning up – scrubbers for power stations, filters, recycling plant – have a rosy future. So do companies that can offer to solve other firms' green problems, by disposing of their waste, for instance. For those companies whose production processes cause the pollution in the first place, the prospect is more arduous. As Chapter 3 (Part II) argues, some measures to reduce pollution undoubtedly save money. Others are expensive.

That does not necessarily mean that companies should fight them. Companies should demand certainty from governments; and they should point out honestly when governments introduce regulations that impose high costs on consumers in exchange for little improvement in environmental quality. Beyond this point, the cleverest companies have an interest in making sure that all their rivals are set the same standards (or taxes) as they face. They stand to do best if the threshold for environmental quality is one that they can comfortably pass, but their competitors cannot. Such companies are the natural allies of green governments.

Reference
[1] See *ENDS*, Report No. 185, June 1990, pages 16–18.

3

ALONG THE PIPE

Given the rising costs of being dirty, more companies see the benefits of being clean. The traditional approach has been "end-of-pipe" solutions, approaches that tackle effluents or gases just before, or even after, they leave the plant. But a new approach is now being developed: one of preventing pollution in the first place. It is cheaper in the long run to rethink the whole of an industrial process than to tack on a bit of extra technology at the end.

As a result, "waste minimisation" has become a catchphrase among the greenest companies whose names are rarely found on labels on supermarket shelves. Of the 100–200 companies worldwide that have made environmental performance their top concern, most are chemical companies. The most radical corporate thinking on the environment is taking place in large chemical companies, in America and Europe, such as Du Pont, Monsanto, Dow, Hoechst, ICI and Ciba-Geigy. Realising that the environment is one of the three or four most important issues facing their industry, their main boards have formulated green strategies and set up sophisticated management systems to meet them. This is hardly surprising: chemical companies in industrial countries typically produce 50–70% of all hazardous waste, either in the course of manufacturing or in the form of their final product. In other industries – especially oil and cars – there are companies that take greenery equally seriously, but they are rarer. But the number of companies and industries that come into the former category will rise as the costs of polluting increase.

These companies have tended to be more interested in making the manufacturing process cleaner than in producing goods for green consumers. They have concentrated mainly on the pollution that comes from smoke stacks and sewage outflows. They have been driven much less by the buying power of shoppers than by the costs described in Chapter 2 (of Part II), and especially the risks of handling and the costs of disposing of toxic waste. Many also claim that being greener has saved them money. Now, just as companies driven mainly by green consumerism have widened their attention from cleaner products to cleaner processes, so these businesses have begun to think more about their products, as well as their processes.

Beyond the rule

A striking aspect of these green strategies is the extent to which they move far ahead of local regulatory requirements. For example, a number of companies have set themselves targets for toxic emissions and for waste generation far more stringent than anything the law requires. Monsanto has pledged itself to cut toxic air emissions by 90% by 1992 and then to work towards a goal of zero emissions. Du Pont has promised to cut toxic air emissions by 60% from 1987 levels by 1993, to cut carcinogens by a further 90% before the end of the century, and eventually to stop emitting them entirely.

These "green leaders" also frequently set standards for their overseas subsidiaries which may be even higher when measured against local standards. Frequently they insist that the company's standards be applied worldwide. For example, Union Carbide stipulates that its facilities in Africa stick to standards consistent with America's Clean Water Act, even though there is no such act in Africa. Johnson & Johnson, an American health-care products company, applies the same standards all over the world. If standards rise in one country, the company claims, they are adopted universally. Dow Chemical has technology centres for various products, part of whose job is to ensure that the same technological standards are applied wherever a new plant is built. One effect is to raise standards in third-world countries.

These policies have their critics. Few economists would regard the goal of zero emissions as a wise one. Better to aim for the point at which the cost of getting rid of an extra molecule of nasty substance overtakes any rational estimate of the benefits to human health or to the environment. That point might come after a few puffs of carcinogens, especially for a plant in a densely populated area. It might be reasonable to aim for a much higher level of emissions in the case of less harmful gases, especially from a plant in the middle of nowhere.

Some industrialists, even in the chemicals industry, think that zero emissions are fine as an ideal but ludicrous as a practical goal. Robin Paul, managing director of Albright & Wilson, a British chemicals-to-household good group, is one such: "Science", he points out, "is getting better all the time at measuring traces of substances in emissions." The chairman of Du Pont, Ed Woolard, made a broader point in a speech in December 1989: "As we move closer to zero, the economic cost which society must ultimately bear may be very high. Or the energy expenditure necessary to eliminate a given emission may have more ecological impact than trade emissions themselves. Society will have to decide where the balance should be struck, and may conclude in some cases that zero emissions is neither in the environment's nor the public's best interest."

Imposing world standards has other drawbac. countries, where it may be harder than simply aimi. the locals. It may indeed sometimes be worse for thir playing by local rules. Excessive virtue may lead western less than they might otherwise have done, leaving the door o. more interested in evading than exceeding their country's gree. company's partner may be the government, which may jib at higher emission standards than its own laws require. Or there may s. no local facilities. IBM found no site in Argentina able to meet its requirements for waste disposal. Its Argentine plants therefore recycle th. quarters of the waste they generate.

Cost-effective cleanliness

Pollution control still mostly means adding bits and pieces to treat whatever the manufacturing process discharges. It may mean installing a dust filter or building a purification plant, essentially transforming one type of waste into another which is less harmful and more manageable. For instance, a dust filter may convert uncontrolled clouds of filthy smoke into clean smoke and a heap of dirt which can be disposed of in a properly run landfill. Such an approach involves no change in the manufacturing process.

For the smallish group of companies most affected by the pressures described in Chapter 2 of Part II, add-on technology is not enough; the costs of being dirty and the benefits from being clean are so high that a new approach becomes worthwhile. The sums being spent, especially in the chemicals industry, on pollution control are staggering. Bayer, a German chemicals group, spends 20% of its manufacturing costs on environmental protection, about the same as on energy or labour. Chevron, an American oil company, expects environmental spending to grow by 10% a year, and sees it glumly as "the only growth area of the oil industry". Albright & Wilson spends half its capital programme on environmental protection projects or products.

As a result, these companies find that it pays to take a more radical approach to environmental protection than the average company. They have been seeking ways to ensure that, in the phrase coined by 3M, "Pollution Prevention Pays" (PPP). 3M claims to have saved well over $482m in the 15 years of its PPP policy. Other companies have now thought up acronyms of their own: Chevron has SMART (Save Money And Reduce Toxics), Texaco has WOW (Wipe Out Waste) and Dow Chemical has WRAP (Waste Reduction Always Pays).

Often simple improvements in process efficiency are looked for at first. Chris Hampson, main board director of ICI responsible for the environment, is quoted in *Managing the Environment*[1] as saying that about a quarter of the company's current environmental costs came from "losses in containment and less than optimum operation of plant". Robert Muirhead, formerly Exxon Chemicals' European safety and environmental control manager, reckons that posal costs are double the actual cost to the company when account made of lost production and operating costs. When future liability for waste is added in, the cost could be doubled again.

3M, which popularised the idea of waste minimisation in the first place, now thinks through the concept in four stages, as follows.

1. Reformulation. Can a product be made using fewer raw materials, so that the company does not have to keep warehouses full of a dangerous medley of substances? Can it be made using different ones which are less toxic? For instance, can a solvent-based coating be replaced with a water-based one?

2. Equipment redesign. Can steam from one process, for instance, be used to drive another?

3. Process modification. Is it helpful to change, say, from batch feeding, which may mean readjusting the pollution-control systems with each new batch, to continuous feeding, with fewer quality-control problems?

4. Resource recovery. Can a waste product be salvaged and reused – as a raw material in another process, or as a fuel, or as something worth selling?

Union Carbide breaks the pattern down in a different way. It is one of several companies that insist that each plant draw up its own waste-minimisation policy. Since 1987 every big capital-investment project has been reviewed for its potential in reducing waste. The company reckons that most of the measures it takes to minimise waste fall into one of three categories: good housekeeping, including reductions in spillages and leaks, and better inventory control so that, for instance, chemicals are bought in smaller quantities; changes in the materials used, switching to less hazardous substitutes; and changes in technology.

The simple virtues of good housekeeping

The simplest waste-minimisation techniques are often of the good-housekeeping variety. Stopping day-to-day accidents may not be as dramatic as preventing another Bhopal, but its cumulative effect on the environment may be just as great. Some companies form techniques to stop accidents after they have had one. Sandoz, for example, Switzerland's second largest chemicals company, spent Sfr150m on measures to prevent a repetition of the disastrous Schweizerhalle fire in 1986, including installing two catchment basins to stop water used in fire-fighting from draining into the Rhine. Shell UK spent £100,000 on a new leak detection system after its spill in the Mersey in 1989. It is better, of course, to make such investments before accidents occur.

Better still is simple waste prevention. Union Carbide has found one of the best ways to stop polluted air escaping from its plants has been simply to set up a regular schedule of checks on components such as pumps, valves and flanges. Keeping these promptly and properly repaired has allowed the chemical company to cut fugitive emissions down to a minute fraction of the levels judged acceptable by the Environmental Protection Agency. Utah-based Geneva Steel reckons it has been able to reduce its emissions to a quarter or a fifth of the allowable maximum mainly by the simple device of teaching workers to take proper care of the doors of its coke ovens. "The workers baby the things," says Joe Canon, its chairman.

Such good housekeeping is likely to be the cheapest kind of pollution prevention. Indeed, it is most likely to be the kind that shows a profit. "Most waste happens because something is not being used properly," argues ICI's Mr Hampson. "Waste may happen because a plant is only 90% efficient in its use of raw materials. The rest is going out in waste. A lot of pollution is associated with inefficiency." As an example, he cites the production of fine denier nylon yarn by ICI fibres division. It is wound in a continuous thread several miles long on to a 25 lb bobbin. Each time the yarn snaps, ICI loses money — and creates waste, because the half-filled bobbin then has to be disposed of. "Our efficiency is currently around 85%," he reckons. "If we can get that up to the low 90s, we will make a 30% increase in profits."

Good housekeeping may stop waste being created in the first place. Beyond that, waste minimisation becomes more complicated. It may involve changes in the quantity or quality of raw materials used in order to prevent waste being created in the first place. Thus Volvo is cutting solvent emissions from car plants by switching to waterborne paints. Sigvard Höggren, vice president for environmental affairs, believes that: "In the long run we must use materials in our processes that do not give rise at all to hazardous emissions." Polaroid is trying to find ways to substitute water for organic solvents in the manufacture of films for cameras. Exxon Chemicals, unhappy about the amount of hazardous waste caused by soil contamination, is rethinking the design of some of its plants. Often, simply using less air or water dramatically reduces the amount of polluted air or water that a plant has to dispose of. The volume of really nasty toxics may be no lower, but it may be easier to handle. Sandoz has been trying to reduce the amount of waste water it generates. Handling fewer dangerous materials is one protection against accidents. Mr Mahoney describes how Monsanto reached that conclusion. "After Bhopal, we found we were handling far more hazardous materials than we needed to."

Uses for waste

Many of the companies that have tried to reduce waste have found ways of recovering and reusing it. This not only means that the company has to dispose of less waste; it may also be able to buy less raw material. For example Chevron produces 10,000 oil samples a month, each contained in a tiny glass vial. Because even a trace of oil on the glass puts the used vials in the category of hazardous waste, the company used to pack them with absorbent material in 55-gallon drums and send them to hazardous-waste landfills at a cost of $5,000 a month. In June 1988 a vial crusher was installed, which broke down the vials and recovered the traces of oil. The oil could be reused, the glass recycled. The equipment cost $20,000, paying for itself by the end of the year.

Chevron also spent huge sums disposing of the mucky emulsion of oil and water left from a plant's waste-water system. It installed a mobile centrifuge to spin the sludge, separating the oil and water and leaving a small cake of solid gunge. The oil is reused as feedstock, the water purified and discharged, and the cake of muck, its volume less than 5% that of the original sludge, is all that still needs to be sent to a hazardous-waste dump.

Polaroid used to use freon, a liquid solvent whose evaporating vapours seem to damage the ozone layer, for cleaning the plastic parts and electronic circuit boards that go into its cameras. In 1988, as the possibility of a ban on chlorofluorocarbons approached, Polaroid installed new degreasers at one of its plants which captured and recycled escaping freon vapours. Polaroid saved a net $75,000 a year by cutting the bill for new freon.

Quite a lot of companies have found markets for wastes that they could not use themselves. Thus Du Pont formerly got rid of 3,600 tonnes a year of a chemical called hexamethyleneimine (HMI), used in making nylon. When it started to look for other methods, it discovered a market for HMI in the pharmaceuticals and coating industries. Now, demand exceeds by-product supply. In 1989 Du Pont had to find a way to make HMI on purpose.

Some companies have relied on the ingenuity of local managers to find ways of disposing of waste. Others have had a more structured approach. In 1986 Dow Chemical set up a management team to pick out potential by-products that were being thrown away, and find ways of reusing them. They took five plants and examined each to see how far primary feedstocks could be replaced with by-product feedstocks. They planned the plant modifications that had to be made and sorted out transport difficulties. As a result, they cut purchases of hydrocarbons for feedstock, made it possible for those plants which had found it hard to get enough feedstock to produce at higher capacity, reduced the company's demand for expensive incineration of waste, and marketed spare ethylene dichloride to other companies.

A Chevron subsidiary, Warren Petroleum Company has found another outlet for its waste. About twice a month it sends used caustic to nearby pulp and paper manufacturers, which use the corrosive liquid in their treatment of wood products. Chevron found these buyers by adding the chemical by-product to a list published each month by the Houston Chamber of Commerce Industry Surplus Chemical Inventory Program. But it is not always the company that finds the outlet. In France waste glucose from the manufacture of prunes d'Agens caused a huge water-pollution problem. The river-basin authority solved it by suggesting that the manufacturers bottle and sell the juice.

A powerful argument for preventing pollution at the earliest possible stage in a process is that it is likely to be cheaper in the long run. Some work by America's Electric Power Research Institute found that pollution-control equipment – cooling towers, scrubbers, electrostatic precipitators – added to a coal-fired power plant after it was built could add 45% to the capital cost and 30% to the operating cost. Integrating controls into the plant at the design stage could save up to half these costs. The plant's complexity was also reduced, and its flexibility and reliability increased.

A practical example of this arithmetic, quoted in *Managing the Environment*,[2] comes from Novo-Nordisk, Denmark's largest pharmaceuticals company. In 1987 the Danish parliament decided that total discharges of nitrogen compounds should be cut by 50% from their current levels by 1993. The company found it had large quantities of waste nitrogen compounds from its Kalundborg plant. One option was to build a large waste-water treatment plant to convert the dissolved nitrogen compounds into gas that could be evaporated into the atmosphere. The company thought that would cost Dkr100m in initial capital investment and Dkr20m–40m in running costs.

"The clean-up solution didn't feel right," says Torben Schjidt Jensen, manager responsible for environmental affairs. "It's a waste to convert nitrogen which could otherwise be used as fertiliser into gaseous nitrogen, which just evaporates into the atmosphere. " Instead, the company halved its nitrogen emissions within two years, at a capital cost of Dkr10m, mainly by converting the leftover nitrogen into fertiliser and distributing it free to farmers. The separated waste water is sent to the local coal-fired power plant and mixed with lime to neutralise sulphur emissions.

Better, but harder

This money-saving raises the unavoidable question: if pollution prevention always paid, why would anybody pollute? Terry Davies of America's EPA provides the answer: "We have a database with a thousand examples of companies doing pollution prevention that pays – but we could clearly do the opposite, and collect examples of where it doesn't pay."

Much pollution prevention yields genuinely high returns that may have gone unnoticed for years: take the parallel of energy conservation, discussed in Chapter 6 of Part I. Much pollution prevention may well cover its cash costs in two or three years. Yet companies may still not undertake it, because the yields may be small in absolute terms compared with those from other more central non-environmental investments. And managers may not want the nuisance of finding out about the best ways of cutting pollution, or the bother of implementing them. Unless companies have other good reasons for making pollution prevention a priority, these costs may mean they see no reward in cleaning up.

In fact, the farther the road is travelled towards zero emissions, the smaller the financial returns will become. The cost of each bit of pollution prevention will rise relative to the amount of cleanness it buys. The "green leaders" are frank about this. "We're going to test the public's willingness to pay," says Monsanto's Mr Mahoney. "There will be a price tag for all this, and in my company it will be hundreds of millions of dollars." Monsanto argues that the main reason that, in spite of large increases in productivity, its gross profit margin has remained stuck at 25% is the cost of the many social programmes (including environmental) it has introduced. 3M's latest initiative, called "Pollution Prevention Plus", comes with a warning that not all future cleaning up will be profitable.

Many companies have hardly begun to think about switching to clean technology. An OECD study[3] reckoned that clean technologies accounted for barely one-fifth of pollution-control investments. Companies, it argued, are most likely to adopt clean technologies when they are changing the production process. Volvo, for example, combined its programme to reduce solvent emissions from paint-spraying with the construction of a new paint shop, at Torslanda. This will have a capacity of 130,000 car bodies, half Volvo's annual capacity at Gothenburg, and will cut solvent emissions by 80–85% compared with a conventional paint shop. The OECD study argues that changes in the production process will be made only if the new process is more profitable than the old; it does not add, as it might have done, that for industries where pollution carries high costs, such changes are more likely to be made partly for environmental reasons.

Clean technology is easier to introduce in new and fast-growing industries. Indeed, because new technology is almost always cleaner than the old sort, any country with low levels of capital investment (such as Poland and Britain) will tend to be relatively dirty. Fast-growing industries have the opportunity and flexibility to build in new technology. But with the important exception of chemicals, those fast-growing industries are often ones, such as office machinery or electronics equipment, which are only moderately polluting. The big polluters – industries such as metals, textiles, clothing and leather, food – are ones where slow growth discourages new investment.

The attractions of the quick fix

By contrast, end-of-pipe equipment has attractions for polluters, the pollution-control industry and regulators. The technology is tried and tested, easily available from suppliers and easily applied. The risks are less: if the device does not work, the company can continue to produce; if, on the other hand, a new process gives trouble, the company's survival may be threatened. Installing add-on technology is a neat public statement of a company's commitment to a better environment, and may be easier for people to appreciate than the adoption of a new technology, which may be one reason those companies that have pursued strategies of waste minimisation spend such a lot of time talking about what they have achieved.

Measuring the costs of environmental protection relative to its benefits are easier with end-of-pipe technology, too. As Mr Höggren of Volvo pointed out in *Managing the Environment*[4] when discussing the clean technology of Volvo's new paint shop at Torslanda, "Let's say it's a total cost of some Skr1.7 billion – how much of that amount is devoted to purely environmental matters? I could never define that." The person in charge of environmental issues may find it hard to persuade those in charge of the production process of the need for change. That is, of course, why dramatic action is often taken after an environmental accident: at that point, the manager in charge of environmental affairs suddenly has more clout.

In the pollution-control industry the drawbacks are different. A few small companies specialise in developing waste-minimisation technology. Generally, though, companies want to sell products which are highly standardised and easily recognisable, rather than processes which need long, specific studies and may be difficult to market. Industry case studies made by the OECD show that new clean technologies may be hard to transfer from one user to another. They may be highly specific to particular installations and particular production techniques. Worse, they lack the particular advantage of add-on technologies, which are likely to be maintained by the company that provides them. The maintenance contract may be worth more than the original product to the company that supplies it. A clean process, by contrast, is simply handed over to the customer. If things go wrong with it, the necessary repairs and adjustments may be much less profitable to the installer.

In many countries various kinds of financial aid are given for pollution control. In Germany, for instance, accelerated depreciation is possible on investments of which at least 70% goes on pollution control. It is often easier for a company to get aid if it uses add-on treatment rather than changes in the production process that hide the treatment technique.

Even regulators may effectively discourage the adoption of clean technologies. In industrial countries permits tend to be given for "best available or practicable technologies" (or BATNEEC), and often include an incentive or even an obligation to use proven "conventional" processes. An industry may see the choice as unpalatable: if it experiments with an unproven process and gets it wrong, the regulator will grumble; if it gets it right and achieves a much higher level of pollution control, the regulator will ratchet up the standards to meet this new level of performance.

Building incentives
Government attitudes are beginning to change. Countries like France and the Netherlands have set up special government agencies to promote clean technologies. The Dutch offer a higher level of state subsidy for clean technologies and product than for add-on technologies, though much of the higher grants have tended to go towards the development of quieter vehicles rather than cleaner processes. Denmark offers state cash to pay for pilot projects in clean technology. In 1983, the year reported by the OECD, only 1.3% of the

available cash was used by industry "which reflects", as it says with masterly understatement, "some circumspection on its part".

Probably the most important incentive to the spread of clean technologies is likely to come through government measures to check pollution. Up to now, such measures have tended to have two characteristics: they deal with one type of pollution at a time, and they require industry to use a method rather than achieve a result.

That is now starting to change. Interest is increasing in the concept of "integrated pollution control", the idea that regulators should take account of all the ways in which a plant generates waste, rather than looking at one medium at a time. Why cut air emissions, if the net result is more water pollution, or more muck dumped in landfills? This attempt to build waste minimisation into the structure of regulation is a cornerstone of the Environmental Protection Act passed by the British government in autumn 1990. Permission for some 5,000 of the largest and most polluting industrial processes will have to be obtained from Her Majesty's Inspectorate of Pollution (HMIP). Its inspectors will expect new investments to use "best available technology not involving excessive cost", and HMIP intends to keep an eye on technologies developed in other countries as well as at home. Existing plant will gradually have to be brought up to a set of standards decided by HMIP. Once companies began to understand what they were in for – and a survey by KPMG Peat Marwick McLintock in May and June 1990 found that even in chemical companies, nearly a quarter of senior managers had never heard of the impending legislation – they began to yelp about what it would cost them. The challenge for HMIP will be to teach British companies that cleaner technology may frequently be cheaper in the long run than the add-on kind.

At the same time, a growing number of countries are talking about setting mandatory waste reduction goals. The American Congress has repeatedly threatened to introduce them. Several states, led by Massachusetts, are in the throes of introducing toxics-use reduction laws, aimed at restricting the amount of toxic chemicals that companies use, rather than the amount they emit. A common provision of such legislation is to require companies to produce plans for reduction. What happens in America may soon happen in other parts of the world.

Making industry clean up is relatively easy. In the EC some 60% of industrial waste is already being reused. But 60% of household waste is dumped. The cleaner large companies make their processes, the more they will be urged to help consumers be clean too. That is the subject of the next chapters.

References

[1] *Managing the Environment*, Business International, 1990.

[2] *Ibid.*

[3] *The Promotion and Diffusion of Clean Technologies*, OECD, June, 1987.

[4] See note 1.

4

THE PROBLEM
IS THE PRODUCT

The better companies get at reducing their waste, the clearer it will be that the problem is the product, not the process. In the best chemical companies effluent accounts for perhaps 4% of output. It is the final user that creates big amounts of waste. Throughout the 1980s companies like Dow and BASF cut effluent per ton of product sold by 10–13 percentage points, but their final sales increased.

So the next obligation on companies will be to consider the impact of their products on the environment all through their lives. That means thinking not just about the extraction of raw materials and the production process, but about the way in which a product is packaged and transported. More important, it means thinking about what will happen to a product when the consumer no longer wants it. This chapter looks at the rise of rubbish; the next (Chapter 5) looks at how companies are starting to take responsibility for the final fate of their products.

Rubbish and economic growth tend to rise in step with each other. This is not surprising, for rubbish is one of the most revealing indicators of consumption. All those natural resources the human race uses end up either in the air, or in water, or on rubbish heaps; those which are not disposed of by factories or flushed down the drain usually end up in rubbish bins.

Only decouple

Society now needs to decouple rubbish from growth, just as the oil price rises of the mid-1970s decoupled energy use from economic growth. But decoupling rubbish will be harder. Measures that reduce rubbish also reduce the initial demands made on raw materials. Indeed, it is through the costs of disposing of rubbish, costs that tighter regulation will help to increase, that society finds incentives to economise in the use of natural resources. Instead of worrying about the finite stocks of coal and oil, society will react to the

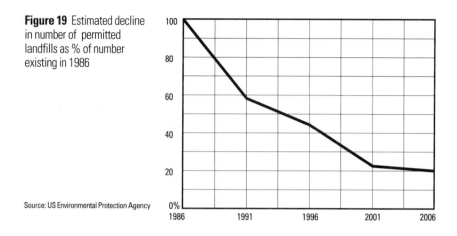

Figure 19 Estimated decline in number of permitted landfills as % of number existing in 1986

Source: US Environmental Protection Agency

finite ability of the planet to absorb waste, and in particular to the finite capacity of landfills and incinerators (see Figure 19).

Because most of the goods people buy end up as rubbish eventually, decoupling rubbish from growth can mean one of only a few things: buying products that use less raw material to serve their function; buying products that can be recycled or reused; buying products that last longer; or simply buying less in the first place. Deep greens would see only one answer: consuming less. That might be achievable if people were to buy reusable products and substitute them for other products that would otherwise have been bought; or if buying longer-lasting products meant making less frequent purchases. Although most people are unlikely to accept it, deep green logic is impeccable. For instance, the Dutch government at one stage were considering whether to alter the code of conduct for advertisers in order to discourage consumption.

More probably, people will go on consuming as much as ever, but demand new technologies and new materials. Take an analogy from the food industry. Some people, finding that sugar and fat are bad for them, manage to drop both from their diets. But others continue to have their cake and eat it, thanks to food technologists who have invented ways of making things sweet and creamy without sugar, milk-fat or calories.

Rather than make big changes in consumption patterns, people and governments will look to industry to help them to consume in less environmentally harmful ways. The attitude of governments to companies will be: "You created this problem. Now you solve it." That may mean looking for products that disintegrate more quickly. "We're looking for products guaranteed not to last,"was the slogan of Wal-Mart, an American supermarket chain. Or, conversely, it may mean finding products that last for longer, or ways to make products more easily recyclable. It could mean selling less – especially of packaging, the obvious way for consumers to minimise waste – or selling products that are less toxic. Or, most radical of all, it may mean thinking in terms of selling an "impact" rather than a product: if a consumer wants a warm house, say, does that mean selling electricity or insulation?

Such innovations will be most likely if governments find ways to ensure that the full costs of waste disposal are reflected in the cost of the product to the customer: through regulations on companies making their products recyclable, which will show up in higher product prices; or by charging people for disposing of the waste they create. Neither happens much yet. Indeed, neither the manufacturer nor the consumer of most products pays any of the costs of disposal (directly, at least). Both will pay more in future.

Where rubbish comes from

Environmentalists think that rubbish is a bad thing. But for the human race as a whole, the increase in rubbish is partly a reflection of improvements in living standards. Take packaging, which is easily the biggest single category of domestic rubbish. In America, packaging accounted for 43% of all municipal solid waste in 1988, measured by weight. If the concept of "waste prevention" adopted by companies applies to consumers, it surely means reducing packaging.

Yes, but packaging frequently increases the value of a product, not just in trivial ways – by looking nice, for instance – but by ensuring better hygiene. The increase in waste caused by the growth in packaging may have been balanced by a reduction in the amount of food people throw away.

Another reason for the rise in rubbish has been the pursuit of convenience. Takeaway meals are an example of greater convenience bought at the expense of more packaging – and more litter in the streets. But the drive for greater convenience has not affected only the food industry. In a number of other respects, waste has been created by consumers' desire to buy products that save time. Food packaging is one manifestation of this: as customers shop less frequently, they want packaging that will extend, say, the shelf life of tomatoes from a couple of days to two weeks. There has also been large growth in single-use products: from throw-away pens and cameras (no time needed to replace the ink or the film) to paper cups and plates in restaurants (no staff needed to do the washing-up).

The fastest growth in bulk of all single-use products in individual households is the disposable nappy, which makes up perhaps 4% of all the solid waste that American municipalities collect in domestic rubbish. One study[1] puts the American market for disposable nappies at $4 billion a year, and their annual "life-cycle" bill (which includes the cost of landfill to receive them, but not of the pollution caused during their manufacture), at an additional $3.9 billion. If the retail price of disposable nappies were doubled to reflect more of their true costs, would the market have grown so fast?

The continued increase in rubbish will of course be partly driven by that most powerful force of all: demography. As the growth of populations in western countries stagnates, the value of human labour will rise, relative to other resources, including natural ones. Both employers and individuals will have an incentive to substitute underpriced natural resources – underpriced because their retail price in no way reflects the costs to the environment of their use or their disposal – for their own increasingly valuable time.

If households put a high value on their time and convenience so, even more, do employers in labour-intensive industries. To Europeans one of the most extraordinary sights in an American café is customers tipping a whole tray-load of paper or foam cups and plates into a bin at the end of a meal. European restaurateurs still choose to go on struggling to recruit washers-up.

Hospitals are another labour-intensive industry which has substituted disposables for human time, with some garish results. American hospitals now generate on average some 13 lb of waste per bed per day, ranging from disposable sheets and dressings to needles and syringes. Many of these objects have helped to ensure higher standards of hygiene, even more essential given the public fear of AIDS; but hospital managers also jumped at the chance to cut their laundry bills. Then in the summer of 1988 medical waste was washed up on American beaches. Now, as Congress and state governments demand tougher standards for wrapping waste and keeping track of its eventual fate, the costs of disposables in terms both of cash and of scarce managerial time are also starting to rise dramatically. Incinerating medical waste (the method used to dispose of 80% of the stuff in America) already costs an average of 30 cents per lb before adding the costs of packaging and transporting. If the incineration has to be done off-site, as it is increasingly, a hospital can easily pay $400 a ton. Not surprisingly, some administrators think back nostalgically to the days of the hospital laundry. Johnson & Johnson, a large manufacturer of health-care products, finds itself approached by administrations, asking for help.

These examples suggest that if waste disposal is underpriced or (as for households) unpriced, people will substitute goods for time. Sometimes, as in the fast-food industry, disposables mean increased convenience for both staff and customers. The response of some fast-food chains to pressure to do something about the litter in the streets has been not to reduce the number of burger boxes or chicken cartons but (sometimes) to send staff on litter patrols to collect discarded wrappings from the streets and (in the case of McDonald's) to encourage customers to sort their wrappings into bins on the premise for recycling. It is easier to try to make waste more manageable for consumers than not to create it in the first place.

Find the bad guys

What matters most: the bulkiness of rubbish, or the safety and speed with which it can be got rid of? Hard to say: yet much rubbish policy assumes one set of answers rather than another.

Ask most people to put the rubbish problem into a single word, and they will generally say "plastics". Plastics are undoubtedly a problem. They

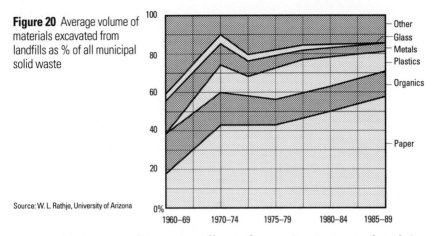

Figure 20 Average volume of materials excavated from landfills as % of all municipal solid waste

Source: W. L. Rathje, University of Arizona

degrade slowly; some of them give off toxic fumes when incinerated; and they are rapidly increasing their share of all waste materials (a direct reflection of the rapid increase in their use, especially in products with short lives). Yet plastics still account for a small part of total municipal waste: 7% by weight in Britain, 8% in the United States.

"Dig a trench through a landfill," says William Rathje, an archaeologist from Arizona who has done just that (see Figure 20), "and you will see layers of phone books like geographical strata or layers of cake. Just as conspicuous as telephone books are newspapers, which make up 10–18% of the contents of a typical municipal landfill by volume. During a recent landfill dig in Phoenix, I found newspapers dating back to 1952 that looked so fresh you might read one over breakfast." High standards for insulating landfills, designed to keep methane gas and nasty smells under control, make a nonsense of the word "biodegradable". Without air, rubbish simply will not rot.

In most industrial countries paper is the biggest single item in rubbish dumps: 33% of household refuse in Britain, 40% of municipal waste in the United States. Even so, it is the plastics industry that is under most pressure to think about getting rid of its product, and especially plastic waste that is packaging. Some of the industry's leaders smell conspiracy. "Newspapers don't seem so interested in the effect of paper on landfills," says the chairman of Du Pont. He is right: journalists rarely tell their readers that one way to produce less rubbish is to buy fewer newspapers and magazines.

Nor would most people think of the contents of the garden compost heap as a big part of the rubbish problem. Yet in America nearly 18% of the weight of municipal waste is garden refuse, and just over 7% is food (and the figure would be higher if so many American kitchens did not have garbage-disposal units in their kitchen sinks). In most European countries the bonfire has not been banned as polluting, and the art of the compost heap remains. But "putrescibles", as the British authorities call them, still account for roughly 20% of household waste.

Cost-effective strategies to reduce the growth of municipal waste ought obviously to concentrate on paper, food and garden sweepings. They don't. True, one other consideration matters: the toxicity of the things that end up in rubbish bins. Waste-disposal authorities increasingly worry about the fact that, while industry has had to adopt more stringent policies to deal with toxic waste, much of what households throw out is just as lethal. A study by Britain's Hazardous Waste Inspectorate reckoned that one-fifth of domestic refuse was hazardous. What happens to waste discarded by individuals may be much more dangerous than what well-run companies and institutions do. For instance, the medical waste that littered America's beaches seems to have come, not from hospitals (which will carry most of the costs of tighter rules for waste) but from drug addicts and people using medical supplies at home. Stricter rules on the way industry handles products such as paint, batteries and pesticides will look bizarre beside dustbins full of half-used tins of paint, discarded batteries and almost-empty drums of garden chemicals.

Even places (such as Massachusetts) that have laws on what can and cannot be thrown into the rubbish bin find it hard to enforce them. Indeed, reducing the toxicity of municipal waste may prove harder than slowing its growth. Manufacturers will be asked to find answers. Some are already doing so. Polaroid has developed mercury-free batteries for film cassettes; Safer (gardening products) markets pesticides based on naturally occurring fatty acids rather than petrochemicals, which it claims are far less toxic; Procter & Gamble has eliminated metal-based inks for printing on packaging.

Making more with less

The greenest way to reduce rubbish ought to be to get people to buy fewer products, or products made with less material. Technology can create products that need to be replaced less frequently. For instance car tyres are a particularly difficult kind of waste to dispose of. Production of tyres in the United States has risen, as people have bought more cars and driven more miles. But the number of tyres per million vehicle miles of travel has declined, mainly because tyres are more sturdily made. A boon to harassed rubbish collectors? Only partly. The new blends of natural and synthetic rubbers that have strengthened tyres mean less recycling of rubber from old tyres. And steel-belted tyres, while more durable than the old kind, are also more difficult to recycle.

While technology also can devise ways to produce more goods from less raw material, it will not come up with waste-saving products unless the costs of waste disposal are reflected in the price. Tyres have become more durable not because the costs of disposing of them have risen (although they are one of the hardest products to destroy) but because consumers wanted fewer punctures and tyre changes. Without clear signals from the market, technologies that appear to be based on fewer raw materials may actually include more.

For instance, the widespread assumption of the 1970s, that electronics would reduce the use of paper, now seems ludicrous.[2] The use of paper by American businesses rose from 850 billion pages to 1.4 trillion between 1981 and 1984. Harvard's computer printers spew out more than 22m pages a year, not including personal and faculty computers; the Rush Medical Library in Chicago in 1982–83 used 188 miles of paper in its photocopying machines.

Indeed, without the guidance of a price structure, new technology is as likely to create more waste as less. For example, microwave ovens have created a new market for film-wrapped packages of things that would once have come in large paper bags. In the days when people bought a pound of green beans in a paper bag, the wrappings accounted for 0.6% of the weight. When they bought the same quantity in a tin, the container was 13.5% of the weight. Once they changed to microwave cooking, the packaging was over 16% of the total weight. A general trend has been to sell more individual portions of food, which reduces waste but means more wrappings, both around each portion and around several portions sold in a pack. Technology has created convenience and saved people time; but waste has increased.

But the advances of technology do mean economies in raw materials. Products become smaller and lighter. Think of toasters, irons and television sets. New smaller products replace bigger old ones: pocket calculators, microwave ovens. The ultimate small-is-powerful is the microchip. The entire global annual production of microchips could fit in a single 747 jumbo jet. But lighter products are often produced on the assumption that, if they break down, they will be replaced rather than repaired, another example of the substitution of environmental resources for human labour. Also, the small new products may be additional, not alternative: few kitchens use a microwave to replace a conventional oven, rather than to complement it. And the tiny microchip, whose manufacture generates a surprisingly large volume of nasty chemicals, sits in a large plastic or metal box.

If the main priority for reducing municipal waste becomes cutting the weight of products, then the simplest solution is to reduce the weight of packaging materials. That is already happening. Reynolds Metal, one of the biggest manufacturers of aluminium cans, has cut the weight of its product by 45% over the years. Some figures produced by Britain's Industry Council for Packaging and the Environment show how dramatically the weight of a number of other kinds of packaging has declined[3] (Table 19, page 200).

But there are still problems. One of the easiest ways to cut the weight and bulk of paper packaging is to substitute plastic. The EPA reckons that corrugated cardboard boxes account for 12% of the weight of America's municipal rubbish; many could be replaced with shrink-wrap film and a plastic base. Several companies are doing just that. Nordyne, a subsidiary of Nortek, an American energy company, transports mobile home air-conditioner and furnace units that are shrink-wrapped with plastic on to pallets, with corners, tops and bottoms protected by corrugated cardboard. Gerber, a baby-food

Table 19 How packaging gets lighter (oz)

	pre-1939	1950	1960	1970	1980	1983	1985	1990
Baked beans can	...	...	...	2.4	2.1	...	...	2.0
Glass milk bottle	18.9	14.0	12.0	...	...	...	...	8.6
Beer can	...	3.2	...	...	...	...	0.7	0.6
1.5 litre PET bottle	...	...	...	...	...	2.3[a]	...	1.5[b]

[a] Including base cup.
[b] No base cup.
Source: INCPEN, "Packaging and Resources", 1989

manufacturer, distributes glass jars in shrink-wrapping on a corrugated base, without cardboard partitions between the bottles.

A German study calculated that to switch from plastic to other materials would quadruple the weight of packaging and double the use of energy during production. As so often with environmental questions, there is no single virtuous answer (apart, deep greens would claim, from simply not consuming): a choice has to be made between two second-bests.

A few manufacturers have found that they can do away with some kinds of packaging entirely. Hertie, a German department store, has changed its policy on direct imports of shirts and no longer requires each to be packed separately in a plastic bag. In the first five months of 1990, that saved 2.7m plastic bags. Migros began in 1985 to sell toothpaste tubes without an outer plastic box. The company's marketing executives were aghast. Unboxed toothpaste tubes would look awful on the shelves. They were right: toothpaste sales dived in the first six months after the change was made. Gradually, in-store signs educated customers. Migros went on to remove excess packaging from everything from yoghurt to drinks.

Manufacturers will often be faced with conflicting choices when they try to reduce the impact of their products on rubbish heaps. If products are more durable, and need to be replaced less frequently, they may be harder to destroy at the end of their lives. If products are designed to be biodegradable, or easily destroyed, they will tend to be lightweight and may therefore not be recyclable. It looks as if governments will pre-empt these decisions. Meanwhile, however, the main way society tackles waste reduction is likely to be through recycling. That promises to be one of the boom businesses of the 1990s. Chapter 5 looks at what is happening, and why.

References

[1] C. Lehrburger, *Diapers in the Waste Stream, A Review of Waste Management and Public Policy issues*, Sheffield, MA, December 1988; quoted in US Congress, Office of Technology Assessment, *Facing America's Trash: What Next for Municipal Solid Waste?*, Washington DC, 1989, pages 116–117.
[2] Robert Herman, Siamak A. Ardekani and Jesse H. Ausubel, "Dematerialisation", in *Technology and the Environment*, Eds. Jesse H. Ausubel and Hedy E Sladovich, National Acad. Press, Washington DC, 1989.
[3] See INCPEN, "Packaging and Resources", 1989, page 6.

5

SECOND TIME ROUND

Many people love recycling rubbish. They acquire a comforting sense of virtue from sorting their tins and bottles. A reason, perhaps, is that it offers something concrete that individuals can do to feel they are being good greens without spending extra money or making big changes in the way they live. The danger is that too much will be expected of a solution which can, at best, make only a modest dent in the accumulation of waste. Indeed, by forcing this fashionable solution on companies, governments may close off other options that might sometimes be more efficient economically – and even environmentally.

Left entirely to the market, some recycling will occur, but at rates that do not reflect the environmental costs of extracting raw materials or disposing of rubbish. It will take place only where demand for the recycled product is strong enough to cover collection costs. Even then, commodity markets are always volatile, and the market for recycled materials, as a marginal material, even more so. In America in 1988 90% of the lead in car batteries was recycled. That fell to 80% in 1989, a direct result of the fall in the price of lead, which reduced the incentive to recycle. The demand for recycled materials is vulnerable, like the demand for all products, to technical change. Technology, or the rising relative cost of human labour, can easily make market-led recycling uneconomic.

Different materials have different optimum recycling rates, different points at which the marginal cost of recycling an extra tin can or glass bottle overtakes the marginal benefits to the environment. Probably the optimum recycling rate for any material has not yet been achieved, let alone passed. But a danger for the 1990s is that fervent enthusiasm among legislators for encouraging recycling will create targets which cost society more to meet – in terms of human time, say, and energy use – than they save by economising on raw materials and waste disposal.

Recycling is not new. For example, people once bought lots of goods, from biscuits to milk, in reusable tins or bottles. As manufacture became less local, and as the cost of labour to clean up the returned containers increased, reusable containers became less economic. They survived only where the rate at which they were returned by consumers was high, and where the cost of returning and cleaning the container was no higher than an alternative form of packaging. Thus returnable bottles are widely used in doorstep milk deliveries in Britain, where the average bottle makes a dozen trips, but less and less for soft drinks bought from groceries, where on average only two out of three bottles are returned to the shop. They survive in the British pub trade because manufacturers can rely on the pub returning them repeatedly, because the customer does not handle them. Japan does better still: two-thirds of all bottles are collected and used an average of three times, while beer and some sake bottles are re-used an average of 20 times. (Though that is changing as the Japanese grow richer: they can now buy a can of sake that heats itself to the correct temperature.)

However, the pressure for recycling now comes not from companies, but from voters. Voters are not always entirely clear why they are keen on recycling. Sometimes they argue that recycling saves natural resources. Certainly it makes more sense to melt down an aluminium can than to mine bauxite and smelt it, using far more energy in the process. But it is less clear that the environment is helped by making less paper from virgin timber: paper is made mainly from commercial forests which are replanted as fast as they are destroyed.

It does make sense to price raw materials at levels that reflect the environmental harm done by their extraction and consumption. Left to itself, the market will generally prefer virgin to recycled materials, if only for their greater consistency of quality. In fact, much raw-material extraction is subsidised, through special tax treatment to encourage exploration and development, for instance. Ending such subsidies would be much the cheapest way to reduce the consumption of raw materials: indeed, it would actually save government revenue

An alternative argument that gained ground in the 1980s is that recycling reduces rubbish. As the costs of disposing of rubbish have risen, driven up by tougher standards and by NIMBYs reluctant to see a new landfill open, so the economic arguments for recycling have advanced. But in many places even well-run landfills are a cheaper option than recycling. In that case, recycling schemes work only if taxpayers subsidise them or if governments force companies to make them work.

"You can do four things with garbage," said Ed Koch, New York's colourful mayor of the late 1980s. "You can burn it. You can bury it. You can recycle it. Or you can send it on a Caribbean cruise." Up to now, burning, burying and the Caribbean cruise have been the most popular solutions. They are now becoming more difficult and expensive. But burying may often remain more efficient than recycling, however much green voters resent the fact.

Recycling makes most sense as an alternative to other ways of disposing of rubbish. The costs of disposing of rubbish have been rising, for reasons that are essentially manmade. In America in particular, the costs of landfill space have soared, especially on the eastern and western seaboards. This is partly because it has become almost politically impossible to open a new landfill; and partly because the costs of running a landfill have risen as the legal obligations on waste managers have grown tougher. Tipping rubbish can cost a city in California or New York as much as $100 a ton. Disposal costs are not much lower in some European countries. In Germany, the Netherlands and Italy getting rid of rubbish can cost $80–100 a ton. Shortage of landfill space has been compounded by the difficulty of opening new incinerators, unpopular with local voters, and by curbs on the export of rubbish, especially to the countries of Eastern Europe. Britain is one of the few industrial countries where waste disposal is cheap. Costs range from around £3–4 a ton to £30–40. Britain's indigenous extractive industries have left plenty of old clay pits with naturally impermeable soil; its sloppy approach to waste regulation has also helped to hold down costs.

How to collect

The costs of running a recycling scheme are determined by two main factors. One is the cost of collection; the other, the market for the collected waste. The economics of collection depend on a number of factors. Who sorts the rubbish? If consumers will do so reliably for free, that is obviously much cheaper than doing so by machinery – and cheaper still than paying others to do it more laboriously. Next, what proportion of the waste can be recovered? The high capital costs of reprocessing some materials (such as plastics) means they need big throughputs to make them worthwhile.

Collection is usually organised in one of three ways. Either the public sorts the rubbish and brings it to bottle banks or other collection sites; or the rubbish is sorted into different bins and left on the kerbside for collection; or all rubbish is collected together and sorted separately. Most North American schemes involve kerbside collection. The household separates its rubbish into special bins which are left at the kerbside for collectors to remove. The rubbish is further sorted – into bottles and tins, for instance – either as the collectors go along, or at a special depot. In Europe, these "collect" schemes are rare and "bring" schemes are more common. People take their sorted rubbish to collection points, such as bottle banks, from which it is picked up, often by specialist contractors. Such schemes are backed up by some mechanical sorting of general rubbish: magnets, for instance, may remove steel cans. A few experiments with "collect" schemes are now under way in Europe, including one in Sheffield and one in Dunkirk.

"Collect" schemes inevitably cost more than the "bring" type; in old cities, with lots of flats and narrow streets, they may also be hard to organise. But "collect" schemes are obviously more convenient. One study,[1] by Britain's Warren Spring Laboratory in January 1990, estimated that "bring" schemes might eventually cut Britain's household refuse by up to 20%. "Collect" schemes have become increasingly popular in America, Germany and Denmark, achieving cuts of 20–25% in household waste – and might perhaps manage 30%.

"Bring" arrangements could probably recover 10–15%, or maybe 20% in the longer term. Central sorting is probably practicable only for metals and glass, and might therefore recover no more than 15%. All told, perhaps a maximum weight of about 40% of the contents of Britain's domestic rubbish bins are technically recoverable for recycling.

Recycling will be cheaper if it draws on the co-operation of a well-motivated public. That is an attraction of involving green groups in schemes. In Britain, Friends of the Earth have helped to launch the "collect" scheme in Sheffield (mentioned already). In France and Germany voluntary groups have been running campaigns to persuade the public to recycle rubbish; the companies that collect the sorted trash pay the groups so much per ton.

One way to increase the supply of recycled material is to make it more expensive for people to dispose of things in other ways. As the price of dumping rubbish in landfills rises, municipal authorities will wonder whether to impose on consumers the incentives that already face many companies: charge them for the volume, or even the toxicity, of their rubbish. Most will hesitate, for fear of encouraging customers to get rid of their rubbish in socially nasty ways (like dumping it on the town-hall steps, perhaps). But at least one municipality already has such a system of charging. Seattle, in Washington State, charges a small flat-rate fee for rubbish services and a larger amount by the bin load, or even the half-bin load, as a way of encouraging people to take part in its recycling scheme.

The scheme is run by Waste Management; 90% of eligible households take part. Nick Harbert, who is in charge, doubts whether Seattle's carefully calibrated scheme of collection charges is the main influence on participation. In San Jose, in California, where he previously worked, 55–60% of households took part, even though it made no difference to their bill for rubbish collection. "That makes me think that a sense of moral obligation is the main thing that drives this programme," he says.

Charging may be less important as an incentive for individuals than it is for companies. Individuals in many countries, including Japan, Germany and America, show an extraordinary willingness to take part voluntarily in schemes to reduce the burden of rubbish. In one Japanese municipality, Zentsuji, citizens sort their waste into 32 separate categories, from rags to paper to appliances, and take it to appropriate collection sites. Sometimes the pressure comes from state laws or bossy neighbours. More often, it seems to be simply a sense of civic duty that makes people willing to sort their rubbish into different space-consuming heaps, to rinse out steel cans, to lug bottles to bottle banks and newspapers to recycling depots. Far from recycling to save themselves money, people are willing to spend time and effort to do it. Many must derive a rewarding sense of virtue, or even pleasure, from being able to make an individual effort to be environmentally responsible.

Indeed, where people are required by law to recycle rubbish, rather than do it out of altruism, it may be that the quality of recycling will suffer. Garden State paper, a customer for New Jersey's mandatory newspaper recycling programme, has reported problems with contamination of supplies. A famous book, *The Gift Relationship*,[2] by a British sociologist, Professor Richard Titmuss, argued that the quality of blood donated under Britain's voluntary scheme was higher than that provided under schemes in America where donors were paid. So it may be that recycling schemes work best if cities or voluntary bodies make it as easy as possible for households, but then allow a warm glow of self-righteousness to be their main reward.

Now, who wants it?

Persuading citizens to sort their rubbish is only a first step. The other big factor in the economics of recycling schemes is the market for what is collected. If the sorted rubbish ends up on a landfill with all the rest of the trash, then all the expense of sorting and transporting (the main cost of all rubbish-disposal systems) will be wasted. Recycling is pointless without a market for re-using materials.

At present, the rubbish which commercial recyclers want to buy is not the rubbish that costs municipalities most to dispose of. In America some 55% of aluminium cans are recycled, and 43% of all aluminium that towns would otherwise have to get rid of. The comparable figures for all aluminium vary from 18% to 40% in Europe and Japan, partly because aluminium is less widely used in drinks containers; Sweden, with the aid of a deposit system, has managed to recover 70% of all aluminium drinks cans. The economic incentives are there, created by the fact that recycling aluminium uses only 5% of the energy needed to extract the stuff from raw bauxite in the first place. So in Britain, where Alcan announced the first plan for recycling aluminium cans in April 1989, recycled scrap already accounts for a third of production.

But while recycling aluminium is highly profitable, it is a minute part of the contents of rubbish bins. Even in America, the world's biggest market for aluminium products, with packaging and cans accounting for a quarter of the industry's output, aluminium makes up only 1% of the weight of municipal solid waste.

Precisely the opposite is true of garden waste and discarded food. Together they account for about a quarter of the weight of waste discarded by American households, and a tenth of what the British throw away. Even as compost they have precious little value, although some American cities have set up municipal compost heaps to try to recycle garden waste. A constant problem is that pesticides and other chemicals tend to get mixed up in lawn clippings and fallen leaves. In some states, including New Jersey, people are not allowed to throw out their leaves with their ordinary rubbish. Few projects are as ambitious as the one begun in Fairfield, Connecticut, where a $3m composting centre was opened in autumn 1989 to create topsoil for parks and landscaping.

If landfill is sufficiently expensive, if collection costs are low enough, and if the value of the scrap is high enough, recycling schemes can be economic. Indeed, some of the big American waste-management companies have already spotted municipal recycling as a growth industry, less fraught with legal pitfalls than disposing of toxic waste. Waste Management, an American giant that runs more recycling schemes than any other private enterprise, reckons that the most efficient kerbside collection schemes cost $70 a ton. Add to that perhaps $40 a ton for a materials recovery facility, to sort and clean the waste, and the costs of a "collect" scheme start at $110 a ton. Of that, perhaps $30–40 can be recovered by selling the scrap. But the remainder has to be met through some system of shared savings or "diversionary credits": the municipality pays the recycler some of the money saved by avoiding landfill costs. If landfill costs $100 a ton, the sums clearly work; if it costs $20, they do not.

Several American cities now use such concepts to spread the cost of recycling. The Waste Management scheme in Seattle pays because it costs the city $75 a ton to dispose of rubbish; it can therefore cheerfully pay Waste Management $51 a ton to collect some for recycling. Chicago, Newark and Grand Falls all separate their paper rubbish, and split the money they save in landfill costs between the recycling business and their own coffers. Britain's Environment Protection Act, passed in autumn 1990, provided for a scheme of diversionary credits. The idea is similar to the concept of shared savings used to promote energy conservation (described in Part I, Chapter 6).

But where landfill costs are not high enough to pay for recycling, governments face a choice. They can use tax revenue to bridge the gap (as some American cities do); or they can make companies meet the deficit. Of course, such subsidies from taxpayers or companies beg an obvious question: if the whole point of recycling is to save landfill costs, why do it if it costs more than well-run landfill? But that is a question voters rarely ask.

Technology strikes back

The market for the collected waste can change, like any other market, with new technology and consumer tastes. One example of the way the market for recycled products can be hit by technological change was given at the annual convention in 1989 of the Bureau International de la Récupération, the trade association of the world recycling industry, by Henri Ubogi, president of the textile-recycling division. Mr Ubogi bemoaned the advent of self-cleaning machinery in the printing and car industries, which had knocked the bottom

Table 20 Scrap value of car hulks

Typical hulk weight	3,150 lb
Steel scrap: 2,250 lb @ $125.00 net ton	$135.00
Non-ferrous: 150 lb @ $0.12 per ton	$18.00
Fluff: 750 lb @ $125.00 net ton disposal	($47.00)
Freight	($10.00)
Processing costs: 3,150 lb @ $30 net ton	($47.00)
Scrap value of hulk	$48.75

Source: Dr J.P. Clark and Dr F.R. Field, " Recycling: Boon or Bane of Advanced Materials Technologies? Automotive Materials Substitution", WRI, Annapolis, 1990

out of the demand for wiping cloths.

A more dramatic illustration of the same phenomenon is provided by the car industry itself. In the late 1960s the usual practice of dumping cars in hideous graveyards was becoming more difficult: space was in short supply, and people hated their appearance. In 1970 President Richard Nixon's environmental message to Congress called for some system to encourage the recycling of junked automobiles. In fact, no government action was needed. The market devised its own system, thanks to the development of two technologies, that turned unwanted car hulks into a useful raw material. The late 1960s saw the transition from open-hearth steel-making to the basic oxygen furnace,[3] a process which used less steel scrap (typically, 28% compared with 45% with open-hearth technology). But at the same time, another steel-making process, the electric-arc furnace, came into commercial use. It was capable of making steel almost entirely from scrap. It could be used on a much smaller scale, which meant the capital costs were lower. Mini-mills, using electric-arc furnace technology, gradually emerged as the most profitable part of the American steel industry (Figure 21). Unlike traditional mills, they tended to be set up near sources of scrap, which kept down the costs of raw materials and of their transport.

The second new technology that the market threw up was the develop-

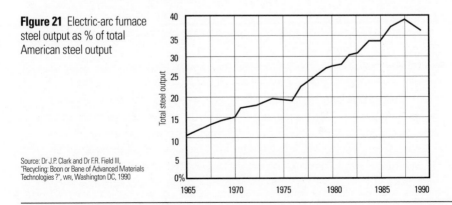

Figure 21 Electric-arc furnace steel output as % of total American steel output

Source: Dr J.P. Clark and Dr F.R. Field III, "Recycling: Boon or Bane of Advanced Materials Technologies ?", WRI, Washington DC, 1990

207

ment of the automobile shredder, a machine that takes a complete car, minus its tyres, radiator, petrol tank and battery, and shreds it into fist-sized pieces. Separators then remove the non-metallic bits and the non-ferrous metals. Put mini-mills and shredders together, and add the boom in demand for steel scrap in 1973–74, and the market had serendipitously devised a solution to the problem of car graveyards. As Joel P. Clark and Frank R. Field say:[3]

> In retrospect, the resolution of this automobile dumping problem seems almost magical. This is perhaps unfortunate, since it perpetuates the myth that technology will always find a solution to any situation, and thus all that is needed is to push technology along through regulatory mandates. As this case shows, while there was much in the way of legislative and regulatory discussion, technological and economic pressures resulted in an efficient solution with essentially no intrusion upon the private sector.

The magic may now be wearing off. The main concern of car-makers during the 1980s has increasingly been to meet foreign competition and to comply with ever tighter regulations on emissions and fuel economy. A good way to increase fuel economy is to reduce a car's weight; a good way to reduce weight is to substitute plastic compounds of various sorts for ferrous metal. The danger with this is not that increases the amount of plastics ending up in the rubbish stream although, of course, ultimately it does. The more worrying fact is that it reduces the value of, and thus the incentive to recycle, car hulks. Car shredders will find that each hulk yields less steel scrap and more shredded plastics (Table 20, page 207). The cost of disposing of the unwanted plastics, often toxic, will go up.

The tale of car hulks demonstrates the two qualities a material needs to be readily and economically recycled, and low collection costs and strong final demand. Steel benefits from both – even steel thrown out by ordinary households can be magnetically extracted from rubbish heaps – with the result that recycling is general everywhere. In Britain, for instance, scrap accounts for 44% of production, although not much of that comes from municipal waste. If recycling is to make a big dent in the amount of rubbish that ordinary consumers throw away, the magic that kept American car hulks out of graveyards for 20 years needs to work for other materials, too.

Making the magic work has proved hardest, so far, for paper and for plastic. Paper is a good example of the sheer complexity of recycling, and of the number of things that have to go right to sustain an effective market. It is far and away the largest single component of landfills: 41% of America's municipal solid waste by weight and 33% of Britain's. Its recycling rate is just under a quarter in America, if industrial scrap paper such as returned newspapers and printing offcuts are not counted. In Europe, figures collected on a different basis show quite large variations in the rate at which waste paper is recovered.

The less homogenous the paper collected, the greater the cost of sorting. High-quality office paper is worth money to recyclers, but takes up far less room in rubbish dumps than newsprint, whose value is low and highly variable. But collecting waste paper is a minor difficulty compared with that of finding uses for it. Popular enthusiasm for collecting newspapers for recycling in the 1980s on both sides of the Atlantic caused a sharp fall in the price. West Germany made waste-paper collection mandatory without first setting up end uses for it. The entirely predictable result was a glut and a collapse in the world price. A surge in collection in America in 1989 led to vast stocks of unwanted old newspapers accumulating in warehouses.

The oversupply spilled over into foreign markets. America, already the world's biggest exporter of waste paper, enormously increased its overseas sales of waste paper in the 1980s. In 1970 only 3% of America's recovered waste paper was sold abroad; by 1987 the amount had risen to 18%. American exports to Europe have been falling, a direct result of a rise in local recycling.

The green consumer's demand for products labelled "recycled paper" has helped to create new markets, and 1989 saw a 20% rise in the amount of waste paper used by British industry. A growing demand for recycled paper could reduce the pressure on landfills. The story so far suggests that two main changes are likely. One is that in industrial countries, paper mills may increasingly be located near centres of population, rather than near forests, to keep down transport costs. Even mills set up near trees may often have capacity to use waste paper as well as virgin pulp. They will invest heavily in de-inking plant and other equipment to improve their ability to salvage waste.

A second possibility is that third-world paper industries may grow up on the basis of paper reclaimed in richer countries. Some 60% of America's exports go to markets in three newly industrialised countries: Taiwan, South Korea and Mexico. They benefit from low labour costs, which allows them to sort paper more finely than richer countries can afford to. They also have relatively new and efficient mills. In Taiwan and South Korea, rising labour costs are likely to limit the competitive advantage in sorting rubbish. But other countries, with still lower labour costs, may take over where they leave off.

Plastics and perceptions

Plastics illustrate a rather different point. Consider this question: which is the more environmentally friendly container for a pint of lemonade – glass or plastics? Glass, the recycler would say without hesitation. America's Office of Technology Assessment (OTA) estimates that glass made entirely from cullet (glass scrap) saves about 15% of the energy needed to make the product from virgin raw materials, and the same amount again by avoiding the costs of mining and transporting the raw material. But the OTA also calculates that recycling pure plastic resins can save 92–98% of the energy needed to produce single virgin resins, although that sum excludes the costs of collecting and transporting the recycled resins. Besides, plastics with their light weight relative to their strength cut transport costs both of raw materials and of retail distribution. They also take up less room in rubbish dumps.

These considerations are deeply embedded in the arguments that will take place over government pressure on industry to recycle. If what matters is recyclability, then it may be (though see below) that glass wins. But that implies that recycling is an end in itself, which is clearly wrong. If what matters is the whole impact of a product on the environment – the collection of raw materials, the use of energy to produce and transport it, and its final disposal – it is not at all clear that glass is superior to plastics; and per litre, paper cartons are friendly than either.

At present glass is an easy material to recycle and plastic one of the hardest. Although both these account for 7% of America's and Britain's solid municipal waste by weight, only 1% of what is thrown away is recycled in America and hardly any in Britain. The reason is partly that the industry is in its infancy. The plastics industry only started to think much about recycling in the mid-1980s, not because it was cheaper (as with steel scrap) but in order to fend off popular criticism. But recycling plastic also poses some fundamental problems. Plastic's high weight-to-strength ratio means that a vast volume of, say, empty plastic lemonade bottles may have to be collected in order to provide a modest quantity of material for recycling. Worse, plastic products are often made of several different resins bonded together. This is especially true for plastic used in food packaging, which may be made up of several plastics used for different purposes. A ketchup bottle may use one plastic on the outside for appearance and strength, another for the middle, and a third designed to resist fats and acids. Not surprisingly, separating this club sandwich for recycling may be nearly impossible, certainly for the householder and probably for the industry. Yet single resins are much more valuable than the mixed variety.

Lots of work is going into developing technologies for separating different plastics, with German and Italian companies leading the field. Wellman, the company which accounts for 75% of PET (polyethylene terephthalate) bottles recycled in America, has embarked on a large research programme to develop sorting technologies for mixed resins.

Most plastic available for recycling is made out of a mixture of resins. Few companies can handle it. A study by the Environmental Protection Agency in 1990[4] identified only 16 companies in the world which were turning mixed resins into structural products such as plastic "timber", three of which were in the United States, although others, some using other technologies, are rapidly being ordered or built. The end-products from mixed resins up to now have tended to be replacements not for other plastics, but for timber, concrete and metals to make things like park benches and building materials. The city of Chicago has already awarded a contract for recycled plastic timbers and equipment for its city playgrounds. A sound-baffling wall, 320m long, has been built with mixed-resin blocks in Cologne. Bales of mixed plastics are being used to build bridge abutments and to protect underground pipes in France.

Here recycled plastics will be different from other recycled materials, which usually become substitutes for the virgin product. Moreover, while a bottle made from recycled glass can be made into another recycled glass bottle, it is not possible with present technology to recycle plastic park benches made from mixed resins. That may well change: but the effect of such recycling is to postpone the eventual problem of disposal, not to solve it.

An alternative to recycling plastic might be to make it more readily biodegradable. Several American states have passed laws requiring the use of degradable plastics: Alaska for beer-can carriers, Florida for packaging for foodstuffs and Oregon for backing for disposable nappies. But apart from markets for these products, created and sustained by regulation, degradable plastics have few uses in which they do better than conventional plastics (surgical sutures is one exception). That has not stopped several companies, including the Ferruzzi group, an Italian chemical giant, from developing new degradables that are based on cornstarch, and so are a logical application of its agricultural interests to its chemicals markets. Recyclers worry about the consequences if degradable plastics are swept up in mixed-bag recycling programmes: will that playground furniture start to droop? And legislators who know about Mr Rathje's excavations are beginning to realise that "degradable" is a slippery concept.

One other possibility might be to incinerate the stuff. A number of schemes either planned or in operation use rubbish to generate energy, and a virtue of plastics as a waste material is its high energy yield. Many such schemes are in Germany; at the start of 1991 the government announced an increase in the price paid by the national grid for electricity generated from landfills. German plastics producers think that incineration with heat recovery is the best way to dispose of their difficult product. In October 1990 National Power, Britain's biggest electricity generator, announced plans to burn almost 10% of Britain's domestic and commercial waste by the end of the century. The company plans to earn 60% of its revenue from waste-disposal fees paid by local councils, which will be saving the fees they would pay for landfill space, and most of the rest from selling electricity. One advantage of rubbish is that, unlike other fuels, it arises near centres of population, which in turn are the main markets for electricity. A disadvantage is that the neighbours of incinerators worry about the fumes; and disposing of the toxic ash left at the end of the process can be difficult. In many countries building new incinerators is becoming harder than opening new landfills.

Recycling the bill
Recycling was static for much of the 1980s after growing rapidly in the

1970s. But because governments consider that recycling is a popular way to reduce rubbish heaps, they have begun to set themselves ambitious targets. Britain's target is to recycle a quarter of household waste by the end of the century; the EC wants to raise the proportion from a third to a half; the EPA from about 10% in 1986 to 25% by 1992. Some American states have even more ambitious targets: Florida's goal is a 30% reduction in solid waste by 1994; New Jersey wants each county to recycle a quarter of its waste by 1991; New York aims to cut its waste stream in half by 1997. It sounds impressive; but in 1989 more than half of all American states recycled less than 5% of their waste streams.

Even with shared savings, companies like Waste Management rarely make much money from running municipal recycling programmes. If governments are to achieve such targets, they may need to step in and give recycling extra encouragement through regulation or taxation.

A first step is that governments should make sure that they are not favouring the use of virgin products over recycled ones. One way and another, they frequently are, and so are indirectly damaging the market for recycled goods. As the first half of this book makes plain, the cost of virgin materials is subsidised in many countries: cheap electricity cuts the price of aluminium; depletion allowances for mining hold down the price of minerals; capital-gains tax relief for forestry makes timber cheaper. One study[5] put the value of such reliefs in the United States at nearly $7 billion in the 1982 fiscal year, although that figure declined dramatically as a result of the tax reductions in 1986. Recycling schemes will always have a better chance of working if raw materials are properly priced, and an even better one if the costs of environmental damage, for instance by mining, pulp-making or commercial forestry, are also included. But if raw materials are not properly priced, then subsidies for recycling will operate just like subsidies for environmentally friendly agriculture: governments will spend one lot of tax revenue to offset the harm done by spending another lot.

Governments can intervene in a number of ways. They can, for example, tax virgin raw materials or subsidise recycled products, either with cash or through government purchasing programmes.

One example of a tax to encourage recycling is America's imposition of a $1.37 per lb levy on virgin CFCs. More widespread taxation in this form might solve the problem faced by Britain's Bird Group, a metals recycler. It has teamed up with Germany's Lindemann, a machinery maker, to develop a technology to extract all the CFCs from domestic refrigerators – not just from the compressor, but also from the insulating foam. In 1990 it reckoned that the scheme would work only if customers were charged a compulsory deposit of $29 per refrigerator. In time, the phasing out of the manufacture of CFCs will drive up their price; a tax or deposit scheme is a way to accelerate what the market should eventually achieve unaided.

There is less urgency about ordinary rubbish. Still, some American states have tried levies on products that cannot be recycled: Florida in 1988 announced that a disposal fee of 1 cent would be levied from October 1992 on any container sold through retail outlets that does not achieve a recycling rate of at least 50%. That fee will go up to 2 cents if the 50% target is not met by 1995. Others have tried banning products, for instance disposable nappies in three American states and in Minnesota plastic drinks containers, polystyrene-foam food packaging containing CFCs and food packaging that will not biodegrade and cannot be recycled.

Another option is that governments could underpin the market for recycled products: the converse of subsidising virgin products. Some American states are starting to consider proposals for favourable tax treatment for purchases of recycled goods. The Dutch government supports the market for recycled paper, just as governments support commodity markets for virgin products in order to ensure stable supply.

Recycled protectionism

One kind of support may be a ban on rival products, such as the Danish restrictions on one-trip drinks containers. That acts as a kind of protection, underpinning the market for a technology that may be more environmentally friendly than the alternatives, but is not on its own more economic.

A way to bring this kind of protection out into the open is through deposit refund schemes (also discussed in Part I, Chapter 5). In the days when children scavenged for lemonade bottles to augment their pocket money, manufacturers found it cheaper to use refillable bottles and government had no need to intervene. But once one-trip bottles become cheaper, a new logic emerges: deposits offer a way to recoup some of the environmental costs that such containers impose on the environment. The consumer has a choice: take the time to return the bottle, or lose the value of the deposit.

Deposit schemes seem to work well with drinks bottles. In Sweden a deposit scheme of about 5p on PET bottles brought a return rate of 60–70%. Experience with deposit schemes for aluminium cans suggests that a recovery rate of 80–90% could be obtained by raising the deposit to around 15p a bottle. Studies in the United States quoted in the OTA's 1989 report[6] suggest that such schemes result in the return of 70–90% of targeted containers, and are especially good at reducing litter. Several states report that they have cut the number of drinks containers dropped along the roadside by as much as four-fifths.

The fact that the government imposes a deposit system does not mean that it has to run or finance it. But allow manufacturers to choose whether or not to charge deposits and they may well decide not to do so. If they do, their products will appear more expensive than those of their neighbours. In Switzerland, where deposits are imposed on glass containers, the market share of aluminium ones, which carry no deposit, seems to be growing.

Recruiting recyclers

Governments increasingly want companies to make the arithmetic of recycling add up. The pattern has been repeated in several parts of North America: suggest that a ban may be put on some products, such as disposable nappies or soft-drinks bottles, unless the industry that makes them "voluntarily" sets up a recycling scheme. This sort of green blackmail has persuaded packaging industries to become involved in paying for, or even organising, recycling schemes. It has been used to try to create markets for recycled products. Its effect has been most dramatic on the plastics industry. Hostility to plastics in legislatures in many countries has led to frantic efforts by manufacturers to find ways of saving their materials from the dustbin.

Because they realise that the future acceptability of their product may depend on whether or not it can be recycled, plastics manufacturers are putting heroic efforts into finding ways to recycle their materials. Manufacturers have rarely become much involved in the recycling of less problematic materials. One exception is a joint venture announced in January 1990 between giant rubbish collectors Waste Management and Jefferson Smurfit, one of America's biggest manufacturers of paper and packaging products, to process and market recycled paper fibre. Such deals are likely to be more common in the plastics industry, where manufacturers have a direct interest in showing that their product can be recycled. In April 1989 Waste Management had already set up a similar arrangement with Du Pont, America's biggest plastics manufacturer, to collect, separate and process recovered plastics. Du Pont has also been working to develop markets for recycled plastics. It has, for instance, persuaded the state of Illinois to test a variety of road-building products made from recycled plastics.

Other plastics manufacturers are also moving rapidly into recycling. Dow Chemical was one of the first. With seven other plastics manufacturers it has formed the National Polystyrene Recycling Company to recycle polystyrene into non-food packaging. Part of the company's raw materials come from 450 McDonald's restaurants, which have installed separate bins to encourage customers to recycle their food containers. The aim is to recycle a quarter of all disposable polystyrene products by 1995, a proportion which would exceed current recycling rates for glass and paper. Reynolds Metal, which already recycles as well as manufactures aluminium, aims to recycle at least as much plastics as it produces. Union Carbide, another plastics manufacturer, is building a plant to recycle plastics retrieved from the states of New Jersey, New York and Connecticut. In Congressional hearings on pollution prevention in April 1990 Ronald van Mynen, the vice president in charge of environmental affairs at Union Carbide, gave a neat example of how to turn the tables on the public sector by complaining that Connecticut had not made it mandatory for consumers to recycle plastic waste. "Union Carbide wants to make plastics recycling work," he told the Senate subcommittee on environmental protection. "And we want Connecticut's plastic waste. We have the experience, the technology and the markets – but we need a steady supply of plastic waste. That's where elected officials and other opinion leaders must exert their influence to educate and stimulate the public to participate."

Other creators of plastic waste are trying different approaches. One is to try to create a market for the waste recycled. Several schemes for recycling have foundered when voters discovered that their recycled bottles and newspapers were being buried or burned, rather than re-used. Another strategy is to design the initial product to make it more suitable for recycling at the end of its life. Plastics are a special problem: New York, Iowa and Massachusetts all admit that less than half of all plastic containers collected are recycled.

Procter & Gamble insist that containers for their liquid soap and bleach are made with a 25% minimum of recycled resins. McDonald's hopes eventually to use recycled burger boxes to fit out new restaurants. Another strategy is to design the initial product to make it more suitable for recycling at the end of its life. Plastics recycling in some European countries has been made simpler than in the United States by the more widespread use of bottles made from PET, a plastic which is relatively easy to recycle. For instance, Colgate-Palmolive is experimenting with bottles made from recycled PET for washing-up liquid. Coca-Cola has been working with a bottle producer and governments in the Netherlands and Germany to develop a single-resin drinks bottle that would be easier to recycle. McDonald's is considering whether all the plastic it uses should be polystyrene, and Heinz has replaced its multi-layered ketchup bottle with one made of PET alone.

An initiative by 25 British firms with an interest in plastic containers is the most dramatic. In 1990 they set up a joint venture called Recoup, aimed at making it possible to recycle half Britain's plastic containers by 1995. It will help to pay for a number of collection schemes for sorted domestic waste, which will then be sorted as far as possible into pure polymers by a sister company, Reprise, at a separation plant which aims to have the world's first automatic process for separating PET and PVC.

If Britain's plastics industry meets its target (extremely tight, considering that in 1990 hardly any plastics were recycled), it will leap far ahead of the recycling rates for other containers such as glass and aluminium. An interesting question is whether that will that make a large difference to the acceptability of plastic containers. Will an investment in recycling old bottles turn out to be really an investment in market share for the new ones?

In North America, it has become common for recycling schemes to involve three partners: the consumer, the municipality and the manufacturers of the products perceived to cause most of the problem. Companies become involved for fear of incurring worse penalties if they do not. Thus it was to save themselves from even heavier obligations that companies in Ontario supported a pioneering recycling scheme. In 1986 the state government threatened to ban some products, such as disposable nappies and some soft drinks bottles, if industry did not "voluntarily" support recycling. The soft drinks industry and its container and container-material suppliers therefore decided to set up a scheme. More arm-twisting subsequently brought in the newspaper industry, grocery manufacturers and distributors, and the plastics and packaging industries.

Let the companies pay

Governments play many versions of the Ontario gamut: threaten a ban or stiff regulations, and the costs of not running a recycling scheme suddenly overtake the costs of doing so. The threat of regulation changes the arithmetic. Newspapers offer one example of such legislation. Californian newspaper publishers have been told to make sure that a quarter of the newsprint they use is recycled. That target will rise to half by the end of the century. In some parts of east-coast America, publishers face an even tighter timetable: Suffolk County, on Long Island, passed the toughest recycling law in the United States in June 1990. It would compel newspapers with circulations of 20,000 or more that are printed or sold in the county to be published only on newsprint containing at least 40% recycled fibres by the end of 1996, or face a $500-a-day fine. New York state's newspapers, including the mighty *New York Times*, are cross: 64 of them had already signed a voluntary agreement with the state to increase the amount of recycled paper they used to 40% by the end of the century – a good example of companies asking to be allowed to do voluntarily what they would otherwise be compelled to do.

The trend in Europe and Japan may be to load the entire costs of recycling on to companies. The pressure in Europe began to build up after the European Court threw out a case brought against Denmark by the European Commission. Denmark banned non-refillable drinks containers, a policy which the Commission said was protectionist. Drinks manufacturers from other EC countries would hardly bother to use the special bottles demanded by Danish law for so tiny a market. In 1988 the court ruled that this was an area where the interests of the environment should take precedence over those of free trade.

The ruling opened the way for other EC members to pursue their own policies on packaging. The greener member states had been frustrated by the ineffectual way the Commission had been trying to put together a directive on drinks containers since 1974. The directive, finally passed in 1985, feebly told member states to draw up whatever programme each thought best to minimise the impact of drinks containers on the environment, by voluntary or legal means, as they preferred.

With *carte blanche* from the European Court, Germany set about protecting its market for refillable bottles, which conveniently also meant protecting myriad small bottlers of beer and soft drinks, many of them in politically sensitive Bavaria. For some time the German government had been struggling to prevent a growth in the volume of one-trip containers, especially non-refillable plastic drinks bottles. To protect the local beverage industries, and to please Germany's powerful green lobby, the government has fought to keep plastic bottles out of the market. In 1977 the government and beverage industries reached a voluntary agreement to try to halt the decline in the use of refillable bottles. When, in spite of the 1977 voluntary agreement, the use of one-trip bottles began to rise in the mid-1980s, the government brought in quotas for different refillable bottles, deposits on the larger plastic ones, and an obligation on industry to accept bottles when consumers returned them.

Liberated by the decision of the European Court, Germany went further. In 1989 a mandatory deposit was put on plastic bottles, which crippled the market for bottled water from France and Belgium: EC rules say that mineral waters must be bottled at source, and lightweight plastic greatly reduces transport costs. France and Belgium now produce mineral water in special glass bottles for the German market.

When the deposit scheme for plastic bottles passed through Germany's green parliament, the public demanded to know why only one kind of packaging was under attack. In 1990 the government obliged. Under a proposal due to pass through parliament in March 1991, tough new obligations were to be imposed. Retailers will be made responsible for recycling packaging. They will have to remove outer packaging before offering a product for sale, or else provide a receptacle so that customers can leave it at the shop rather than take it home. There will be signs in shops to make customers aware of their rights to remove packaging on the spot.

These obligations will be waived for manufacturers and distributors who take part in a "voluntary" recycling scheme which will pick up used packaging, sort it, and pass it free of charge for recycling.

The government has laid down tough targets. By the middle of 1995, 9–42% of all packaging materials must be collected and recycled. Thereafter, the proportion rises to 64% for plastics, paper and board, and 72% for glass, tinplate and aluminium. No recycling scheme has ever achieved such targets. Moreover, the system will be paid for entirely by industry. There will be no recycling credits, as in Seattle, to help split the cost with municipal taxpayers who no longer have to pay tipping charges. Instead, companies will pay a levy linked to the number of dots on their product packages. The cost is likely to be immense. In theory, it will cost DM10 billion–DM15 billion to set up the scheme and then DM2 billion a year to run it. That sum will be met by selling companies the right to put a green spot on their packaging, guaranteeing that it can be recycled. Companies in turn will add 2 pfennigs to the cost of each product marked with the spot.

In practice, manufacturers fear that the cost may be vastly greater, and that they may end up carrying it. They also argue that the scheme covers all packaging (while North American ones tend to go for three or four easily handled wastes); all households (while North American schemes concentrate on houses rather than flats); and starts with no guarantee of final markets for the recyclables. Germany's glutting of the European market for recycled paper may now be repeated in many other commodity markets.

Foreign manufactuers fear that the scheme may be protectionist. German retailers have undertaken to do their best to encourage their suppliers to join the scheme, and may eventually be reluctant to carry products not marked with the green spot. They have not, however, explicitly agreed to exclude non-participants for fear of breaking the cartel laws.

What Germany does, Japan has been considering. Desperately short of dumping grounds, Tokyo metropolitan district has been refusing to accept large items of domestic waste such as television sets or refrigerators. A rash of illegal dumping has followed. Private contractors have been shipping waste to Japan's northern island, and local authorities there are in revolt. So the Japanese ministry of health and welfare has tried to persuade manufacturers to take more responsibility for the final fate of bulky electrical appliances such as old fridges, washing machines and television sets, either by recovering the appliances themselves or by sharing the disposal costs. So far the ministry has been fought off by the employers' organisation, the Keidanren.

Now for Brussels

Other European countries are now racing after Germany. Denmark, which already taxes one-trip packaging, plans to increase the tax, and is debating a ban on PVC. Italy is threatening to introduce taxes from 1993 on materials that do not meet recycling targets of 50% for metals and glass and 40% for plastics. Unlike the German targets, the Italian ones will partly count incineration towards the recycling total. Switzerland has recently introduced regulations for drinks bottles, laying down recycling targets that must be met by 1993. Sweden is proposing a ban on one-trip bottles made of PET. Dutch industry was given until the start of April 1991 to put forward proposals for a 10% cut in packaging by the end of the century.

What frightens Europe's industry most is the awful prospect that the EC Commission, anxious to improve on its earlier directive on beverage containers, might seize on Germany's scheme as a model. The Community has already begun to take a tougher line on manufacturers' responsibilities for the final fate of their products: plastics manufacturers are being told "voluntarily" to take responsibility for the collection and recycling of plastic bags. Plastics manufacturers were invited by the EC Commission in 1987 to come up with credible ideas for managing plastics waste. In 1989 a sense of self-preservation drove the Association of Plastics Manufacturers in Europe to put together a plan to recycle all separately collected plastics by 1995, backing the target with an investment in recycling plant.

Early in 1991 the Commission had yet to give its blessing to the German scheme, although Dr Klaus Töpfer, Germany's environment minister, said he would not ask for it and would take no notice if EC approval were withheld. The Commission had decided to draw up a directive to cover all packaging, rather than just drinks containers. It hoped to have a draft ready to hand to the Dutch when they took over the Community presidency in July 1991.

Much rubbish about recycling

Germany's recycling plan is a clear demonstration of the danger of putting too much emphasis on the most complicated of all answers to waste disposal. It is the equivalent of America's command-and-control regulation of air pollution: government lays down a single technological solution to a problem that might more economically be solved in other ways. If carried beyond a certain level, recycling begins to generate large economic and environmental costs of its own.

The packaging industry is particularly keen that any new scheme should not involve collecting recycled materials faster than it can build markets for them. That is what the German plan looks certain to do. But the industry also argues, with obvious logic, that recycling is not necessarily the best way to achieve green goals. Indeed, recycling may make it harder to achieve other, greener goals. In recent years, containers have become lighter. That cuts transport costs (and fuel use), and reduces the space taken up in landfills. On the other hand, light materials may be harder to collect for recycling; and refillable bottles have to be heavy enough for repeated use.

A more sensible approach would be to ensure rigorously green pricing of all virgin raw materials or the products made from them; to make sure that waste disposers pay the proper price for the right to tip; to encourage municipalities to pay diversion credits; and then to hunt for ways to let industry decide the best way to reduce the rubbish it creates. One possibility might be a scheme based on tradable permits (described in Part I, Chapter 5). If manufacturers were told that their contribution to municipal rubbish had to decline by a certain number of tons by the end of the century, they could share out permits on whatever basis they chose. Companies that managed to remove their products from the waste stream fastest (by making them recyclable, perhaps, or by reducing their packaging or weight), could sell permits to other companies who found it harder. The question of deciding which method was most appropriate for each kind of waste could be left for companies, not governments, to decide. Green organisations could always buy up some of the permits themselves and destroy them if they wanted to reduce rubbish tips more quickly.

The greatest gap in the present headlong rush to recycle is that governments act on one side of the market without keeping an eye on the other. It is easy to set deposits at a rate which encourages consumers to return their bottles or batteries; harder to make sure that there is a sensible way to recycle them. Developing markets for recycled products will be a much greater challenge to both government and industry than getting people to sort their rubbish or to bring it back.

Given the pressure behind recycling, one of the big entrepreneurial opportunities of the 1990s is likely to be the need to find new uses for rubbish. As in all new markets, there will be a time lag while companies adjust. It will take time to develop new technologies, to build new markets, to establish new sources of supply. But by the end of the century corporate activity in some industries, from plant location to the colours on the package, will be influenced in one way or another by the garbage glut.

Take back the computer

Recycling fever is starting to spread beyond packaging to other consumer goods. The determined Mr Töpfer has announced plans to introduce compulsory deposits on cars. The German government will eventually consider a plan to impose on manufacturers an obligation to take back used cars, if the industry meanwhile fails to think up a recycling scheme of its own. Manufacturers have begun to think harder about ways of dealing with the plastics they use. General Electric (GE) has reached an agreement with European car dismantlers to take back GE plastics from junk cars. America's Society of Automotive Engineers has developed a standard labelling system for polymeric components to help identify parts when a car is dismantled. Volvo has similarly begun labelling the plastic components of its cars, so that their composition will be clear when they reach the ends of their lives. Several car makers, including Volkswagen and BMW, are experimenting with reverse assembly or dismantling plants, which separate car components according to their construction material. BMW is building a special plant in southern Germany to produce a recyclable car.

After cars, computers. The German association of computer manufacturers has formed a project group to think about disassembly before Mr Töpfer does, so that it can put a proposal to him rather than vice versa. Another proposal on the government's drawing board would force tyre manufacturers to take back and recycle used tyres.

Companies' obligation to dispose of products will change their thinking. It will encourage them to band together, as plastics manufacturers have done in America and Europe, to form joint schemes for research, recovery and recycling. New alliances will emerge. For example, several plastics manufacturers, in America and in Germany, have teamed up with waste-management companies to collect and recycle plastics: Du Pont with Waste Management; BASF, Bayer and Hoechst with a number of smaller German waste collectors.

Companies are starting to take into account the final fate of a product when it is being designed. Plastics manufacturers and their customers are moving away from complex bonded layers of resins which are lightweight but hard to recycle, and away from composites, designed to do specific jobs efficiently, towards heavier, less efficient, single resins. Mail-order companies in America now pack their goods in popcorn rather than polystyrene foam beads. Enlightened car manufacturers are trying to use a narrower range of materials, especially plastics. GE is designing some of its appliances to make them easier to dismantle. Migros, Switzerland's biggest retailer, sells toothpaste in naked tubes, with no encasing cardboard or film.

The final fate of a product will become an integrated part of its initial design. That is something new: how many manufacturers in the 1970s considered whether their wrappings could become filler for ski jackets or bedding for farm animals? As Eberhard von Kuenheim, chairman of BMW, puts it, motor engineers will have to become concerned "not only with the construction, but with the destruction" of cars. They need to find ways "to reduce the need to extract new raw materials from the earth, and to reduce the amount of material which we must dispose of". Many manufacturers of many different products may eventually find that strategy thrust upon them.

All this would be more impressive if governments were clearer about their reasons for encouraging companies to recycle. When, in 1987, a commission set up by the Australian government looked at a proposal to levy deposits on glass drinks bottles, it found that a scheme which would cost industry and consumers A$200m–350m ($154m–270m) would cut the costs of litter collection by A$2m–4m, and reduce waste-disposal costs by about A$26m. "For consumers to judge that container-deposit legislation would be worthwhile," commented the commission with masterly understatement, "they would need to place a high value on the total of those benefits which the commission could not quantify." If governments are doing what their electors want, people must be willing to pay plenty for the pleasures of recycling rubbish, rather than disposing of it in other ways.

References

[1] P. Bardos, J. Burton, C.J. Burlace, R. Derry, A. Ikuwe, W. Pendle, H. J. Prosser and A. R. Tron, "Market Barriers, Materials Reclamation and Recycling", Warren Spring Laboratory, Department of Trade and Industry, 1990.

[2] Richard M. Titmuss, *The Gift Relationship: From Human Blood to Social Policy*, Allen & Unwin, London, 1971.

[3] Joel P. Clark and Frank R. Field III, "Recycling: Boon or Bane of Advanced Materials Technologies? Automotive Materials Substitution", paper for Towards 2000: Environment Technology and the New Century, a symposium sponsored by WRI and OECD, Annapolis, 1990.

[4] EPA, *Methods to Manage and Control Plastic Waste*, Report to Congress, Washington DC, 1990.

[5] Quoted in US Congress Office of Technology Assessment, *Facing America's Trash: What Next for Municipal Solid Waste?*, Washington DC, 1989, page 198.

[6] *Ibid.*, page 318.

6

MANAGING GREENLY

Companies that take the environment seriously change not only their processes and products but also the way they run themselves. Often these changes go hand in hand with improvements in the general quality of management. Badly managed companies are rarely kind to the environment; conversely, companies that try hardest to reduce the damage they do to the environment are usually well managed.

Why the link? Perhaps the main reason is that concern for the environment means adding a new layer to management. Companies whose strategy was maximising profits and ensuring survival now find they have acquired social obligations and the need to worry about their impact on the natural world. These ends may conflict with each other. What happens, for instance, when the demands of the environment turn out to be incompatible with the demands of the consumer for quality or convenience?

Even when there is no conflict, these goals demand a tolerance for ambiguity that irritates conventional managers. Ulrich Steger, whose Institute for Environmental Management at the European Business School in Oestrich-Winkel, Germany, is the first of its kind in the world, argues that "environmental management needs state-of-the-art management tools to manage complexity". Another management guru, Don Simpson of the Banff Centre for Management in Canada, speaks of the need to develop "the skills to deal with multiple stakeholders" and to "think in networks, not hierarchies".

Total greenery, total quality

The directors of those companies that have tried hardest to improve their environmental image speak with an impressive conviction. Ralph Saemann, a director of Ciba-Geigy, sets out his vision of corporate environmental responsibilities in language as emotional as any campaigning green politician. He speaks of the need for a new corporate culture, to foster environmental conviction from the bottom up, and of the need for "empowerment", a term beloved by green activists but alarming to conventional businessmen because of its overtones of increasing the influence of lobbyists on corporations. Some directors of American companies (but no British) speak with equal openness and passion.

In American management terms, environmental responsibility has become an aspect of the search for total quality. The concept that defects in the production process cost most to remedy if a product has left the factory gates, was born in America, exported to Japan and reimported into best managerial practice. Recalling faulty cars, for instance, is costly and embarrassing. Less embarrassing, though still inefficient, is to put right the defects before the car is shipped. Best of all is to aim for total quality and zero defects: to prevent mistakes from occurring in the first place.

Close parallels may be drawn between aiming for total quality and cradle-to-grave environmental management. For example, just as remedying defects is most expensive once a product has left the factory gates, so cleaning up after an environmental accident is most expensive and costly in terms of reputation. Cheaper is end-of-pipe technology to remove pollutants at the end of the manufacturing process. Cheapest in the long run, and safest, too, is pollution prevention: cutting down on the toxics used in a plant. Kenichi Taguchi, a Japanese exponent of the total quality concept, argues that an important aspect of the quality of a manufactured product is the total loss caused by that product to society. He argues that the aim should be to minimise the "societal loss" made by each product. One kind of "loss" is a failure to satisfy customer needs; another is the loss suffered by the environment as a result of the production, use and disposal of a product. Indeed, some managers wonder whether traditional definitions of quality, that apply to customer satisfaction, ought to be broadened to incorporate environmental criteria and to extend to all who are affected by a product from its cradle to its grave.

Such visionary thoughts help managers to build into their own reckonings all those costs that are otherwise not captured in the price mechanism. Many of these costs, as previous chapters have argued, are already being incurred by companies, in the form of siting problems, potential damage to reputation, sudden changes in regulations and customer tastes. Such costs are expected to rise, and they need to be incorporated into management strategies.

The pursuit of total environmental quality helps to explain why so many of the most earnestly green companies (especially Americans), search for the Holy Grail of zero emissions, the green equivalent of zero defects. Those companies that do not feel comfortable with the policy of zero defects ("I prefer 'continuous improvement'," said the chairman of one large British chemicals company), do not like the idea of aiming for zero emissions either.

The pursuit of quality may explain why some companies insist on setting common green guidelines for subsidiaries all over the world. Just as a well-run company would not willingly set lower quality targets for third-world plants, so those that take environmental management seriously want common goals for greenery. That strategy is possible only where environmental policy is a centralised responsibility. American multinationals often impose detailed environmental operating disciplines on their subsidiaries, both in the United States and abroad. British companies, which often have more decentralised managerial structures, find such an approach too rigid. That may change. ICI, whose decentralised approach thwarted the top management's desire to take the lead in phasing out CFCs, decided in 1990 to ask each of its sites to draw up an environmental improvement programme and to report regularly to the centre on their performance against a set of quantifiable objectives.

No cookbook

How in practice does management differ in the most environmentally serious companies from the rest? The answer is complicated by the fact that no single set of rules – no one cookbook – tells managers how to set about being truly green. This may be because it has taken business schools (at least outside Germany) so long to grasp the importance of environmental management as a subject. Certainly the number of packed conferences on the subject run in 1990 and planned for 1991 suggests that managers are eager to learn.

The first and essential step is a clear statement of corporate principles and objectives spelled out with the full backing of the board. These then need to be broken down into detailed rules to cover all activities. Compliance with the rules must be regularly monitored and the results presented to a senior executive with responsibility for environmental performance. The gathering and dissemination of information is central. A key element in this strategy is the environmental audit and its integration into corporate policy (see pages 231–235).

But would-be-green companies have other characteristics which set them apart from the dirtier kind. One interesting example is Johnson & Johnson, which demonstrates the close links between a company's environmental policy and its attitude to its employees. Johnson & Johnson's policy grew out of its "credo", a statement of corporate goals laid down in the 1940s by General Johnson, a remarkable man, who founded the company in the 1930s. He believed that "factories can be beautiful" and that "we ought to pay our employees what they are worth". His "credo" laid down that the company's first responsibility was to its customers, its second to its employees. The community came third on the list, and shareholders last of all.

This fine vision became clouded over the years. In 1978 at a series of meetings its managers round the world said,"The credo is all very well, but all the chairman wants to know about is the profit for the past quarter." In 1982 the company had a traumatic experience when supplies of its pain-killing drug, Tylenol, were found to have been tampered with and contaminated.

Part of the company's recovery has been driven by the development of a new environmental programme based on the "credo". It starts from the proposition that, in the words of Jack Mullen, vice president in charge of corporate affairs, "If you are in the health-care business, you can't play games with your employees' health and safety." A programme has been set up which involves making sure that all parts of the company are obeying government and corporate environmental rules. It is now building links with local communities (some educational, some financial) and continuing the environmental education of employees. It is also trying to cut packaging and make as much use as possible of recycled and recyclable materials. Possible new products are studied for their impact on the environment from every point of view, including their use of raw materials, manufacturing process and packaging.

Johnson & Johnson's experience illustrates a number of features common to companies anxious to improve environmental performance. Like some other companies, it has built its environmental programme on the foundations of a corporate disaster. Near-catastrophe influences boards to accept large budgets for environmental-protection programmes. It shows, too, how environmentally conscious companies attend to their employees' welfare, since these are the people most likely to be hurt by a sloppy environmental policy. Probably bad employers cannot be good environmentalists. Finally Johnson & Johnson's example demonstrates the crucial importance of securing the whole-hearted backing of the board, and putting a board-level director in charge of environmental policy. No company can pursue a coherent green policy unless everybody sees that the board backs it up to the hilt.

Worker power

A prerequisite for effective corporate environmental policy is the need to harness the enthusiasm of employees. A company's employees may also be its neighbours. For example, most of the people who work for Geneva Steel, in Utah, also live near it. They use the ski resort 15 minutes away from the mill's coke ovens. They must be the world's best-educated steelworkers, with an average of one year of college education each. Many of them, like their chairman, Joe Canon, are hard-working Mormons. All this gives the workers a strong sense of environmental responsibility. The company is one of the few steelmakers in the world with a good environmental reputation – and one of the world's most profitable.

Mr Canon is unusual in the steel world in many ways. First, he is in his early forties, like most of his managers, and so 20 years younger than most steel bosses. His managerial style is flexible and informal. Second, he began his career as a regulator working for the EPA. So he understands how regulators work – even if he finds them as maddening as other industrialists do. Third, his company is profitable, and he has a controlling stake in it. All these may explain why he has been able to bring forward the timing of some large investments – replacing an old and inefficient open-hearth furnace with newer and much less polluting technology – mainly on environmental grounds. "We began more than a year before the state wanted us to," he says, "but we would have had to make the change eventually. The alternative would be to sue and fight. Litigation is expensive."

One consequence of Mr Canon's known enthusiasm for greenery has been that employees have found some good answers to environmental problems. The company used to cool its steel in freon, an ozone-depleting substance. One of the laboratory workers waged a war with the purchasing department to persuade them to try using a much more expensive silicon-based alternative. Her trump card was to argue, "Joe Canon wants us to think about the environment." When the department capitulated, it emerged that a barrel of freon evaporated within a month, but the silicon-based coolant could be used over and over again. "It turned out to be cheaper, after all, and we're no longer discharging 55 gallons of freon a month," said Mr Canon triumphantly.

Involving employees in environmental policy is not just a way for a company to appear a caring employer. It may also make it possible to push through policy changes that would otherwise meet with inertia or resistance. Board enthusiasm may be hard to translate into action from middle management but once workers become environmentally committed, the constituency backing reform in a company will be larger and more powerful. Workers may start to make new green demands too. Workers at Hercules BV's Rijswijk offices are given a folder each day in which to put paper for recycling. Hercules is a company that takes the environment seriously. As its employees grew greener, they began to press management to do something about phenol emissions, which smelt nasty but were not considered threatening to health. The company managed to eliminate them within a year.

The other green consumers

Employees may be the people most affected by companies' environmental policies, but its other neighbours come close behind. Green issues have brought a new emphasis to the ways companies handle their links with those who live around their plants as well as pressure groups.

As ICI's Chris Hampson said: "We've had operations on Teesside for more than 50 years. Once, people were grateful for the wealth we brought. Now, they are pleased with the jobs, but don't want dirt in their rivers. Our own people find they get attacked by their neighbours, if we are regarded as polluting."

Large amounts of management time are devoted to building links with local people. When, for instance, British Petroleum wanted to build an oil platform in Poole Harbour, a beauty spot in the south of England, the development director of the oil field spent more than a third of his time trying to allay the worries of local people. Giving people a feeling that they have some control over what happens to their environment is a way to win friends and planning permissions. The company carried out extensive environmental research, ran computer simulations to study tidal flows and sand movements, and drew up six different options for public debate.

One American waste-management company found sites in six towns, and then told each one that they were one of the options. Were they interested? Approached this way, a couple of towns said yes. In France there is much less public opposition to the sites of new nuclear-power plants in America or in the rest of Europe. In 1978–80 local people were offered cheap electricity. Envious American companies fear that such a tactic, if they tried it, would be called bribery. So it is; but another way of looking at it is as a rational bargaining away of some environmental rights for cut-price fuel.

The bargaining is usually of a more discreet sort. Sensitive companies may invest management time and some cash in being nice to the local community: a donation to the local boys' club here, an open day there, a sports centre across the road. Most companies do a bit of this sort of thing; but chemical companies tend to try harder. Dow Chemical, for instance, adopts sections of beaches and highways to keep them litter-free, and runs special collections of household hazardous waste. Its Michigan division has given $25,000 to the local Audubon Society to study bird populations on the Great Lakes. Companies also produce as much public information as they can. All Dow Chemical's main sites have visitor centres and run plant tours. In the north of England, the visitor centre at Sellafield, British Nuclear Fuel's main site, has become the biggest tourist attraction for miles around.

Those frightening lobbyists

The groups most courted and feared by managers are the green lobbying organisations like Greenpeace and Friends of the Earth which can, with a single press release, condemn a product or a company. The more responsible groups realise that this power is both a strength and a weakness. After years of protesting, they find themselves suddenly asked by companies and governments, "All right, then, what do you want us to do?" Being asked to set out practical environmental priorities is very much harder than holding demonstrations or boycotting products.

Some green groups have begun to build links with companies. Raymond van Ermen of the European Environmental Bureau, an umbrella body for Europe's green lobby, says that his organisation is often approached by business federations and European companies with requests for a dialogue. Greens and businesses are already talking at national level; the new emphasis is at EC level. Green groups want better access to corporate information, and to product research at an early stage; companies want to get a feel for the way green groups will be pushing regulators.

Such rapprochements pose delicate problems for both sides. Green groups proliferate: American companies face – at one estimate – 18,000 of them. Which to talk to? Pick the wrong one, and jealousy may make the others more hostile. The green groups, too, walk a narrow line. When Loblaw, a Canadian retail chain, introduced a line of 100 environmentally friendlier products early in 1990, many of them were endorsed by Friends of the Earth and Pollution Probe. Mr Nichol, president of Loblaw, argues that the co-operation of green groups was what brought green consumerism to Canada within a matter of months. The executive director of Pollution Probe did television commercials with Loblaw, arguing that non-disposable nappies were the greenest way to wrap up a baby, but that Loblaw's disposables were the next best thing. In the uproar that followed, he was forced to resign.

In America plenty of green groups still suspect anything a company wants to do. Some lobbying groups deliberately target environmental leaders. Mr Jerry Martin, director of environmental affairs at Dow Chemical, claims that his company was told by Greenpeace: "We're picking on you because you're a leader. If we can move you, we can move the whole industry." Subsequently, he says with relief, Greenpeace shifted its attentions to Du Pont.

But other groups have begun to help companies devise better environmental strategies. One of the leaders has been the Environmental Defense Fund (EDF). In August 1990 the EDF set up a six-month task force with McDonald's to look for ways to reduce the amount of waste the company creates. The agreement specified that EDF should receive no money for its work, and be free to use whatever means it liked, including litigation, to pursue solutions it believed in, whatever McDonald's were to decide; it also precluded McDonald's from using the agreement with EDF in advertising. The deal was promptly attacked by the grandfather of consumer campaigns, Ralph Nader. "Grassroots environmental groups are not convinced that McDonald's is serious about creating a better environment," he announced.

In the future green groups will diversify. Some will concentrate on providing services to their members, in the form of information, recycling or campaigning; others on building bridges with companies. Indeed, companies may come to see that they have something to offer the campaigners. Shell has drawn up an elaborate range of scenarios for future energy demand, including one picturing a sustainable world, which it intends to share with interested green groups. Well-informed campaigning is in everybody's interest.

Keeping customers satisfied

The green consumer is essentially a retail market. But some companies claim that their industrial customers are beginning to put a value on greenery. 3M found in a survey in the late 1980s of business attitudes towards suppliers that nearly 20% of respondents rated "concern for the environment" as the most important quality, followed (17%) by value for money. In some industries the pressure to be green is changing the relationship between companies and their customers. ICI, for instance, now offers to take back contaminated sulphuric acid from its customers in the oil industry and clean it up. Mr Hampson sees this as a chance to strengthen ties with customers: "Customers will increasingly want to deal with suppliers who can solve their environmental problems. Disposing of our customers' waste products is a way for us to link ourselves more closely with them."

Dow Chemicals has also turned a responsibility into an opportunity. It is developing a concept called "product stewardship", designed to make sure that its products are safely distributed, stored and used by its customers. In 1989 Dow launched an even bolder scheme. Most of the chlorinated solvents the company sells are replacements for ones that have leaked into the air or water. Dow's Chemaware solvent-recovery project is designed to help customers reduce this leakage, and to collect and reprocess used solvent, getting rid of the residue in an environmentally acceptable way. The company reckons that the Chemaware programme will eventually mean a big drop in its solvent sales. It went ahead with the project, though, partly because it saw what had happened with CFCs. A failure to prevent leakage has led to a ban and to the development of other products that will do the same jobs at much higher cost and less efficiency.

Some companies have seen a chance to offer customers a new, greener service for CFCs. Toyota has pioneered a scheme to drain and reprocess the CFCs in customers' car air-conditioning systems for free, rather than let them leak out to damage the ozone layer. ICI and Du Pont both have schemes to recycle CFCs. Du Pont will ship containers anywhere in America to collect CFC-11 and CFC-12 (the two main kinds used in refrigeration and air conditioning), as long as there is a minimum load of 500lb. The customer simply has to meet the cost of filling the containers. Neither Du Pont nor its customers make money from recycling – yet; though Du Pont expects to do so as the supply of CFCs dwindles and recycling becomes more profitable. Suppliers are realising that they may be able to offer customers a service that will tie them in more closely, and thus they will eventually increase profits even as the volume of sales diminishes.

Greenery is also encouraging companies to build links with each other. Ed Woolard of Du Pont points out that: "One alternative to recycling waste ourselves is to form relations with other companies: we won't lose responsibility for the waste, but they will help us handle it." The search for an alternative to ozone-gobbling CFCs has led to new levels of corporate co-operation: product companies have got together to test toxicity, and have run joint recycling schemes. Plastics manufacturers have set up some research cooperatives to look for better ways to recycle their materials. The problem of disposing of heavy metals in batteries has led Phillips, an electronics group, to join other companies in the Netherlands involved in battery manufacture and distribution to set up a body to try to recycle 80% of nickel cadmium batteries.

Such clubbing may also make it easier for small companies to make room for the environment. Big profitable companies with spare room and management capacity understandably find it easier to be green than small ones, though the most ingenious technology for cleaning the environment often comes from small firms. A survey by Baum, a German club for companies that aims to spread green ideas, found that many small companies were not even obeying environmental rules, let alone pursuing green policies. One of Baum's aims is to spread greenery by getting bigger firms to chivvy their smaller suppliers.

More facts, please

No management tool is more powerful than information. When boards of directors realise what volume of wastes are being emitted, their attitude to greenery often changes dramatically. The British subsidiary of Rhône-Poulenc decided to build a computerised waste-accounting system, to keep track of the waste each plant generates and the costs of disposing of it. The data go back to each plant every month. "The first time I did this," the manager in charge of the system told the newsletter *ENDS*, "there was quite a sensation. I was besieged by calls saying 'Are you absolutely sure?' It was a revelation. They were jolted from blissful ignorance about their true product costs."

In America nothing has galvanised senior management as much as Title III of the 1986 Superfund Amendments and Reauthorisation Act (SARA). Title III insists that companies report all the pollutants they emit, which goes farther than the draft directive on environmental information agreed in 1990 by the EC council of ministers, which will affect new plants but leave existing ones largely unaffected. Complying with SARA Title III was an eye-opener for many chief executives. "It is painfully clear", says Fran Irwin of the Conservation Foundation, "that companies had no idea what they were releasing – no idea."

"Unless you measure something, you don't really control it," says Mr Hampson. The environment directors of some European companies wish that their firms were obliged to collect and publish as much data as their American rivals. Quite apart from opening eyes, the data are formidable management aids. They set out sensitive figures in a form that directors can translate into corporate policy. It makes it possible for chief executives to set goals for subsidiaries: get your reported emissions down to such-and-such a level, or lose a bit of your bonus.

Union Carbide, for example, sets managers targets for health, safety and environment. Failure to meet them can mean loss of pay. "One guy failed twice and is no longer with us," says Cornelius Smith, the vice president in charge of the environment. "Another is rumoured to have lost 80% of his bonus when he got a fail. But the measurement is a litmus test of good management. Good environmental programmes usually point to the presence of a good manager." ICI has also decided to make greenery a factor in management rewards.

Companies are developing new ways to build greenery into accounting procedures. At 3M Robert Bringer, vice president in charge of environmental engineering, has been looking at setting prices for raw materials, such as hydrocarbon solvents that cause particular pollution problems, to reflect more closely their environmental costs. And General Motors, as part of a broad review of the way internal pricing affects incentives, has been considering charging prices that reflect the high costs of disposing of pollutants. In the paint shop, for instance, such a system might encourage engineers to look more closely at the way paint guns are purged. As companies do more work on activity-based costing in order to set better price signals, environmental costs are likely to fall closer to the point at which they are incurred. "That way," points out Dr Bringer, "at least the company gets to keep the money."

Send for the auditors

For most green companies an environmental audit is essential. This process was first developed in the United States in the early 1970s as a way for a company to check that it was complying with environmental legislation. Specialist environmental auditors check compliance and examine sites or plants that are being bought or sold to ensure that they carry no surprise Superfund liabilities. After the Bhopal disaster, companies became anxious to ensure that their overseas subsidiaries met the same standards as their parent company. American multinationals started to audit abroad. That has brought the practice to Europe, where it has acquired a different role. Because environmental liabilities are less severe in Europe, companies see auditing as a way of discovering how they could be greener, and demonstrating to the outside world that they take their responsibilities seriously. They may also want to look at broader environmental issues, and particularly at where their raw materials come from. In America, too, environmental auditing is increasingly seen as a way to make sure that a company is protecting itself against criticism, rather than merely as a defence against legal liabilities.

First into the field were chemicals and petrochemicals companies. Arthur D Little, a management consultancy, developed environmental, health and safety auditing for Allied-Signal, an American chemicals giant, after a series of pollution incidents involving a pesticide called Kepone. In the early 1980s chemicals and petrochemicals companies accounted for four-fifths of Arthur D Little's worldwide clientele.

The range of companies calling in environmental auditors widened in the late 1980s, although most are still in manufacturing. Ron McLean of Arthur D Little says that in 1988 all his clients were subsidiaries of American firms. By 1990 home-grown European firms accounted for a third to a half of his business. One British consultant, SustainAbility, found that 30–40 companies had asked for help within a month of starting to undertake audits (with PA Consulting Group, a management consultancy).

One example of the way audits work in practice is provided by Union Carbide. A bureaucratic, stuffily managed company, Union Carbide was scarred by the Bhopal disaster and then frightened by a takeover bid. Part of a dramatic improvement in management has been a strong emphasis on environmental policy, which has been a corporate requirement since 1987.

Responsibility for day-to-day environmental management is in the hands of individual plant managers, who may spend more than half their time working on health, safety and the environment. The objectives they pursue are monitored and enforced through a system of audits, presided over by Cornelius Smith, who in turn reports directly to the company chairman.

Union Carbide's auditing teams look not only at subsidiaries but also at some facilities used by the company, such as overseas terminals. Sometimes the company pools auditing of hazardous waste sites or terminals with other chemical companies. This is another example of the joint enterprise that environmental policy encourages. A tough follow-up procedure ensures that the auditors' recommendations are systematically put into effect.

The auditors may be retired senior members of staff. Companies with long experience of auditing prefer to use either their own staff or a mixture of employees and outside consultants. Allied-Signal puts its high-flyers to work with hired consultants, seeing auditing as a wonderful way to get to know how the whole company operates. BP creates teams of people drawn from different parts of the group in different countries. Besides reviewing compliance and environmental management, BP conducts "issue audits". In 1989 it examined its activities in tropical rain forests; in 1990, its impact on wetlands.

Can we help you?

The number of consultants eager to offer audits has increased. In 1988 Environmental Data Services drew up a directory of environmental consultants operating in Britain. There were 125. In 1990 it published a second edition. The number had almost doubled (see Figure 22). Accountants of the ungreen sort see this as a splendid new opportunity. Every European conference on environmental auditing is now either promoted or attended by a bevy of men in pin-striped suits eagerly discussing sustainable development and waste minimisation.

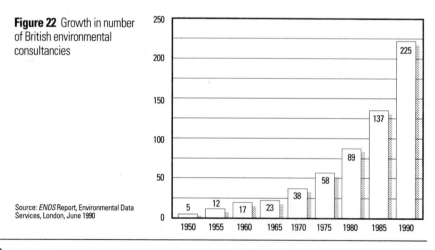

Figure 22 Growth in number of British environmental consultancies

Source: *ENDS* Report, Environmental Data Services, London, June 1990

What does audit do?

People have widely different expectations of the purpose of an audit. The International Chamber of Commerce argued in a position paper published in 1989[1] that the purpose of environmental audits "is to provide an indication to company management of how well environmental organisation, systems and equipment are performing". Conventional auditors tend to see it as a tool to test how well a management system works, to make sure that national and corporate regulations are being properly applied and check on exposure to environmental risks. Some companies see it in terms of laboratories, technologists in white coats and figures for emissions – as a way, in other words, to monitor the reduction in sources of pollutants. Some audits do both. For instance at Royal Dutch/Shell, an oil and petrochemicals group, the auditing looks at environmental-management systems and performance, as well as at various environmental indicators, such as the quantity of wastes produced, the number of spills reported and deviations from effluent or emissions limits.

In future, audits may look more closely at the life cycle of products. Retailers, anxious to buy greenly, will want information from suppliers about the environmental impact of the raw materials and manufacturing processes used to make the products on their shelves. Similar information will be needed for eco-labelling schemes. Investors in green equities will start to demand green information at annual general meetings and in company annual reports.

Green lobbyists are interested in environmental audits. The proponents of the Valdez principles want signatories to carry out an audit and then to publish the results. Britain's Labour Party is wondering whether to make audits compulsory for companies. The European Commission is working on a proposal to insist on them, which is due for publication in 1991. The Commission is thinking of limiting the obligation to large firms and suggesting a three-year reporting cycle. But when audits start to become political, rather than management tools, problems will start to emerge.

Standards for the standard-setters

The question of what exactly constitutes an audit will become more pressing. When environmental auditing stopped being purely compliance auditing, it came to mean different things to different companies. The trouble with the loose use of the term "audit", argues Nigel Haigh, director of the London office of the Institute for European Environmental Policy, is that it "gives the whole process an imprimatur of respectability by drawing a false analogy with financial audits".

The question of who should be allowed to conduct an audit is also important. Growth on both sides of the Atlantic has meant that green auditing has attracted some firms with no expertise. Established firms, anxious to preserve their reputations (and profits), are starting to think about drawing up a com-

mon methodology, agreed standards, and even lists of accredited practition-
ers. But auditors at Arthur D Little think it may be easier to standardise the
methodology of audits than to draw up an agreed checklist of environmental
standards.

Accountants have begun to think about external environmental auditing.
In Britain the Chartered Association of Certified Accountants sponsored a
report on the greening of accountancy by Rob Gray of the University of East
Anglia.[2] He suggested two possibilities. One cautious version suggested disclosure in the annual report of a firm's environmental policy, of its spending
on environmental protection, of future spending, including contingent liabilities, of compliance with legal standards, and of statistics for discharges,
emissions and waste. A more radical alternative, beginning with the concept
of sustainable development (see Chapter 2 of Part I), would try to build on
the distinction between manmade and natural capital. Green accountancy
might re-categorise business assets, so that annual accounts would reflect
diminutions in natural capital as well as depreciation of the more conventional sort. The Association has asked Mr Gray to develop criteria which
could form the basis of new environmental accounting standards, which
might eventually be prepared by the Accounting Standards Committee. If
environmental auditing is to be compulsory, it will need some such common
set of rules.

Perhaps a report from the environmental auditors will become as much a
part of a company's annual report by the end of the century as the report from
its financial auditors. A few bold companies have already begun to publish
external accounts of their environmental achievements. In 1989 the Caird
Group, a British waste-disposal company, circulated a summary of an inde-
pendent environmental audit of all its waste management operations to its
shareholders. Even more dramatic was the publication in 1990 of two reports
by Norway's Norsk Hydro, a large chemicals and fertiliser manufacturer, one
for Norwegian readers and the other for an international audience. The more
detailed Norwegian report (according to Environmental Data Services) sets
out details of emissions and discharges against authorised limits; describes
environmental-impact assessments carried out by the company and by official
bodies on corporate activities; and discloses some potential liabilities, such as
serious mercury contamination in the soil beneath one plant. The company
has subsequently asked each of its plants to prepare inventories of overall
waste generation. These will provide a baseline for subsequent improvements. Quarterly reports of plant emissions and of any spills or incidents are
also being centrally collected. In this way, the collection of information for
publication is likely to serve as an impetus to better environmental management.

Norsk Hydro is, so far, unique. Not many companies are likely to see the
compulsory publication of such a report as an opportunity. Indeed, insisting
on the publication of audits, or even on their conduct, will undoubtedly alter

their effect. Auditors and audited both claim that audits are far more useful when senior management backs them than when they are considered to be merely an obligation. What matters, after all, is not whether an environmental audit is carried out, but what action is taken to follow up its findings. Besides, just as no company would append to its annual report full details of its auditors' review of its financial position, so none will willingly publish a full review of its environmental activities. The EPA, pressed by the green lobby to insist on the publication of environmental audits, takes the view that published ones would be less frank than those conducted for internal consumption.

In time, companies may come to do one audit for public consumption, and another – or several more – as aids to internal management. Rather than press for compulsory auditing, politicians and lobbyists would do better to press for more disclosure of information on the materials companies use and the wastes they create.

References

[1] International Chamber of Commerce, "Environmental Auditing", Paris, 1989.
[2] R. H. Gray, "The Greening of Accountancy: The Profession after Pearce", Certified Research Report No. 17, Chartered Association of Certified Accountants, 1990.

7

GOING GREEN TOGETHER

Most companies will be only as green as governments make them. That is another way of saying that companies are not altruists. They will do what is required of them, and what they perceive to be in their self-interest. That is as it should be. It is not the job of companies to decide what values ought to be attached to natural resources and what the priorities of environmental policy ought to be, any more than it is their job to decide what share of national income should go into education, or what the speed limit should be. The setting of environmental priorities and their translation into price signals and regulation is government's role.

But government can do its job more effectively, and clever companies can profit, if both understand their mutual interest in environmental regulation. The rules government sets – whether through market-based instruments or command-and-control – are essentially a form of domestic protectionism. They work like customs barriers. They keep out of the economy those companies that cannot meet them. Dirty power stations are penalised, just as customs barriers penalise third-world textile manufacturers. They raise prices in much the same way as customs barriers: electricity becomes more expensive if power stations have to invest in scrubbers, just as shirts are dearer because Bangladeshi imports are kept out.

Here, though, the similarities end. The companies that lobby most vigorously for protection from cheap foreign imports are the weakest: those who cannot cope with competition at the bottom end of the market. The weakest companies will be those lobbying hardest against environmental intervention. They will be the ones to shout loudest that tough environmental rules will make it impossible for them to compete with companies from dirty countries abroad.

Market leaders will see things rather differently. The challenge is to get government to set standards at a level that they can meet, but their competitors cannot. They will see foreign competition differently, too. Realising that worldwide environmental standards will improve over the years, they will see the advantage of an assured home market, protected by tough standards, in which to develop path-breaking environmental technologies. These will then have eager markets abroad, as other countries raise their own standards.

Governments in countries with a tradition of state corporatism understand this function of regulation. In Japan and Germany the concept of technology-forcing regulation is familiar. In countries such as Britain and America, where government has become wary of intervening to tell industry how to do its job, the concept seems more novel. Only gradually are governments coming to realise how industry's environmental leaders can reduce the costs of raising standards. If one company has developed a cleaner technology, then it costs a country less to raise standards to the level that technology can deliver. From the company's point of view, the past costs of investing in developing the technology have to be offset against future benefits from selling it. From the government's point of view, though, the balance of costs and benefits looks better: the costs of a standard that can be met with an existing technology are far lower than the costs of one for which no appropriate technology has yet been developed.

A green alliance

The potential green alliance between companies and governments is a delicate one. Protectionism is always a dangerous path and green protectionism is no exception. The greenest companies will want government intervention designed to give as much support as possible to their particular answers to environmental problems. Government's interest is in raising standards, but leaving the terrain open for many different technological solutions to blossom. Large companies with lots of political clout may see the alternative to, say, CFCs to be another chemical; or the alternative to cars running on leaded petrol as cars running on lead-free. They may collude with governments to set standards that benefit their particular brand of greenery.

However, small companies less wedded to particular technologies may come up with quite different solutions through lateral thinking, rather than building on their existing product base. They may find answers in mechanical processes rather than chemical ones, or in biotechnology rather than engineering. Environmental innovation generally comes from "outsiders": small companies, suppliers and foreign firms. It is important to foster their inventiveness, rather than suppress it.

The idea of building an industry around government regulation is an uncomfortable one for companies to stomach. Business schools do not think that environmental policy is an important component of what managers are taught, except in Germany. The preferred areas of study are innovation in finance, marketing and management, rather than the less visionary concept of how to make the most of government regulations. Generations of managers have therefore been trained to think of government regulation, if at all, as an incidental inconvenience rather than a central fact of corporate life that might be turned to an advantage. "There's no single required course on business regulation in the United States," asserts Paul Portney of Resources for the Future. "I'd bet my mortgage on it." Most managers therefore think of green regulation as something to fight. A characteristic of American small companies that have spotted environmental niches is how often they turn out to be run by former regulators, often "graduates" of the EPA.

A better way

The more governments intervene in markets, the more important it is that they do so in benign ways. Most pollution controls, in most countries, work through standard-setting. The usual goal is best available technology. Enforcing that goal has two implications: it means an extraordinarily high degree of government intervention in industrial investment decisions; and it rules out decisions about whether the costs of imposing a standard exceed the likely environmental benefits.

Taken literally, "best available technology" suggests that if a better technology exists, companies should use it, however expensive it may be. This has led the British environment department to try to build into its new system of pollution controls the broader concept of BATNEEC, "the best available technology not involving excessive cost". But to judge whether costs are excessive may involve pollution inspectors in even more intervention, wrangling with company finance departments, as well as with engineers.

Britain's new controls, introduced in the Environmental Protection Act of 1990, bring a further problem. In the past, government pollution inspectors have tended to work out in cooperation with industry the standards it has to meet. To escape accusations of excessive cosiness, and to try to ensure that uniform principles apply, Britain's pollution inspectors have decided to try to distance themselves, and to draw up guidelines for companies without their collaboration. However, companies insist that they know better than government inspectors what does and does not work. Britain's tradition of collaboration is very much a hallmark of European pollution policies, and is distinctly different from the more adversarial relationship of government and companies in America where, policies dubbed "command-and-control" have frequently set out not just the goal in terms of pollution reduction, but the technology by which companies must attain it. That removes from companies any incentive to find cheaper ways to meet a given pollution standard.

Standards are rarely a good way to encourage innovation. They are easier to apply to new products and processes than to existing ones. In the pharmaceutical industry, this "new-source bias", which is particularly strong in America, has reduced the number of new drugs brought on to the market compared with other countries. Bizarre though it may seem, there are more examples of environmental standards being used to protect dirty old industries than to encourage new clean ones. Robert Crandall, of the Brookings Institution in Washington DC, has collected examples. Electrical utilities are one; metal smelting is another. In both cases, tighter emissions have been set for new entrants, mainly in southern and western states, but not for older, dirtier enterprises in the Midwest. This dirty protectionism, he argues, is partly a reflection of America's political system, which gives two Senate seats to old industrial states which have lost population as well as to the fast-growing new ones. States where industrial jobs are being lost frequently back high new standards because they know they will apply mainly to newer industries in rival states.

Raising standards may depress sales. Thus each time emission standards on American cars have been tightened, car prices rise and the average age of the car fleet creeps up. In the mid-1950s the average American car was six years old; in the late 1960s, 5.5 years; by 1987, 7.6 years. That may partly reflect a slower rise in incomes, encouraging people to replace their cars less often. It may also mean that cars have become more durable so that they need replacement less often. But it probably also reflects tighter emission standards. For part proof, compare the smaller rise in the average age of American lorries, whose emissions are less heavily regulated: the fleet was 7.7 years old in the late 1960s, and eight years old at the end of the 1980s. Higher emission standards mean not only that cars become smaller and lighter and have lower performance. They also make cars more expensive. By the mid-1980s, reckons Mr Crandall, higher environmental and safety standards accounted for almost 20% of the cost of a new car in gadgetry and in extra fuel consumption over its lifetime. Safety standards represented only one-fifth of that figure.

As environmental standards tighten, diminishing green returns set in. As the clean air legislation wound its way through Congress in the summer of 1990, General Motors was vociferously arguing that yet tougher controls were a daft way to cut emissions. Why spend millions developing more fuel-efficient engines, when the cost per mile of fuel had halved in the 1980s in real terms and stood, on the eve of the Gulf crisis, at 2 cents, its lowest level ever? A carbon tax would be better. What conceivable interest could a car manufacturer have in pushing for a carbon tax? Easy. It would not only be the most cost-effective way to reduce emissions; it would also shift most of the cost from purchasers of new cars to the users of existing vehicles. Indeed, it might provide a positive incentive for drivers of old, smoky cars to trade them in for a newer, more economical model.

Unocal, a Californian oil company, found an ingenious way of making this very point. To celebrate its centenary in 1990, the company offered to buy up 7,000 pre-1971 cars for $700 apiece. Its tests showed that they each emitted more than 60 times as many hydrocarbons as a 1990 model. Unocal swore the scheme was not intended to make a point about Los Angeles air standards. But the point was there: money spent on helping the dirtiest to clean up buys more greenery than money spent on the clean.

In spite of all the drawbacks, companies often prefer standards to the use of economic instruments which, as Chapter 5 of Part I explained, are almost always the most cost-effective ways to reduce pollution. Why? Partly because they are a known quantity, and appear to be fair to everybody in a given industry (though in fact they are not). Partly, as Chapter 5 also pointed out, those economic instruments that raise revenue do so by taking money from companies. Green taxes fall on companies that have reached a minimum pollution standard, as well as those that have not. But if green taxes are combined with schemes to pay money back to the least polluting (of the sort described in Chapter 6 of Part I), then good green companies will see them as a way to make money. They will also applaud tradable permit schemes (as long as the permits are not auctioned, in which case they will work like green taxes). Permits (described in Chapter 5) offer the greener companies an ideal way to increase their profits.

Bring in the market

In America, which has more environmental regulation than any other country, there are various schemes which try to create incentives for industry to throw its weight behind a cleaner environment. In most cases, such schemes bear the stamp of a handful of imaginative environmental lobbying groups who see the power of green market forces, and especially of the EDF, one of the rare green groups whose policy is influenced more by economists than by lawyers.

America's new clean air legislation, based on ideas developed by the EDF and by Project 88,[1] a highly influential study of economic answers to green problems, sets an absolute cap on emissions of sulphur dioxide and nitrous oxide by power stations. It then gives companies permits to emit a certain amount of the gases each year, and allows them to buy or sell these permits. The aim is to encourage those power stations which can clean up most cheaply to do so, and then make money by selling spare polluting capacity to those for whom cleaning up is expensive.

If tradable permits introduced under the new clean air legislation are a success, a whole new industry may grow up around them. They are already encouraging a new kind of trader. John Palmisano, whose company AER*X has been arranging trades in pollution permits under an older, less satisfactory bit of clean air legislation, looks forward to a big increase in demand. He is a former EPA official and is now the only specialised broker in the business. Most permit trades under the old legislation were put together one at a time by attorneys. After the new clean air bill came before Congress in 1990, other firms became interested.

Successful pollution-permit trading will require unusual combinations of skills among brokers. Mr Palmisano employs engineers with experience of working in regulatory agencies. Other companies are now putting together broking skills, engineering expertise and an understanding of environmental regulations, in the hope of benefiting from the new legislation. They will then approach companies, offering to cut their emissions and pay for it by selling their spare emission rights. "My best client is the finance manager," says Mr Palmisano. "Not the pollution-control manager, who is probably an engineer with a strong not-invented-here attitude." He emphasises the importance of making sure that no cheating takes place, for cheating devalues the permits. "I make sure that everything that goes through here is completely kosher," says Mr Palmisano.

More light, less power

Another environmental group, the Conservation Law Foundation, helped to devise a framework for electricity pricing in Massachusetts and Rhode Island that has provided one utility, New England Electric, with an incentive to sell its customers less electricity, rather than more. Over the next 20 years the company plans to cut the demand for its product by one-third below the level it would otherwise reach, by investing in a variety of conservation measures on its customers' premises. The logic is that explained in Chapter 6 of Part I: utilities expect a payback on new generating plant of 12–13%, but their customers look for rates of return of 30–40% on investments in energy conservation. It should therefore make better sense for a utility to invest in insulating its customers than in building new power stations.

New England Electric offers to pay part or all of the cost of insulating buildings or installing high-efficiency lightbulbs or cooling systems. In the mid-1980s the company used to carry out energy audits of customers' buildings, but left it to the customer to decide whether to carry out the work. What has brought it into the energy-conservation business in a big way is a change in the way state regulators allow it to calculate its prices.

A first step was to allow the company to pass on some of the costs of cutting customers' electricity bills to its customers at large. That was moderately helpful, but provided no incentive to do the work. In 1990 the rules changed. Not only can it pass on, through higher electricity prices for all customers, the cost of making such investments; its rates also guarantee it a proportion of the savings made by its customers. That concept of "shared savings" has made it more profitable for the company to invest in energy conservation by its customers than to build new generating plant. "We add the cost of conservation into the rates in the year we spend the money," says New England's chief executive John Rowe. The principle is that today's electricity prices should reflect future environmental costs. The practical consequence has been marginally to offset the depressing effect on energy conservation of the fall in real energy prices in the late 1980s.

The size of the energy-conservation programme is still quite small: the company spends 4% of its $65m revenues on it, which is large in proportionate terms but small compared with some utilities in California. But by the end of 1991 New England Electric expects to have saved over 300MW in five years by energy conservation. Apart from shared savings, the company benefits in two other ways: from a good press, vital in conservationist New England, and from avoiding the burden of building new plant. That burden is not just one of debt; building a new plant means fighting with green community groups who do not want a power station in their back yards, and fighting with regulators for a rate increase to cover the costs. New England Electric has not built a new plant since the early 1970s; by the late 1980s capacity was becoming tight. Shared savings, coupled with buying power from outside suppliers, have relieved the pressure.

In other American states, regulators are finding similar ways of giving utilities an interest in energy conservation. In 1990 California and New York were considering shared savings. Wisconsin was the first state to give utilities a way to capitalise investments in conservation in their rate base, earning 2% on investment in conservation than in new supply.

America's utilities are far more regulated than most industries. The creation of financial incentives for utilities like New England Electric to invest in energy conservation is entirely dependent on the regulators. The thinking behind such schemes, though, has come partly from campaigning organisations: EDF in California and the Conservation Law Foundation (CLF) in New England. "CLF found that it knew how to beat up utilities, but not how to make good things happen," says Mr Rowe. "We began as adversaries, but then realised we weren't getting anywhere by fighting."

A third example of using the market to encourage industry to be green is California's Proposition 65. This was another EDF brainchild, but owed nothing to cooperation with industry. Indeed Californian companies lobbied vigorously against it. Its aim is also to create incentives for industry to be green, rather than bludgeon it with bureaucracy.

Proposition 65, which became Californian state law in 1986 and came into force two years later, places an obligation on companies to warn the public, consumers and workers if they are being exposed to chemicals believed to cause cancer or birth defects. Governments everywhere have long found it hard to reach agreement with industry to curb the use of chemicals with possibly dangerous side-effects if they are already in common use. Dealing with new chemicals is easy; those on sale raise immense difficulties. California had found it a long, slow task to persuade companies to agree with the state government on levels of risk for exposure to chemicals. The law has shifted from government to companies the burden of proving the exposure limits below which the chemical poses no significant risk of harm. In its first two years, say the law's supporters, more safety limits were established under Californian state law than the federal government had set in 12 years. The need for a big bureaucracy has gone.

Indeed, as no company wants to have to put health warnings on its products, some have had an incentive to find replacements for ingredients that would otherwise not meet the safety limits. The food industry has stopped using lead solder in tin cans, the single biggest source of dietary lead in the state, rather than warn customers that lead might cause birth defects. Gillette reformulated some colours in its liquid-paper correction fluid to avoid having to label the product. One of the incentives in the law which companies understandably found hard to swallow was a bounty-hunting provision for consumers: private citizens can take a company to court if they find that it is not complying (even if they have not suffered personally as a result), and receive a quarter of any fines levied. No comparable provision makes citizens reimburse part of a company's costs if a case fails.

Green barriers to trade

As national environmental policies develop, companies worry increasingly about their impact on their competitive position. Companies are affected in two distinct ways. First, one government may set environmental product standards that one industry may be best placed to meet. That will help to keep out rival products. The point applies with some kinds of economic instruments, too, such as obligations on companies to run recycling schemes. Secondly, governments that set high environmental standards (or impose steep green taxes) on processes will drive up the costs for companies, which may then have to think of decamping to other countries with lower standards.

Both these have caused particular difficulties for the European Community, which wants simultaneously to remove barriers to the movement of labour and capital between its member states, and to be seen as a good green organisation. These two goals conflict and are likely to do so increasingly not just in EC trade, but in world trade at large.

National product standards notoriously obstruct free trade. The European Court of Justice took a landmark decision in 1979 to prevent West Germany banning French *crème de cassis* (a blackcurrant liqueur) on the grounds that its alcohol content did not meet German regulations. A standard accepted in one EC country, the judgment implied, should generally be accepted in another.

But environmental product standards are different. How different was tested for the first time in 1986 when the EC Commission hauled Denmark before the court over a law introduced in 1981 which required that beer and soft drinks be sold only in returnable bottles, with a compulsory deposit. Brewers from other countries grumbled that the costs of recycling bottles wiped out the profit to be made in Denmark's small market. Eventually the Commission took the case to court, arguing that the Danes were imposing a disproportionate level of environmental protection.

In September 1988, however, the court backed Denmark. Its judgment, that in some circumstances environmental considerations should take precedence over free trade, has had important consequences. It encouraged the Dutch to propose financial incentives for motorists who bought cars that would meet the EC's deadline for exhaust emissions ahead of the deadline, which had been set only after prolonged wrangling among EC countries. The

Dutch decision blew a hole in an elaborate compromise. Partly because it was clear that the European Court might uphold the Dutch decision, and partly because elections to the European Parliament were looming, EC ministers hastily agreed to a tighter timetable and to tougher exhaust standards.

The court decision also led the Germans to introduce the deposits on large plastic bottles and the package-recycling scheme described in Chapter 5 of Part II. The deposit scheme is designed to protect both the environment and Germany's many small brewers; under the recycling scheme, German retailers will increasingly stock only products certified as recyclable or biodegradable by a German company, set up by German manufacturers for the purpose.

The best way to reduce the impact of these schemes on free trade is to make them international, rather than national. Sometimes (as with refillable bottles) that may be difficult. It may be easier with eco-labelling. Already, more than 10% of environmental product labels in Germany are held by foreign firms (including 14 from the Netherlands, 11 from Austria, 33 from ten other West European countries and some Japanese car manufacturers and American chemical companies).[2] The EC is anxious to introduce an EC eco-labelling scheme. An alternative that would be unpopular with the greener countries would be to agree on mutual recognition of national green labels.

Shut out the dirty world

Multinational companies are going to find themselves facing different environmental product standards in different countries. They will therefore have to lobby governments to harmonise on standards that they can meet. As a result, the environmental standards set in the largest markets will tend to spread to smaller ones. California's standards on car emissions have, after a lapse of time, become America's; Germany's packaging laws threaten to become Europe's.

The EC negotiations on controls on car emissions were long stalled by an argument between those countries whose car industries specialised in big cars and were already fitting catalytic converters to the cars they sold to America, and those which tended to sell smaller cars, on which catalytic converters were less economic. The emission standards which the greener EC countries wanted Brussels to set could be achieved only by fitting three-way catalytic converters and sophisticated fuel-injection equipment. They would discourage the development of the fuel-efficient lean-burn engine with an oxidation catalyst, which Britain hoped would be a better, cheaper answer. The main drawback to the lean-burn engine was that it was still on the drawing board.

In the event it was not the attitude of Europe's car manufacturers that broke down opposition to standards requiring three-way converters. But since that decision the British government has been lobbied hard by Johnson Matthey, a British company which is also the world's biggest manufacturer of autocatalysts, to bring in tax incentives to encourage motorists to switch early to catalytic converters. The EC debate showed that, in order to win industrial backing for tougher standards, it may be necessary to back one technology against another: existing technologies are a cheaper basis for environmental reform than those which are still bright ideas.

Ozone friendly profits

An even more striking example of congruent interests in green standards has been that of chlorofluorocarbons (CFCs). In September 1987 the countries that signed the Montreal protocol agreed to cut CFCs by half by the end of the century. That was a brave move since commercial alternatives to CFCs had not yet been developed. A year later Du Pont, the world's main manufacturer of CFCs, announced it would go much farther, and stop making CFCs by the end of the century. As Chapter 7 of Part I described, the industry's support for the protocol was crucial to its success. Mexico, the first country to sign it, is one of three third-world countries in which Du Pont makes CFCs; Brazil, the most populous signatory, is another. When, early in 1990, the American government refused to commit new cash to help third-world countries switch to alternatives to CFCs, it was producers and users of CFCs in America who protested loudly enough to get the decision reversed.

Why did industry take this line? Du Pont's initial decision to abandon CFCs was taken, some outsiders think, partly because the company feared being sued by people who contracted skin cancer and blamed it on the damaged ozone layer. But Du Pont, and other big producers and users of CFCs, are investing immense sums in developing substitutes. *Managing the Environment* records a manager from ICI, one of the first companies to develop such substitutes, saying "The risks involved in this investment are horrendous. We are going out with a product which is less efficient than the one we are replacing, costs five times as much, and the only reason is because of the environmental imperative. We've never been in a market quite like it before."[3]

Profits from increasingly scarce CFCs will accrue to the manufacturers; so will profits on the substitutes. Users will carry most of the costs of adapting. Having invested over $3 billion in developing substitutes, the large chemicals companies now have powerful incentives to make sure that the ban on CFCs is watertight. Their representatives were influential bystanders at the second conference of parties to the Montreal agreement in London in 1990, at which the main challenge was to increase the number of third-world signatories.

A major issue for India (see page 136) was the amount of technical assistance that western companies would provide to make CFC-substitutes in India. Both Du Pont and ICI were encouraged by their respective governments to try to pacify the Indians. Given India's cavalier attitude in the past to intellectual property rights, both companies are wary of giving India the technology to make CFC-substitutes or even selling it, at least until they can be sure that India will not pinch the technology and export it. A more probable option would be a joint venture, which would allow the Indian government to take a share of future profits. Both companies have a vested interest in making it as easy as possible for third-world countries to acquire technologies for using CFC-substitutes, and in getting western governments to foot the bill.

Makers and users of CFC-substitutes also have a strong interest in making sure that the timetable for the Montreal agreement leaves them with time to earn a decent return on their huge investment. This is the flip side of the companies' vigorous support for the protocol. It creates a potential problem. The two main groups of substitutes now under development, known collectively as hydrofluoroalkanes (HFAs), both have worrying environmental side-effects. One group, the HCFCs, are essentially CFCs in which some of the ozone-damaging chlorine is replaced by hydrogen. The remaining chlorine would do some damage to the ozone layer, though much less than CFCs. HCFCs are easy to use in air conditioning, refrigeration and foam-blowing. But some of the greener countries (which generally do not have chemical companies developing CFC-substitutes) want limits to the use of HCFCs written into the Montreal protocol. The other compounds, HFCs, are CFCs in which all the chlorine is replaced by hydrogen. They are likely to be used mainly in refrigeration and leave the ozone layer unscathed. But they add to the greenhouse effect – not as much as CFCs, but enough to worry environmentalists.

Manufacturers of CFC-substitutes point out to governments that the cost to society of phasing out CFCs will depend largely on how quickly the change has to take place and how confident users can be that new technologies will not have to be quickly replaced. A study[4] carried out by America's Department of Energy in 1989 reckoned that to phase out CFCs by the end of the century would cost $19 billion–34 billion in equipment write-offs, assuming (too pessimistically) that no commercial recycling market were to develop. If limits are placed on CFC-substitutes, the costs will be higher. Users will stick with CFCs for longer, in the hope that other substitutes will come along before the ban eventually bites. Manufacturers may charge more for substitutes to insure against limits on the time they have to recoup their development costs.

The argument over curbing the growth of CFC-substitutes shows that environmental protectionism has its drawbacks. Better, though, to have a protocol on CFCs in exchange for protecting the market for substitutes than no protocol at all. And better for manufacturers to win an international agreement, forcing competitors to adopt the same standards, than for individual countries to move alone. The agreement reduces the risks to manufacturers who are developing CFC-substitutes; the development of substitutes, in turn, reduces the costs to society of banning CFCs.

The costs of being cleaner than the rest

Of all the incentives for companies to support tough environmental policy, none is greater than the promise of larger markets abroad. And of all the arguments they deploy against it, none weighs more heavily with government than the danger of losing foreign markets to dirtier companies. Can both perceptions be right?

They can, but not equally. Consider two points. First, such debates tend to blur the line between the products companies make and the processes they use to make them. Companies that take the lead in making green products will find plenty of eager customers abroad. But when governments force companies to employ greener processes, they will drive up the costs. Companies may also, serendipitously, find that the technologies they develop to bring down the costs of complying with high environmental standards for processes have a lively overseas market. But that will not always be the case, if only because green processes are often specific to a particular industry, or even to a particular plant.

Japan and Germany, two countries whose industries have long been required by government to invest in green technology, illustrate the way tough green rules can pay off. They are both big and growing exporters of pollution-control equipment. Japan allocated a staggering average of 14% of industrial investment to pollution control in the 1970s. As a result, it found itself technologically well ahead of other countries, selling plant for scrubbing flue gases to European countries. Germany, during that decade, devoted only 5% of investment to environmental spending. Since then, its air-quality standards have risen. German manufacturers have developed desulphurisation equipment which they now sell to Japan. By contrast, Britain's first flue-gas desulphurisation plant on a coal-fired boiler is not due to be commissioned until 1993. As regulators insist on best available technology, even if made abroad, one country's advance will bring rapid growth in world demand.

OECD studies[5] of the impact of environmental regulations on economic activity show that regulations may sometimes force old plants to close faster than they might otherwise have done. But they also create new industries, new jobs and new markets. Investment in pollution control may go hand in hand with modernisation, and may spur innovation in industries where the pace of change has previously been slow. Spotting the benefit in individual industries is easier than seeing the overall picture: the costs of regulation are easy to identify, the benefits more indirect and diffuse.

For most companies the costs of environmental regulation of their processes are tiny compared with other considerations, such as labour costs and proximity to markets. Although more is spent on pollution control in America, Japan and a few European countries than anywhere else, these costs are usually small relative to total capital investment and operating costs. In no country are pollution-control expenditures by government industry together more than 3% of gross national product; in most industrial countries the average is below 2%.

Some will depart

While some industries will gain world market share because of tough environmental regulations, others will lose. In industries where the costs of environmental regulation are higher, some companies undoubtedly shut down, or move to less regulated markets. That generally means moving to a third-world or developing country, rather than to another industrial one. The richest ones are those that have the toughest pollution controls; and the most successful industrialising countries are becoming fiercer about pollution, especially to foreign firms.

A bigger threat than a loss of investment is that of competition from producers based in countries with weaker regulations. Such competition may be strongest with semi-processed products such as steel or chemicals, where the corporate customer cares more about the quality and cost of the product than the circumstances in which it was produced. It is notable, for instance, that hardly any non-ferrous smelters were built in industrialised countries in the 1980s. It has proved hard also for developed countries to keep out some materials from manufactured goods which they have banned, such as PCBs (polychlorinated biphenyls), in finished goods imported from abroad. But such goods are likely to sell best at the bottom end of the market. At the top of every market customers will continue to pay a premium for products whose suppliers can offer some sort of pledge of their greenery.

Comparing environmental standards is difficult. What matters is how standards are enforced, and that may be hard to measure. Raymond Kopp and two colleagues[6] from Resources for the Future found that policies on air and water varied little among OECD countries, and were converging. Differences were greater for hazardous waste mainly because no European country had legislation as rigorous as America's Superfund. European countries also tend to define hazardous waste more narrowly: Britain lists 31 substances and France 100 compared with some 500 on the list published by the EPA. Because environmental policy in Europe will increasingly be dictated by the EC, and because policy-makers on each side of the Atlantic tend to emulate each other's successes, the convergence is likely to continue.

Much greater differences exist between the old industrialised countries and the new. The most thorough examination of how these differences affect competitiveness was carried out by Jeffrey Leonard in *Pollution and the Struggle for the World Product*.[6] Mr Leonard scrutinised the overseas investment patterns of American companies and concluded that only a small number of American industries had been driven abroad by environmental regulations. They fell into three categories. There were manufacturers of some highly toxic products who had not yet developed safer substitutes or changed their technologies to meet American standards for health and safety at work. They included makers of asbestos, benzidine-based dyes and some pesticides for whom regulations had disrupted or halted production in the United States. Then there were some basic mineral-processing industries, such as copper, lead and zinc whose relocation abroad had been encouraged by requirements in some countries that minerals mined in a country be processed there too. A third group consisted of chemical companies, which, said Mr Leonard, had gone abroad to produce or purchase "intermediate" organic chemicals to process in the United States.

Mr Leonard found some signs in the investment and trade figures that there were moves abroad in two sectors – chemicals and minerals processing – where pollution abatement spending as a proportion of all new plant and capital spending was between one-and-a-half times and double that for manufacturing industry as a whole. But he argues that the industries most likely to flee to escape pollution controls are those with dying markets. They are the ones with least incentive to install expensive pollution controls, or to develop substitutes. Healthy growing industries – even the makers of polyvinyl chloride and acrylonitrile, feared by environmentalists but in solid demand in the mid-1980s – stayed put. They adjusted to environmental controls, rather than escape them.

A Faustian deal

The industries fleeing environmental regulation went to a handful of places. Apart from the rich countries of Europe and Japan, the bulk of all overseas direct investment by the chemicals and metal-processing industries went to Ireland and Spain in Europe, and Mexico and Brazil in the third world (see Table 21, page 250). Such bargains were explained by an old Irish politician who said, "All my life I've seen the lads leaving Ireland for the big smoke in London, Pittsburgh, Birmingham and Chicago. It's better for Ireland if they stayed here and we imported the smoke." In the 1970s Ireland regarded its laxer pollution rules as a potential attraction for American companies; Spain made a special pitch for chemicals and metal-processing firms; Mexico attracted footloose small companies across its border, like pesticide manufacturers and companies using asbestos for textiles and building supplies.

Often, tighter regulation in developed countries is followed by a brief period before substitutes appear; such emigrant companies take advantage of these windows. Eastern Europe's sloppy pre-revolutionary environment rules seem to have helped it to sell cheap chemicals to America. As American regulations have cut off the market, new markets have opened in the third world.

More recently, according to Mr Leonard, industrialising countries have begun to bargain more fiercely with incoming multinational firms. People in developing countries are more likely to complain if they think a foreign company is polluting than a local one. In 1989, for instance, ICI was forced to close a plant in southern Taiwan making methyl methacrylate after local fishermen complained that a subcontractor was dumping waste acid near the coast. Occasionally a company may make an investment and then be forced by local environmental opposition to shut it, as Raybestos Manhattan was forced in 1980 to shut a plant in Ireland's County Cork making asbestos brake pads. More often, though, tough regulations are weakly enforced, or are enforced on multinationals but not on local companies or subcontractors,

Table 21 Direct investments by American chemical and mineral processing industries in rapidly industrialising countries, 1980 and 1984 ($m)

	Chemicals		Mineral processing	
	1980	**1984**	**1980**	**1984**
TOTAL by American companies outside Canada, Japan & industrialised Europe[a]	6,633	6,533	2,160	1,757
TOTAL in under-industrialised Europe[b]	1,362	651	115	118
TOTAL in Ireland and Spain	1,250	621	98	113
% total under-industrialised Europe in Ireland and Spain	91.8	95.4	85.2	95.8
TOTAL in less-developed countries	4,462	4,275	1,652	1,390
TOTAL in Brazil, Mexico	2,094	2,021	952	1,095
% total less developed countries in Brazil & Mexico	46.9	47.3	57.6	78.8

[a] Excludes Ireland, Spain, Portugal, Greece, Turkey. [b] Includes Ireland, Spain, Portugal, Greece, Turkey.
Source: H. Jeffrey Leonard, *Pollution and the Struggle for the World Product*, CUP, 1988

who may therefore "launder" multinational muck.

Can green trade be free trade?

The clash between national environmental standards and free trade will become more important. Countries may hesitate to use trade barriers to protect the jobs of their workers, arguing that to do so raises the prices that everyone pays for goods in the shops for the benefit of a smallish section of the population. To keep out, say, Bangladeshi shirts may keep British or American shirt-makers in business, but means that American and British poor have to pay more for their shirts.

Environmental protectionists feel no such scruples. They will argue that green policies benefit the whole community – and future generations, too. So they will find it easy to persuade governments to keep out products from dirty countries. Setting tough standards will be the first step. Environmental restrictions are accepted as reasonable (provided they do not discriminate in favour of one country or against another) under the rules of the General Agreement on Tariffs and Trade (GATT), which govern world trade. The next step, though, may be the imposition of green tariffs, introduced under pressure from regulated companes as environmental rules tighten. A new form of protectionism will spring up: bans on imports of goods made by dirty processes, using suspect materials. Already the United Nations Environment Programme has discussed the possibility of introducing a levy on dirty trade, and using the proceeds greenly. And the Montreal protocol to phase out CFCs includes provisions for countries that comply to ban products containing CFCs from other countries and even products whose manufacturing process involves the use of CFCs. That may yet set an awkward precedent for the embryonic treaty on global warming. If products manufactured with CFCs can be banned, why not penalise countries that fail to curb their consumption of fossil fuels?

Free-traders will fret. Yet green trade barriers may have a logic of their own. They may be the only way that one country can put real pressure on another to make sure its companies shoulder the costs they would otherwise impose on the environment. When only the national environment suffers, dirty countries can reasonably retort that what they do with their own rivers and hillsides is nobody else's business (though just wait for the green protectionists to reply, in turn, that their concern is for the dirty country's future inhabitants). When the environment of other countries suffers, though, the logic of green protectionism is stronger.

For, as the final chapter of Part I explained, countries that agree to curb planet-threatening pollution have few ways to avoid free riders, those less virtuous countries who benefit for free from the self-restraint of others. Green protectionism offers a double benefit: a way to discourage free riders, and a way to win the backing of clean companies by ensuring an international return on their investments. In that way, green protectionism may amount to much the same as offering a special subsidy to clean companies, not just to those in the country that sets the standards, but to those that try to export to it. They all enjoy a protected market.

The main theme of this book has been that cleaning the environment needs government intervention. That can be done in cost-effective ways, and in expensive ways. Some intervention is deeply harmful. Some is expensively unnecessary. But some is essential, and has already made the industrial countries nicer places to live than they might otherwise have been.

Companies must make sure that government intervention is conducted in ways that reward the cleanest and greenest. Industry's ingenuity can hugely reduce the costs of tackling environmental problems: by inventing substitutes for CFCs, by developing energy efficiency, by finding sustainable uses for rain-forest products, by reducing the rubbish heaps of the world and by inventing simple, reliable forms of contraception. Harnessing that ingenuity by the skilful design of environmental policies is the challenge for governments. Together, wise government and inventive industry could be a formidable alliance for a greener world.

References

[1] Project 88, *Harnessing Market Forces to Protect Our Environment*, a public policy study sponsored by Senator Tim Wirth and Senator John Heinz, Washington DC, 1988.

[2] Peter H. Sand, *Lessons Learned in Global Environmental Governance*, WRI, 1990.

[3] *Op.cit.*

[4] "Assessment of the Impacts Associated with a Total CFC Phase-out", a study by Putman, Hayes & Bartlett Inc, for the US Department of Energy, Washington DC, 1989.

[5] *Environment and Economics*, Paris, 1984.

[6] Raymond J. Kopp, Paul R. Portney, Diane E. De Witt, "International Comparisons of Environmental Regulation", *Resources* No. 11, Fall 1990, pages 10–13.

[7] Cambridge University Press, 1988.

A CHECKLIST
FOR COMPANIES

Now, how should the sensible company chairman turn the ideas in this book into action? Here are a dozen suggestions to start off with.

•1•
Put the most senior person possible in charge of environmental policy.
A member of the board should have clear responsibility and there should be a well-defined management structure. All the golden intentions in the world are pointless unless the chairman cares and is known to care.

•2•
Draft a policy and make it public.
Do not make it woolly. If possible, include clear targets with dates. That will not be possible unless you also:

•3•
Measure.
Nothing concentrates the mind like numbers. In particular, discover what wastes you are creating and what energy you are using.

•4•
Institute a regular audit to check on what is happening.
While an outside consultant may be a help with Numbers 1–3 above, this one can be home-grown. Pay particular attention to the follow-up: there is no point in knowing what is wrong if nothing happens to fix it.

•5•
Communicate.
Tell everybody – your workers, your shareholders, local people, green groups, the press – about your environmental problems and how you are solving them. When possible, involve them in helping you to choose solutions.

• 6 •
Consider ways to reduce the range of materials you use that could do environmental harm.
Do you really need so many toxic chemicals?

• 7 •
Think about the materials in your product.
If you had responsibility for disposing of it when your customer threw it out (and one day, legislators may well dump that burden on your firm), could you do so? In an environmentally benign way? If not, consider changing the design and materials you use.

• 8 •
Remember that you may be able to make a business opportunity out of disposing of your product when the customer has finished with it.
If your customer brings back used paint drums or old refrigerators, it offers a chance to build a new link and to make your customer dependent on you in a new way.

• 9 •
If you invest in a country where environmental standards are low, do not expect them to stay that way.
If one country finds a way of forcing companies to clean up, others will follow. Better assume that standards everywhere will rise rather than risk an expensive and disagreeable surprise.

• 10 •
Accept that green regulations will tend to converge upwards.
What is compulsory in the most energetically environmental markets (California, Germany, Scandinavia) will probably reach your home market, too. If you accept the highest standards before they are compulsory, you steal a market advantage.

• 11 •
Be flexible.
When making investments or designing products, remember the speed with which environmental understanding can change.

• 12 •
Remember that greenery is often a proxy for quality in the eyes of your customers, your workers and your managers.
A truly green company is unlikely to be badly managed. Conversely, a well-managed company finds it relatively easy to be green.

Index